The American Religious Debate
Over Birth Control, 1907–1937

# The American Religious Debate Over Birth Control, 1907–1937

*by*
KATHLEEN A. TOBIN

McFarland & Company, Inc., Publishers
*Jefferson, North Carolina, and London*

**Library of Congress Cataloguing-in-Publication Data**

Tobin, Kathleen A., 1957–
    The American religious debate over birth control, 1907–1937 /
by Kathleen A. Tobin.
       p.     cm.
    Includes bibliographical references and index.
    ISBN 0-7864-1081-7 (softcover : 50# alkaline paper) ∞
    1. Birth control — United States — History.   2. Birth
control — Religious aspects — History.   3. Church and social
problems — United States — History.   I. Title.
HQ766.5.U5T63   2001
363.9'6'0973 — dc21                     2001037048

British Library cataloguing data are available

Manufactured in the United States of America

*McFarland & Company, Inc., Publishers
  Box 611, Jefferson, North Carolina 28640
    www.mcfarlandpub.com*

`'\06`

# Contents

# Preface

This book began as a research paper for a course on religion in the United States during the Depression, taught by Martin E. Marty at the University of Chicago in the fall of 1988. I entered into the project with preconceptions about the Catholic Church and birth control that are common in the United States, notions that I realized later were entirely too simplistic. In fact, my objective at that point was simple — I wanted to see what the Church had to say about birth control during this economic crisis, when millions of American families were struggling to make ends meet. What I found out was that the subject of birth control had provoked a heated debate in that period, with many denominations taking part publicly and privately. I also learned that at the beginning of the debate, which gained tremendous momentum in the 1920s, little had been said about contraception, but essentially all denominations opposed it. Yet, by 1931 many denominations condoned its use, and the Catholic Church had become known as the enemy.

I soon came to realize that the real story — a book-length story — lay in that shift and that major questions remained. When birth control advocates brought the idea to the nation's attention, why did so many denominations come to accept it, while others did not? And while the Catholic Church was not the only one to maintain its position against the use of "artificial barriers" to prevent conception, why did the American public come to view it as the opposition? The answers are quite complicated and not entirely based on doctrine or theology but on historical circumstances setting the stage for the debate. This book only begins to provide answers, as each denomination's struggle with birth control is a story in itself. But it is my hope that it serves to shed some much-needed light on the subject.

Dr. Kathleen A. Tobin

# Chapter One

# 1907–1921:
# The Cultural Environment

*Archbishop Hayes regards birth control as a sin against the divine law and destructive of society. The Methodist Church denounces round dancing as a sin against the divine law and destructive of society. Let us suppose that the Mayor of the City of New York were a Methodist, that the Chief of Police were a Methodist, and that the Methodist hierarchy had a very potent, if not controlling influence in the city administration. Let us suppose that an association of dancing masters called a public meeting in the Town Hall to discuss the question, Is Round Dancing Moral? If the police interfered, broke up the meeting, drove the speakers from the state, and arrested the chairman, it is easy to imagine the protest that would go up all over the city, not less in the City Hall than anywhere else, over such puritanical despotism, and such a violation of the Constitutional liberties of the American Citizens.*
—*The Outlook,* November 30, 1921

The above quote describes an incident perhaps most symbolic in the religious argument over legalizing contraceptives. As birth control activist Margaret Sanger was about to speak on the topic "Birth Control: Is it Moral?" to a crowd gathered at New York City's town hall on November 13, 1921, she was arrested. Within days she pointed to Archbishop Patrick Hayes as the man behind the police action and intensified her condemnation of the Church's opposition to the birth control movement. At this point in history the Catholic Church's official stand was no different from any other denomination's official stand. Yet birth control advocates succeeded in portraying the Church as their enemy.

Today the perception of the Catholic Church as the enemy of the movement does not merely linger. Rather it is still so powerful that it suggests that the Church is, was, and always has been the sole critic of birth control. The truth is, however, that all major denominations in the Judeo-Christian world condemned contraception until this century. So what happened

1

in recent history to provoke such a massive shift? And why did some denominations transform their teaching, while others chose to maintain their traditional positions? The reasons are numerous and complex but are all related in one way or another to the intensity of change taking place in American society and how denominations would respond to that change. The response was not a quiet one, nor was it confined to the pulpit. Rather it emerged as a public and often political battle.

If the birth control issue had emerged simply as a question of whether individual couples should be allowed to choose whether to prevent pregnancy, the debate would have unfolded in a far different manner. In fact, that question had been examined and re-examined by religious figures and moralists for millennia. What made the twentieth century birth control debate unique were religious questions regarding society and the human race and the value American culture placed on the use of science and engineering to improve the human condition. The nation was undergoing vast social changes, particularly in its northern urban regions, but this time various authorities and experts believed human beings might finally have the power to bring society under control with the modern understanding of science. This is the atmosphere in which denominations took a stand on birth control in early-twentieth-century America, but complicating the picture was the political nature of religion during this period in which conflict was the rule.[1] On the subject of preventing pregnancy, the churches would not remain silent, as this concerned the creation of life itself. But when religion became involved this time, the arguments became politicized, pitting denomination against denomination and ultimately non-Catholics against Catholics.

## *Contraceptives*

Although much of the religious rhetoric opposing the legalization of birth control following World War I would reflect "antiscience" views directed specifically at contraceptive devices, there had been little technological advancement in recent years. Through the ages couples used a wide variety of methods to prevent pregnancy, many still being used in 1900. Determining which methods of birth control were used and with what degree of effectiveness is tremendously difficult in part because the details of sexual activity remained secret but also because knowledge regarding the prevention of pregnancy was kept and circulated among women.[2] However, historical references, from public condemnations to personal journals, do shed some light on what was available.

*Coitus interruptus* and periodic abstinence were used, as were vaginal suppositories (made from any one of a variety of metals, herbs, or ointments) and condoms, made of animal intestines or cloth.[3] Nineteenth-century developments in manufacturing and the development of vulcanized rubber brought greater accessibility to what were termed "artificial contraceptives" and "barriers." Condoms and pessaries (similar to the diaphragm of later years) were widely available by 1850, as were douches, spermicides, and vaginal sponges. Law did not prohibit the sale of these at that time; however, their use was not considered "proper," so they were often advertised and sold discreetly. Condoms were readily prescribed for incontinence, pessaries for uterine support, and douches for purposes of feminine hygiene.[4] Although the medical community understood their intended use by couples as preventives, there had been relatively little research done regarding effectiveness. The rhythm method, or abstinence from intercourse in relation to periodic fertility, had been studied in France and the United States,[5] but until the late 1920s there was virtually no research conducted on spermicides being sold, and many were essentially worthless.[6]

Even though the standard methods of the late nineteenth century were somewhat less effective when compared to those of the present day, a growing segment of the American public was willing to take chances with them, and the birth rate showed a steady decline. As their popularity grew, Victorian moralists began a crusade, contending that no decent woman should be interested in such medical knowledge or devices. In his raid against merchandising of obscene materials in 1873, postal agent and secretary of New York's Society for the Suppression of Vice, Anthony Comstock, succeeded in making the distribution of contraceptives and contraceptive information illegal.[7]

The society had been founded by a group of self-appointed crusaders who worked to enforce laws suppressing the trade and circulation of "obscene literature, and illustrations, advertisements, and articles of indecent and immoral use."[8] In 1873 they were successful in passing the "Comstock law," which made it a felony to

> sell or lend, or give away, or in any manner exhibit, or ... offer to sell, or lend or give away, or in any manner exhibit ... publish or offer to publish in any manner, or ... have in [one's possession], for any purpose or purposes, any obscene book, pamphlet, paper, writing, advertisement, circular, print, picture, drawing or other representation, figure, or image on or of paper or other material, or any cast, instrument or other article of an immoral nature, or any drug or medicine, or any article what

ever for the prevention of conception, or for causing unlawful abortion, or ... advertise same for sale.[9]

Such moralism took hold in Great Britain as well, with the establishment of the White Cross Society by the Church of England in 1883. This society focused its efforts on social purity by promoting abstinence and a "respect for womanhood."[10] In the United States, however, the prohibition of contraceptives set the stage for a public battle, and Comstock was singled out as the opposition, serving as the object of Sanger's attacks until his death in 1915.

Sanger's preferred method of contraception for her clients was the diaphragm, which she discovered on a trip to Europe in 1913. She became fascinated with this device, which originated in Holland and had been used in France for forty years. Like the condom, various materials had been used in such a manner through the ages, but the development of vulcanized rubber and mass manufacturing made the diaphragm more practical and widely available. Combined with the use of a spermicidal jelly, Sanger believed them to be very effective, while placing reproductive choice under the woman's control. Because importing diaphragms violated the Comstock law, she considered smuggling some through U.S. customs on her return trip by hiding them in her girdle. Instead, she made headlines the following year by launching her magazine *The Woman Rebel*, where she could describe her birth control philosophy, and by publishing a "how-to" manual called "Family Limitation." Sanger's challenge to the Victorian Comstock law was underway.[11]

The influence of Victorianism in the nineteenth century was immensely powerful in that era's debate over contraception. But the controversy was shaped by a number of issues, including concerns over the declining birth rate among America's "good stock" and the tremendous number of casualties among the nation's young male population during the Civil War. In this "age of progress" when United States economic development, global competition, and territorial expansion depended on population growth, any attempts to prevent pregnancy or birth within "desirable" demographic cohorts would meet with criticism.[12] The essence of these arguments would take on a new life after the turn of the century, as new issues arose and America entered a modern era.

## Marriage, Family, and the Modern Woman

The era in which Sanger first challenged the Comstock law was marked by an intensified struggle for female suffrage and women's rights. In this environment feminists argued that the day had come when women should be valued as humans, or at least as women, rather than as mothers. In addition, some activists challenged traditional notions of the "morality of women," which portrayed them as pious bearers of children rather than as sexual creatures. Though some of the feminist arguments were considered far too radical for the time being, Victorianism was clearly giving way to the idea of the "modern woman." The woman of the new century would soon have the right to vote, be very much involved in social reform and developing an American philosophy of social justice, and in this age of science and modernism, demand more control over her own life.

One of the advantages of the modern woman was the greater opportunity to attend college. The controversy over higher education for women continued, especially in the form of coeducation, but the number of female college graduates continued to rise.[13] Many of the graduates became involved in community work, some through their churches, some through emerging women's clubs, others as social workers or social scientists. In some sense the positions they held remained within the "woman's sphere" and were segregated from men's roles. But the "New Woman," first noted during the 1890s, was attempting to break the bonds of Victorianism. Historian Rosalind Rosenberg describes her this way: "Her distinguishing characteristics were her independent spirit and athletic zeal. She rode a bicycle, played tennis or golf, showed six inches of stocking beneath her skirts, and loosened her corsets. She expected to marry and have children, but she wanted a life beyond her home — perhaps even a career."[14] Access to contraceptives and the ability to plan pregnancy and control family size would certainly benefit this woman.

Birth rates among the upper middle class which gave rise to this kind of woman had already been decreasing, but contemporary studies showed that women wanted better access to contraceptives. Mary Roberts Smith, a former professor of history and economics at Wellesley College, conducted extensive research beginning in 1892, inquiring into the sexual attitudes and behavior of "normal women." Smith found that women were reluctant to engage in sex, that they suffered from "sex anxiety," in part because of fear of pregnancy. To them, abstinence appeared to be the only viable preventive, as they reported the other methods used generally faulty: withdrawal, douching, even condoms. Periodic abstinence, or what came to be known as the "rhythm" method, was unreliable, as they depended on nineteenth-century medical authorities who disagreed on the timing of the "safe period." In fact, most authorities claimed that a woman was most fertile just before, during, and after her menstrual period, the opposite of what is known to be true today.[15]

The practical discussions of contraceptives in Smith's research are significant, but so too, are the discussions of "sex anxiety." The rise of a bolder modern woman, in conjunction with the rise of psychology, contributed to a kind of examination of sex and sexuality that had not existed before. Psychologists labeled Victorian attitudes toward sex as superstitious and unscientific, claiming that sexuality was a positive, energy-producing force that should not be restrained. Only the most free of the free thinkers suggested that uninhibited sex extend beyond the institution of marriage. It was understood that enjoyable and frequent sex should be heterosexual and between a husband and wife. Sanger and some of her more radical colleagues were among those who promoted "free love" in the early years of the birth control movement but eventually directed their efforts toward providing contraceptives to married couples. This trend forced further discussion of marriage itself. In the age of the modern woman, and rising divorce rates, birth control advocates suggested that alleviating "sex anxiety" by diminishing the fear of pregnancy would in fact strengthen marital bonds.[16]

The nation's churches would react to new notions of sexuality, the more conservative ones formulating close links between female immorality and contraceptives. But both conservative and liberal would take one position or another in addressing the very real changing roles of women and changing ideals of marriage and family in general. The traditional family unit had historically been viewed as the cornerstone of society, and any clear disruption in the "normal" family might be viewed as a threat to society. As the divorce rate climbed, the birth rate among the native population fell, and women demanded more independence, social scientists placed the American family under a microscope to determine any links to the ills in society at large.

America's religious leaders would often support these efforts and draw their own conclusions about the purpose of marriage and the family in society and the eyes of God. As the birth control debate advanced, they often centered their internal discussions on the place of procreation within marriage. However, the significance of the debate's social context cannot be ignored, for it is the social context that gave rise to this new kind of discussion in the first place. By the era of the birth control debate, religious leaders placed significant value on social stability and family stability. As they watched Sanger and others promote the legalization of contraceptives, they wondered how it might affect the American family unit, which already appeared weakened. At the same time, however, there existed serious concerns about society at large, and churches couldn't help but become involved.

# The Movement and Social Control

The idea of social reform in early-twentieth-century America was embedded in the larger understanding that scientific principles could and should be applied in an effort to alleviate social ills.[17] In the past the prohibition of contraceptives was intended to rein in women who were considered "out of control." However, birth control advocates of the twentieth century would promote the distribution of contraceptives as part of a plan to bring stability to an urbanizing and industrializing society that was perceived as growing and changing in a manner that was "out of control." Though social ills, and measures to deal with them, had been recognized for centuries, "experts" now widely agreed that the modern age had ushered in a previously unmatched level of scientific understanding, and by using the scientific method and proper planning, problems could be addressed more effectively.

Though to some extent Sanger promoted legalizing contraceptives as a women's rights issue, she was a prominent player in the larger story of social control. In this society some of the most educated and influential were promoting eugenics—the engineering of a better human race—to solve the nation's and the world's problems. Though eugenicists and birth control advocates began their work in separate camps, and did not support each other publicly or wholeheartedly early on, it was in this philosophical environment that Sanger went to work.

Very much a reformer, Sanger worked diligently as a nurse in New York City before the First World War and became aware of the hardships of poverty-stricken immigrant women who had more than their share of health problems. Sanger attributed their ill health in a large degree to the number of years of their lives spent in incessant childbearing, a situation that she maintained had caused the early death of her mother. She subsequently began to work toward what she thought would ease the difficulty of their lives, which she reported very often included self-induced abortions. During her birth control campaign, she often told the story of Sadie Sachs, a Jewish immigrant woman residing in Hell's Kitchen who died after she attempted to abort a fetus with a coat hanger. Following the birth of her last child, Sachs reportedly asked a physician how to prevent future pregnancies, to which he replied, "Just tell your husband to sleep on the roof." Sanger later recalled that the witnessing of Sachs' death was a life-changing experience:

> When I finally arrived home and let myself quietly in, all the household was sleeping. I looked out my window and down

upon the dimly lighted city. Its pains and griefs crowded in
upon me, a moving picture rolled before my eyes with photo-
graphic clearness. Women writhing in travail to bring forth little babies; the babies themselves naked and hungry, wrapped in
newspapers to keep them from the cold; six-year-old children
with pinched, pale, wrinkled faces; old people in concentrated
wretchedness, pushed into gray and fetid cellars, crouching on
stone floors, their small scrawny hands scuttling through rags,
making lamp shades, artificial flowers, white coffins, black coffins, coffins interminably passing in never-ending succession.
The scenes piled up one upon another. I could bear it no longer.
As I stood there the darkness faded. The sun came up and threw
its reflection over the roof tops. It was the dawn of a new day
in my life also. I was resolved to seek out the roots of the evil,
to do something to change the destiny of mothers to whom mis-
eries were as vast as the sky.[18]

Historians have found no proof that Sadie Sachs really existed, but the
repeated telling of the story gained much support for Sanger's cause.[19] Her
accounts shed light on the desperation of women who faced unwanted
pregnancies and helped gain support for legalized contraception as a means
to prevent abortion. In various accounts Sanger said the poor women were
aware that middle- and upper-class women had knowledge of methods to
avoid conception, of which they had learned through private conversations
with their doctors. Sanger wanted to give them the same advantage.

Sanger was not the only one actively supporting an increase in the
availability of contraceptives in the second decade of the twentieth century, but she became the most widely recognized. Another worth noting
was physician Robert Dickinson, who conducted extensive research and
advised newly married couples to periodically abstain from sexual intercourse and to plan and space children. He also maintained that inexpen-
sive methods, such as contraceptive jellies, could be effective if women
were better educated regarding their use. Other notable physicians of the
nineteenth and early twentieth centuries, including Clarence J. Gamble,
Charles Knowlton and Alvin Kaufman, had supported the use of contraceptives and had been instrumental in advancing the birth control movement. Still, the American Medical Association remained conservative until
the 1930s when Sanger appealed for its support in challenging the Comstock law in court.

Wealthy Chicago socialite Katherine Dexter McCormick had demonstrated her concern for health issues, especially those affecting women and
children, and helped fund a number of birth control causes. Chicago, facing issues similar to those in New York, such as unbridled growth and an

influx of immigrants, was the home of a birth control movement based on comparable philosophy and led largely by physician Rachel Yarros.[20] Mary Ware Dennett, an activist in the women's suffrage movement and founder of the Voluntary Parenthood League, worked to educate women about contraception as primarily a women's issue and was viewed by Sanger as her strongest competitor. Dennett challenged her for leadership of the birth control movement following World War I, criticizing Sanger's radical tactics of breaking the law, choosing, herself, to reform the law through legislative efforts. The disagreement between Sanger and Dennett later intensified as Sanger began to court the American Medical Association for support. Dennett saw Sanger's position during the mid–1920s to allow physicians to prescribe contraceptives for contraceptive purposes without fear of legal retribution as benefiting physicians. Dennett consistently maintained that it was more important to give the power of reproductive control directly to women.[21] Yet Sanger won out, drawing significant attention in spearheading the birth control movement.

Before the war Sanger's work centered primarily on attempting to import diaphragms, pessaries, and condoms from Europe, where their manufacture and sale were legal, and on distributing information directly to women in New York, and through the mail to women in other cities. In 1914, following a trip to France to study contraception, she wrote about it in the *Woman Rebel*, coining the term "birth control." Even though she had not outlined contraceptive methods, she endorsed widespread birth control, particularly for the working classes, and the publication was declared "unmailable" under the Comstock law. This incident was the first of her many battles with the legal system. Significant encounters followed the distribution in 1915 of her instructional pamphlet entitled *Family Limitation* and the opening of her first birth control clinic in New York in 1916. By that time she had succeeded in drawing the nation's attention to her cause.[22]

## Malthusianism

Sanger's attempts to legalize contraceptives cannot be isolated from larger social movements already in place in Europe and America. One of the most influential of these was Malthusianism. Thomas Malthus first brought his theories to light in 1798 in his *Essay on Population*, which asserted that rapid population growth had adverse effects on the human race and society.[23] A resurgence of Malthusian teachings in a twentieth-century movement of "neo–Malthusianism" addressed the political and social upheavals of Europe, contending that overpopulation was responsible for disease, starvation, and ultimately the outbreak of World War I. According to neo–Malthusians, these developments would, in turn, increase the death rate, thereby limiting population growth.[24] But to those who revered scientific knowledge, the scientific method, and the potential for engineering in this new age, humans were perceived as having greater power to keep these forces under control. To proponents of science there would be a more humane way to address the problem of overpopulation, and that was to promote birth control.[25] In his *Essay on Population* Thomas Malthus never endorsed contraception, only delayed marriage. But twentieth-century neo–Malthusians often claimed that Malthus would have condoned contraception if he had foreseen future problems, making him the "unwitting founder of the modern birth control movement."[26]

The reasons for the resurgence in Malthusianism are numerous, but the outbreak of World War I gained special attention. A century earlier Malthus had argued that war served as a check on population growth, but in this new era of science and progress the educated were unwilling to accept war as inevitable. They instead looked to Malthus's argument that overpopulation led to competition for resources and ultimately into war. Strengthening their position, the scientific community now added the arguments of Charles Darwin, who, according to the prominent neo–Malthusian Charles Drysdale, "has shown beyond the possibility of dispute that over-reproduction leads to a constant struggle for existence. Animal life is one perpetual conflict, and man too has been in a constant state of war — the impelling force being really, although not always ostensibly, the need for food."[27] Opponents would argue that the scientific knowledge available in this modern era could address food supply and distribution rather than birth control, that World War I broke out in Europe, where birth rates had been declining, and that even if resources were in short supply in some parts of the world, this was not true in the United States. Yet Malthusian sentiment would prevail among the upper classes.[28]

The subject of class was evident in early Malthusian philosophy, and it gained even more attention during the late nineteenth century, as Marxists examined all aspects of the workforce's struggle. From its inception Malthusianism had incorporated economic arguments addressing labor supply and poverty, and those factors were re-examined through socialist eyes when it became clear that the concerns over population growth centered on birthrates of the working class and that birth control was being directed toward the working class. Some socialists argued that an abundance of workers allowed for increased exploitation by industrial capitalism and recommended preventing pregnancy as a means of rejecting future exploitation. Countering this argument were socialists who maintained that a reduction in the birthrate would weaken the proletariat, both in spirit and in numbers.[29]

Numbers were always important in Malthusian arguments, but the concerns never stopped with sheer numbers. As anthropologist Eric B. Ross notes in his book *The Malthus Factor*, "There had always been in Malthusianism an implicit presumption that the poor were not really the equals of the more privileged."[30] From the beginning Malthusians demonstrated their concerns about breeding among the lower classes. But added concerns over the characteristics believed to be inherent in some groups of humans would shape Malthusianism into a movement that easily incorporated eugenics, or the belief that a better race of humans could be engineered through proper breeding. Eugenic ideals— before the "science" of eugenics had been established — are found in some of the basic teachings of early-nineteenth-century Malthusians who published and distributed contraceptive information before the Comstock law. Some of the most active proponents were associated with utopian communities in the United States— as inherent in both Malthusianism and eugenics is a strong sense of utopianism — the perfectability of humanity and community.[31]

## *Race Theory*

Also fundamental to the birth control debate were recent global developments in race theory — better understood as scientific racism. Praised by conservatives, notions of inherent superiority and inferiority among the races justified the social, economic, and political dominance of northern European white races in the world and of white Anglo-Saxon Protestants in the United States. But it was also advocated by liberals who equated science with modernity and progress. Academics conducted extensive studies of the nature of race, providing what they considered scientific evidence of qualitative differences among the various peoples of the world. By the early twentieth century, to question race theory was to question science.[32]

One of the earliest links between race theory and the birth control movement is seen in the intellectual exchange and love affair between Sanger and H. G. Wells. Wells, an influential British social theorist, essayist, and novelist based much of the world's history on racial differences, dividing humans into numerous racial categories.[33] According to Wells, the late nineteenth century marked a period when the enlightened people of the superior races could seriously begin using science to promote progress. But he and other European racial theorists, particularly in Britain, France, Germany, and Italy, saw this progress increasingly threatened in the early twentieth century because of race degeneration caused by unmatched multiplication of the inferior races.[34] Wells also held strongly to the notion of free love, which may have inspired the love affair with Sanger and influenced the aspect of sexuality in the move to legalize contraceptives. But it was his social/racial theory that was most evident in the birth control movement. The influence of his theories of progress is particularly evident in Sanger's *The Pivot of Civilization*.[35] In this work Sanger promoted extensively the notion that science and birth control should work hand in hand — not so much in the development of new birth control technology, but in further scientific research into race degeneracy that would provide insight into new solutions to social problems. In her words, experts were finally coming to understand that "a *qualitative* factor as opposed to a *quantitative* one is of primary importance in dealing with the great masses of humanity."[36]

Race theory carried special weight in America, as theorists warned of the dangers inherent in recent immigration trends, and it was often linked to the American eugenics movement.[37] Experts often made broad statements about the quality of the Anglo race and the strength of America based on its Anglo heritage. For example, Stanford University president David Starr Jordan, one of the nation's strongest advocates of eugenics, extolled the glories of Britain, claiming that British historical strength lay partly in its tradition of primogeniture. As power was handed down to the eldest son, the quality of the race was maintained, as the first born in a family was generally of better quality. But more important, the most significant qualities of individuals were bred in the "blood" and the "bone," from generation to generation, regardless of environment: "Wherever the Englishman goes, he carries with him the elements of English history.... Thus, too, a Jew is a Jew in all ages and climes, and his deeds everywhere bear the stamp of Jewish individuality. A Greek is a Greek; a Chinaman remains a Chinaman. In like fashion the race traits color all history made by Tartars, or negroes, or Malays."[38]

Though many argued that immigrants were not inherently or necessarily inferior, contemporary studies of race categorized humans according to racial quality and pointed to the questionable racial origins of immigrants pouring into the country from Southern and Eastern Europe beginning around 1880. An early public commentary on the demographic changes in the United States with regard to these races appeared in the *Atlantic Monthly* in 1908. According to author William Z. Ripley, who had written the definitive work, *The Races of Europe*, the races prevalent in the

United States could be divided by general physical characteristics into the following: Mediterranean, Alpine, Slavic, Teutonic, and Jewish; and he subsequently commented on the percentage of foreign born in the nation and the birth rates of the foreign born.[39] Madison Grant, referred to as the "high Priest of racialism in America,"[40] placed his hope in the Nordic race and warned of the "dangerous foreign races ... [who] in the insidious guise of beggars at our gates, [plead] for admittance to share our prosperity. If we continue to allow them to enter they will in time drive us out of our own land by mere force of breeding." In his introduction to Lothrop Stoddard's 1920 book *The Rising Tide of Color against White World-Supremacy*, he continued: "The great hope of the future here in America lies in the realization of the working class that competition of the Nordic with the alien is fatal, whether the latter be the lowly immigrant from southern or eastern Europe or whether he be the more obviously dangerous Oriental against whose standards of living the white man cannot compete. In this country we must look to such of our people — our farmers and artisans— as are still of American blood to recognize and meet this danger."[41] Stoddard himself concluded that immigration of centuries past had been beneficial: "Migration peopled Europe with superior white stocks displacing ape-like aborigines, and settled North America with Nordics instead of nomad redskins." However, recent immigration, in which the United States had been "deluged by the truly alien hordes of the European east and south," would have a detrimental effect on American culture, institutions, and religion.[42] Henry F. Suksdorf maintained that the Anglo-Saxon race that provided the best characteristics of America, acknowledging that immigration of Germans, Scandinavians, Dutch, and Celts undoubtedly had some effect on "shaping the physical, intellectual and moral character" of the nation, though not necessarily detrimental. However, the recent influx of immigrants from southern and eastern Europe presented imminent danger. According to Suksdorf, "It is the imperative duty of the statesmen and legislators ... to invite and admit immigration from progressive countries only."[43]

Virtually all race theorists placed Africans and Asians in the lowest categories, but they did not appear to threaten American culture at this point in history, at least not the urban culture of the northern and northeastern United States at this time. The threat of Asians had already been addressed through the Chinese Exclusion Act of 1882.[44] African-Americans had been sufficiently kept "in their place" through Jim Crow Laws and denial of voting rights and had not yet threatened to change demographics in northern cities because mass migration had just begun.[45] Consequently, the majority of attention was directed at southern and eastern

Europeans. The most virulent American race theorist of the early twentieth century was Madison Grant, who in his 1916 *The Passing of the Great
Race* demonstrated little concern for Asians and blacks. Rather, his attacks
were directed at the new immigrant of inferior quality that threatened
American culture.[46]

It is important to acknowledge the power of race theory as a contributing factor in the birth control movement, which would in turn draw
reactions from the religious forces present in the United States. When taking stands on birth control, religious spokespersons would often touch on
race theory, at least indirectly, because of its prevalence in discussions of
population. But race theory is even more directly connected to the religious debate over birth control, as race categories reflected natural denominational divisions. The Nordics and Anglos of northern Europe were
notably Protestant, while the Alpines of central and eastern Europe, and
the Mediterraneans of southern Europe were notably Catholic and often
Jewish. The dividing lines between superior and inferior races would also
serve as a dividing line between Protestants and non–Protestants.[47]

## *Eugenics*

Though Malthusian arguments reflecting numbers and resources continue to influence birth control policy even today, it was the eugenic ideal
of Malthusianism and the emergence of the new "science" of eugenics that
had the greater influence on population theory and policy in the early years
of the twentieth century. In this age of science many believed that "scien-
tifically proven" methods of management, which could be applied to the
workplace, social service organizations, and home economics, should also
be applied to population. To many, progress had laid the groundwork for
understanding who was fit to produce offspring, and eventually they saw
that contraceptive technology could aid in producing a more civilized
race.

The study of eugenics began late in the nineteenth century as an out-
growth of Darwin's theories of natural selection and Austrian Augustin-
ian monk Gregor Mendel's experimentation with heredity and genetics in
plants. Darwin's descriptions of survival of the fittest had been embraced
by the scientific community, as well as by social and economic theorists who
applied the principle to domestic and global trends. However, observers
questioned the possibility of applying the findings to humans when they saw
what appeared as an imminent takeover by the "unfit." Eugenicists blamed
inefficient breeding. The good stock had practiced family limitation,

through whatever means, while the inferior stock was breeding dispro-portionately.[48]

British anthropologist Sir Francis Galton, a cousin of Darwin, laid the foundations for the "science" of eugenics with his works *Hereditary Genius* (1869) and *Inquiries into Human Faculty* (1883),and founded the Eugenics Society in 1908. The eugenics movement gained momentum in the early twentieth century in Britain, Germany, and the United States as the result of the increased concern over the "quality" of the human race. All of the major universities were supporting breeding experiments in plants and animals and requiring courses in eugenics. By 1910 Mendelian genetics was widely accepted in the study of humans, and eugenicists worked under the assumption that all important characteristics were bio-logically determined.[49]

By 1911 the movement in the United States was being led by some of the nation's most prominent and influential men, as seen from this list of officers of the Eugenics Section of the American Breeders' Association: David Starr Jordan, Stanford University; Alexander Graham Bell; Luther Burbank; W. E. Castle, Harvard University; Charles R. Henderson, Uni-versity of Chicago; and Adolf Meyer, John Hopkins University.[50] Much of the sentiment of this organization can be seen in the writing of Charles B. Davenport, who served as secretary, in his opening paragraph of an arti-cle for *Popular Science Monthly*:

> It does not seem right that there should always be about 3 per cent of our population on the sick list, that our alms houses should support over 80,000 paupers, not to mention the hun-dreds of thousands that receive outdoor relief or are barely able to earn a living; and that there should be 80,000 persons in prison. It ought not to be that the nation should have to sup-port half a million insane, feeble-minded, deaf and blind and that a hundred million dollars should be spent annually by insti-tutions in this country for the care of the sick, degenerate, defective and delinquent.[51]

The continued decline in the birthrate among the "well-bred" and the comparatively high birthrate among the lower classes gave further strength to the movement in the United States.[52]

In addition, new scientific understandings of epidemiology suggested that syphilis and other venereal diseases were being transmitted to off-spring at a record pace, contributing to what eugenicists considered a decay of the human race. Applications of similar conclusions concerning hered-ity to instances of "feeblemindedness" and "criminality" were also on the rise. The drive for professionalization and further legitimization of social sciences such as sociology and psychology also played roles in this focus on scientific understanding and betterment of family structure and function, and many of the proposed solutions were based in eugenics. In 1911 the New York State Board of Charities established a Bureau of Analysis and Investigation with regard to eugenics, in order to gather statistics regarding the "dependent, defective and delinquent classes."[53]

The American Sociological Society had formed in 1906, and much of its early discussion surrounded Social Darwinism and eugenics.[54] To Social Darwinists of the late nineteenth century, natural selection should work to eliminate the unfit.[55] After the turn of the century Social Darwinists claimed that charity toward the poor and weak had "virtually suspended the selective death rate.... Instead of allowing nature to kill them in the old way, we, on the contrary, protect and preserve the unfit to the best of our ability." Adding to the problem were statistics pointing to a declining birthrate among the upper classes, while the lower-class birthrate remained high.[56] This concern over charity increasingly drew Catholicism into the debate as Catholics were viewed as overly sentimental and unrealistic in giving to the poor. By the early twentieth century, the idea of supporting the "well-born" over the "dependent" had become prevalent among some British and American Protestants who viewed Catholics as short-sighted and contributing to the degeneration of civilization.[57]

In addition to charity, socialist tendencies were blamed for undermining natural selection.[58] Social Darwinists would naturally oppose socialism in the world of economics, for they saw natural selection as reigning supreme in a good system of free market capitalism. When applying their theories to society in general, they saw socialism as a directive to aid the lower classes—a segment of the population that should be allowed to die off.[59] But by the turn of the century, Social Darwinist arguments were losing out to the power of the eugenics movement. First, notions of scientific engineering, planning, and social control prevailed throughout American society; and second, the "high level of propagation" among the "unfit" was viewed as a failure of natural selection, which called for human intervention.[60] For Progressives, racial improvement was an important element of social reform and deserving of special attention.[61] Much of the argument over birth control was rooted in disagreements over which form this human intervention should take.

Sangerists argued that legalization of contraceptives was the solution and tried to persuade the Eugenics Society to join their campaign. Sanger claimed: "Birth control ... is nothing more or less than the facilitation of the process of weeding out the unfit [and] of preventing the birth of defectives.... If we are to make racial progress, this development of woman-hood must precede motherhood in every individual woman. Then and then only can the mother cease to be an incubator and be a mother indeed. Then only can she transmit to her sons and daughters the qualities which make strong individuals and, collectively, a strong race."[62] But eugenicists argued that legalizing contraceptives—what they often referred to simply as neo–Malthusianism — would be more destructive because availability might encourage parents of "worthy hereditary qualities" to limit their family size even more than they already had and because "defectives of the lower types do not greatly limit sex indulgence by the fear of having children, nor do they resort to artificial means to prevent conception."[63] Other possible solutions considered by eugenicists were laissez-faire, euthanasia, and polygamy — all of which they denounced: laissez-faire because it was ineffective, euthanasia because it was undesirable, and polygamy because it was morally impractical in American society. They did propose, however, various means of sterilization, segregation, and public education regarding the purpose of marriage.[64]

One of the most widely used measures, and considerably radical by today's standards, was involuntary sterilization. In order to prevent the propagation of the unfit, in particular convicted criminals, numerous states, beginning with Indiana, passed sterilization laws. Eugenicists had convinced legislators that criminality and other undesirable traits were passed on genetically, and though segregation of those exhibiting criminal behavior would aid in preventing a new generation of criminals, vasectomy, castration, and tubal ligation were better guarantees. Between 1905 and 1922 thirty bills allowing the sterilization of institutionalized persons were passed in eighteen states, and tens of thousands of mentally disabled or mentally ill were sterilized.[65]

The fact that sanctioned compulsory sterilization could exist to the extent that it did in the United States is a tribute to the powerful influence of eugenics theory, but as widespread as they were, sterilization programs did not proceed without criticism. Still, not even the most severe critics seemed to consider the practice barbaric. Rather, they referred to it simply as "negative eugenics" and made alternative suggestions for "positive eugenics." Many considered the segregation of the mentally ill or disabled from society, by placing them in institutions a more rational solution. Others sought solutions in the prevention of marriage of the unfit. But that, too, was considered negative eugenics.

When the lower class was considered in more general terms—the poor, unemployed, even immigrant, others sought solutions to simply limiting their family size in one way or another.[66] To birth control advocates, this would require the legalization of contraceptives. But critics considered this a form of negative eugenics as well.

The only true method of "positive eugenics" was the call for higher birth rates among the upper class. Early in the debate, after demographic fears intensified but before birth control advocates had made any headway, proponents argued that the upper classes should take note of their own falling birth rates and have more children. One of the most prominent spokesmen for such a position was Theodore Roosevelt, who maintained that propagation was a primary responsibility of the better stock. Roosevelt condemned the conscious restriction of the birthrate on any level as "race suicide." [67] He also viewed it as unrealistic: "[I]mprovement must be wrought mainly by favoring the fecundity of the worthy types and frowning on the fecundity of the unworthy types. At present we do just the reverse. There is no check to the fecundity of those who are subnormal, both intellectually and morally, while the provident and the thrifty tend to develop a cold selfishness, which makes them refuse to breed at all."[68] Roosevelt's comment that there was "no check to the fecundity" of the inferior did not lead to an endorsement of legalized contraceptives. Rather he believed, as did many eugenicists, that availability would likely result in a further decrease among the superior.

But others viewed Roosevelt's call for middle- and upper-class women to breed more as unrealistic. Feminists such as Charlotte Perkins Gilman were tuned in keenly to contemporary discussions of class and family size and rejected notions of "forcing" upper-class women to have more babies.[69] Gilman's solution for improving the quality of humans did not lie in more prolific breeding by "desirables" nor in restricting the family size of "undesirables." Rather, her answer lay in improving the conditions of the city. Furthermore, she deplored the condemnation of the "other class," claiming "humanity is *one*; a living tissue; and our need to make better people is the most vital, the most personal need that can be shown to any human soul."[70] Interestingly, this is essentially the same position that the Catholic Church would ultimately take.

## *Public Education—Eugenics and Marriage*

Whatever the solution might be, public education was viewed as fundamental. This eventually took many forms, but incorporated early on was sex education for the nation's youth. Social workers and charity administrators supported programs to teach teenagers and young adults about sex and sex hygiene, both as a means to curb the spread of venereal disease, which was understood as a major contributing factor in race degeneracy, and to help them become aware of the "responsibility of parenthood."[71] Teaching the "responsibility of parenthood" served as the means to bring the science of eugenics from the academic world into practice within the general population. As a result, sex education programs were developed among the working class in urban areas, in response to the social ills of the city.[72] As early as 1910 Dr. G. Stanley Hall, president of Clark University and ardent supporter of the eugenics movement, recommended sex education in the schools, as well as in organizations such as the Young Men's Christian Association, to encourage the "betterment of the race."[73] Some even encouraged that Sunday schools take on the responsibility of teaching, as this was one of the duties of religion.[74] One of the first public objections to the widespread call for sex education was heard from a Catholic spokesman, not because of the content, but because of the manner in which it was being presented. According to Rev. Richard H. Tierney, S.J., a professor of philosophy at Woodstock College in Woodstock, Maryland, this should not consist merely of the imparting of information but should include the teaching of the virtues of self-control, modesty, and a reverence for women.[75] This sentiment prevailed among many Catholic and conservative non-Catholics, while liberals and moderates viewed the situation as serious enough to warrant candid discussion.

Writing articles for popular magazines of the day was another method eugenicists used to encourage the public to participate in better breeding. Examples are seen in two 1912 *Ladies' Home Journal* articles entitled "What Is Meant by Eugenics?" and "When a Girl Is Asked to Marry: Why It Is the Most Important Moment in Her Life," urging positive eugenics through "proper marriage." The articles noted that we should also "do all we can to discourage the mating of persons whom Nature had stamped as unfit."[76] Some of the most blatant appeals for eugenics measures, whether because of the feared decline of the race, perception of future generations of criminality, or the financial and social costs of maintaining degenerates, called for the regulation of marriage as a necessary and practical solution.[77] Havelock Ellis, a prominent British social theorist, researcher in the field of sexuality, and intimate friend of Sanger had urged marriage regulation as early as 1906. He promoted eugenics noting that the once held belief that the "Anglo-Saxon would increase and multiply until he covered the whole earth is a thing of the past." Ellis called for stricter marriage laws, claiming that procreation should not be left to chance, and said that in order to ensure responsibility in choosing a mate, couples should appear before a board of examiners.[78]

This emphasis on marriage became the heart of much of the religious debate over birth control. First, most advocates of legalized contraceptives, for as radical as they might have seemed at the time, were promoting the use of artificial means of preventing pregnancy only among couples who were married. Second, discussions of the ideals of marriage, the purpose of marriage, and the prevention of marriage were inspired by social scientists but considered the ultimate responsibility of the churches. Americans continued to look to clergy to perform wedding ceremonies, and as the secular and spiritual examinations of marriage flourished, clergy would speak to individual couples, congregations, and the public at large about marriage. In reaction to the rising divorce rate, parish priests, ministers, and rabbis, as well as clerical authorities and theologians, addressed the "ideals of marriage." In reaction to the growing public debate surrounding birth control, they examined their own doctrines regarding procreation, while taking into account modern ideas about companionship and conjugal love when they addressed the "purpose of marriage." And demands from secular society regarding eugenics forced clergy to become involved in the "prevention of marriage." Ultimately, what mainstream religion and the dominant American culture would condone was a kind of marriage that allowed for some control over conception that would benefit society.

## Eugenics and Contraception

Marriage regulations served as only one solution, and a limited one. Soon the use of contraceptives would be promoted as an additional means to prevent degeneracy. Though the Eugenics Society did not officially condone the work of birth control advocates until the 1930s, members from both camps held similar philosophies. While it is true that birth control, or reproductive choice as we know it today, has been an important factor in women's liberation, the eugenics aspect of the birth control movement cannot be denied. The very term "birth control," coined by Sanger herself, carries with it a strong sense of social control, as opposed to the term "voluntary motherhood" used by Mary Ware Dennett.

But in looking at statements by birth control advocates of the period, we see more direct and obvious connections than that. Margaret Sanger's discussion of birth control, in the first issue of her monthly, *The Woman Rebel* in March 1914, promoted it as a right denied to the lower middle class. "The woman of the upper middle class has all available knowledge and implements to prevent conception [but] the woman of the lower middle class is struggling for this knowledge."[79] In the same issue Sanger's friend and associate, the socialist Emma Goldman, presented a more radical position in an article entitled "Love and Marriage," in which she decries the demands of "king, president, capitalist and priest" to preserve the race. Goldman, like many other socialists, maintained that high birthrates among the working class acted to serve the needs of the capitalist class. At the same time, however, she agreed that this birthrate was contributing to race degeneracy: "Woman no longer wants to be a party to the production of a race of sickly, feeble, decrepit, wretched human beings, who would have neither the strength nor moral courage to throw off the yoke of poverty and slavery."[80]

In the following issue *The Woman Rebel* described the prevalence of unfit among the working class, proclaiming, "Statistics tell us that more than 150,000 children in the United States, under 5 years of age, die each year, the greatest number by far being the offspring of working women. It is the foreign women who maintain and increase the population in America. The higher woman goes into social and intellectual life, the less is she inclined to become a child-bearing machine for any flag."[81] And, "If all the children could be gathered together from the orphanages, jails and reformatories, together with the crippled and feeble-minded, the child victims of the cotton and silk mills and the sweated home industries, this huge army of little victims would open the eyes of the working woman to the realization that she must take the matters into her own hands and decide whether she wants to add to this number of unfortunates."[82]

Throughout *The Woman Rebel* there are references to religion in general standing in the way of progress by maintaining superstitions and promoting ignorance among the people. The publication's subheading, "No Gods, No Masters," symbolizes the atheism promoted by many radicals and most socialists of the period. But ultimately the Catholic Church in particular would incur the wrath of the birth control movement.

At this point Catholic spokespersons became more defensive in their position, as they perceived birth control advocates as attacking groups of people represented among their members. After publication of *The Woman Rebel* was prohibited, Sanger continued similar portrayals of the lower class and by 1919, even though she resisted supporting the eugenics movement publicly, claimed that "all our problems are the result of overbreeding among the working class."[83] Three years earlier in Chicago, when the Chicago Woman's Club denied her an audience by turning down her offer to speak, she responded by speaking to a group of fifteen hundred in the Stockyard District instead. She noted the importance of enlightening "the women of the stockyards, the women of the factories. ... I am interested in birth control among working women chiefly."[84]

Marie Stopes, the most celebrated birth control activist in Britain, was strongly influenced by both Sanger's work and eugenicists.[85] Stopes saw widespread disease and disability among the lower classes and believed that society would benefit if they could be persuaded not to breed.[86] In her 1920 book, *Radiant Motherhood*, Stopes wrote that "the middle and superior artisan classes" who paid taxes were reduced to "the position of ancient slave and allowed to [have] but one or two children as the result perhaps of a lifetime of valuable service ... while on the other hand society allows the diseased, the racially negligent, the careless, the feeble-minded, the very lowest and the worst members of the community to produce innumerable tens of thousands of warped and inferior infants."[87]

Throughout her career Stopes met with opposition from clergy who condemned birth control. The feeling was mutual. Never an admirer of the Catholic Church, Stopes grew increasingly anti–Catholic — her feelings exemplified in the following poem:

> Catholics, Prussians,
> The Jews and the Russians,
> Are all a curse
> Or something worse ...[88]

## The State of Religion in America

It is impossible to remove religion from the discussion of preventing conception because of the subject's very nature. But more important, the character of religion in early-twentieth-century America itself played a tremendous role in helping to shape the debate. While numerous factors within the complex religious atmosphere of the United States made the debate a multifaceted one, there were two primary forces at that time deserving of particular attention. First, religion was playing a primary role in tackling social problems; second, the religious environment in this period was one that created more conflict than consensus.

Following the Civil War, Protestantism in America had been notably influenced by modern industrial society, the changing urban condition and the development of scientific thought.[89] In many respects church leaders found themselves responding to the ills that had emerged in the nation's cities. Initially, they stayed within the existing framework of traditional Christian doctrine when establishing children's aid societies, for example, or inner city missions. But the movement gained momentum, developing into an ambitious program of social reform. This movement was referred to as social Christianity, or the social gospel, in which the nation's leading Protestants sought to create a Kingdom of God on earth. Though not the first such attempt in Christian history, American Protestants viewed this nation as having all the necessary elements to make it possible: egalitariansim, democracy, abundance of resources, wealth, and Christianity.[90]

By the late nineteenth century, socially conscious Protestants incorporated science, scientific management principles, the value of expertise, and the establishment of committees and agencies to carry out their reform programs. They embraced the notion that God had given humanity the gift of science and that humanity should use it to improve society. This was rooted in an acceptance of Darwinism, that the human species was continually evolving, that life on earth was continually getting better, that humanity was progressing. To these Protestants, science and religion were not at all at odds with one another; rather God was forever present in the human process and the achievements of human beings — the immanence of God, they called it. By the turn of the century, the nation's leading Protestants viewed themselves as the spiritual guides of progressivism and modernism.[91]

But they did not represent all Protestants, and the deeper their convictions became embedded in modernism and the belief that they represented themselves as holding the world's future in their hands, the deeper the battle lines were drawn between themselves and their critics. The "establishment" denominations were primarily seven: Congregationalists, Episcopalians, Presbyterians, Baptists, Methodists, the Disciples of Christ, and the United Lutherans. They are considered "mainline," representing a majority in the Federal and National Councils of Churches, formed to unify America's denominations and to direct social programs.[92] Because of their programs of social action, these "establishment" denominations were also referred to as "liberal" denominations — for they spearheaded progressivism and therefore liberalism.[93]

But for the sake of clarity, it is important to recognize that there were denominations more liberal than those. The Unitarians and Universalists, for example, more readily adapted teaching and transformed positions to reflect a changing society, and though fewer in numbers, they would be instrumental in the religious shift toward condoning the use of contraceptives. Furthermore, it is essential to recognize that there were numerous divisions among the major denominations, particularly among Baptists, Methodists, and Presbyterians. The clearest divisions lay between Northern Baptists and Southern Baptists, Northern Methodists and Southern Methodists, and Northern Presbyterians and Southern Presbyterians. The northern denominations tended to be more involved in addressing the cities' social ills, naturally because the nation's primary urban centers were located in the north, but, very important, through their social action they tended to embrace modernism. This placed them in direct confrontation with their southern counterparts, who tended to be fundamentalist, adhering to literal translations of the Bible and rejecting doctrinal changes in response to a changing world, which wreaked of modernism. Since the antebellum period, when southern Protestants split over the abolitionist controversy, most insisted on adhering to the spiritual nature of the gospel and rejected "worldly" applications.[94] Though some historians have argued that southerners did participate in carrying out the social gospel, in dealing with such issues as child labor, education, and prisons,[95] others have contended that fundamentalists in general, and premillennialists such as Jehovah's Witnesses, Seventh Day Adventists, and Pentecostals, were hostile to social reform and that the resurgence of fundamentalism that the United States experienced in the first two decades of the twentieth century was a reaction to the modernist approaches of social gospellers.[96]

Regarding developments in the cities, Southern Baptists did comment on the

> appearance of a teeming and crowded population in the poorer districts of the city, made up in part of Americans who are dragging in the mire of godlessness, the moral and religious standards of the fathers, and in part of foreigners who have never known a pure Christianity, and have not lived according to the ideals of our American Christian civilization — a teeming and crowded population which increases and spreads rapidly, spreads out in all directions, touches the life of the city at many points, and wherever it goes carries the taint of its low standards of life and morals.

Their solution would not lie in birth control, rather in evangelization: "Evangelize these foreigners and you evangelize the cities. Evangelize the cities and you evangelize the nation. Evangelize the nation and you do much to evangelize the world."[97]

Complicating the picture were the Northern Baptists, Methodists, and Presbyterians who were fundamentalist and wished to focus on the spiritual, sparking serious debate in urban America.[98] America's Lutherans, numerous and divided, did not generally engage extensively in social reform, choosing to emphasize personal ethics rather than social ethics. The complicated nature of Lutheranism and social policy in the United States stemmed from historical developments, as well as doctrinal differences. For example, Lutherans failed to become involved in the social gospel movement because many of them were foreign born, which would have made them recipients of the social gospel, except for the fact that they lived primarily in rural areas. In addition Scandinavian Lutherans supported prohibition, but German Lutherans would not.[99] And the fundamentalist Missouri Synod Lutherans resembled conservative Christian Reformed who, along with other fundamentalists, publicly decried the social gospel.[100]

Second only to Catholics in demanding attention in the religious birth control debate were Episcopalians. Episcopalians were not remarkably numerous nor particularly aggressive in their politics or social action,[101] but they were an integral part of the worldwide Anglican Communion, which represented the Church of England, Church of Ireland, Church of Wales, and the Scottish Episcopal Church, as well as the Protestant Episcopal Church in the United States and the Anglican Churches in the British dominions and colonies. Representing the Anglo upper class around the globe, the Anglican Communion made some of the earliest pronouncements supporting eugenics, Malthusianism, and race theory, which fed into the birth control movement.[102]

America's religious diversity eventually molds the public debate over birth control and the legalization of contraceptives into one of both theological and political depth, as the major players continually attack and are called on to defend their positions. As mainline Protestant America pushes toward a modernist approach, ultimately seeing birth control as a solution to society's ills, fundamentalists will hold onto their traditional criticism, seeking biblical quotations to support their claims. But although the theological and doctrinal aspects of the debate are instrumental in the shift toward legalization, the influence of America's religious-political atmosphere in this period, particularly reflecting immigration trends and changing demographics, cannot be denied. For example, place into this already complex mix American Judaism.

Jews had been arriving in America, largely from Central Europe, since the early years of colonization. Their faith had been challenged from time to time by evangelical Christians and controversy over "Sabbath laws," for example, instituted in the nineteenth century, but they generally "fit" into American society.[103] Very important, their numbers had not been large enough to pose a threat to Protestant America. However, that would change. Beginning in 1881 and 1882, pogroms against Jews in Eastern Europe spurred a new great migration to the United States. This wave of institutionalized anti–Semitism, in combination with poverty and dislocation during World War I, contributed to a four-decade-long flow of Jewish immigration. In 1880 approximately 250,000 Jews lived in the United

States, but by 1920 nearly 2,000,000 more had arrived.[104] These numbers contributed to the perceived threat to the traditional American population.

Furthermore, these new Jewish immigrants were different from their predecessors, who were generally liberal Reform Jews and who had dispersed throughout the United States, often into rural areas. The new immigrants, on the other hand, were more conservative, holding more tightly onto their religion and their Eastern European culture, and remained primarily in the cities of the northern and northeastern United States. To the native population they appeared very "ethnic" and far less likely to assimilate, and to a large extent this was true.[105] Meeting their needs was the newly formed conservative branch of Judaism. The attitudes of Reform Jews had become too liberal in some eyes, to the point that Jews had mixed so well into American culture that they appeared to have lost their faith altogether. On the other hand, they were not willing to conform to the ways of the Orthodox, who had largely arrived during the seventeenth century. The compromise was a new denomination — Conservative Judaism.[106]

The existence of three branches of Judaism adds to the complexity of theological debate in the United States that would carry over into questions of contraception and birth control. Orthodox pronouncements would resemble fundamentalist Christian pronouncements, with adherence to traditional teaching. Reform discussion and decisions would reflect the modernist shift, adapting birth control teaching to the present day. Conservatives would lie somewhere in between. But again, theology cannot be isolated from the political and social nature of the Jewish contraceptive debate. Reform rabbis, and the liberal Jewish leadership in general, resembled many Protestant social gospellers, as they took their humanitarian role very seriously, using Scripture and science to improve society.[107] More important, Jewish identity itself, particularly by the turn of the century, could not be confined to "religion." Rather, with the rise of race theory Jews became identified more clearly as members of a particular race.[108] Anti-Semitism in the United States was never as intense as it was in Europe, where it became government-sanctioned.[109] In American race theory Jews were simply included among the inferior races— those not Anglo-Saxon or Nordic.[110]

American Catholicism was undergoing its own examination of modernism, attempting to come to terms with Darwinism and modern scientific thought, as liberal Catholic spokesperson called for the Church in the United States to "adapt itself to the values of the modern American republic, including separation of church and state, and liberty of conscience and religious belief."[111] By 1919 a papal official claimed that "Rome now looks to America to be the leader in all things Catholic, and to set an example to other nations."[112] The Church was under constant attack for standing in the way of modernism, but it did not fit into the camp of fundamentalism. Strong fundamentalist denominations, Southern Baptists and Southern Methodists for example, were strongly anti–Catholic. Modernists criticized Catholic doctrine, viewing it as dogmatic and unchanging. But doctrine did not serve as the primary point of contention. In the birth control debate, the Catholic position differed little from that of any other denomination early on and from that of fundamentalists later. The biggest fear lay in the potential power of the Church as a political force.

## Religion and Immigration Fears

The politics of the Church in America met with scrutiny from the early settlement of the primarily Protestant British colonies. Maryland was established in 1642 as a place of tolerance — the only official Catholic colony in North America — while prejudice against Catholics, ranging from distrust to condemnation, persisted in other colonies from Massachusetts to the Carolinas. Protestants were suspicious of the Church for a number of reasons, including its preservation of a strong hierarchy — viewed as authoritarian and undemocratic by its very nature. This criticism of authoritarianism fed into modernist condemnations of the Church in the early twentieth century, as democratic ideals shaped the battle cry of Progressivism. But historical developments in America resulted in more serious anti–Catholicism during the first century of nationhood.[113]

First, the era of intense nationalism and national pride, which fed American strength and expansionism during the mid-nineteenth century, glorified everything that was American. National borders and presidential authority helped to define American patriotism. As a result, the political roles of the Vatican and the pope were called into question. For traditionally Protestant America, the allegiance of the nation's Catholics was unclear at best, for religiously they appeared to be under an international directive. As the percentage of Catholics in America began to rise in mid-century, this fear grew even stronger. Beginning in the 1840s, a new wave of immigration began in the United States, stemming from the potato famine in Ireland and political upheaval in Germany. Many of the hundreds of thousands of newcomers were Catholic,[114] giving rise to significant anti–Catholicism by the 1850s, manifesting itself in a national political party referred to as the "Know-Nothings."[115] And in subsequent decades the number of Catholic immigrants continued to rise.

American industrialization and European economic and political problems encouraged a continual flow of immigrants in the latter part of the century, changing America's demographic makeup tremendously, especially in the cities. By just after the turn of the century, public reports warned of a growing Catholic influence in America, further questioning the allegiance of Catholics and the Vatican's view of America. According to an *Independent* editorial of 1913, the form of American government "has been and still is formally condemned by the church of Rome," which had "repeatedly attacked the free will of the people."[116] Vatican appointments of three new American cardinals, bringing the total number to four, drew criticism from the nation's Protestants. The move was referred to as a "crushing defeat for modernism,"[117] while others warned that the "last battle of the Reformation" would be fought on American soil.[118] Boston's *Zion's Herald*, a voice of New England's Methodists, viewed the appointments as a strategic move by the pope to make the United States the "first Catholic nation of the world." It called on Methodists to "meet the challenge," because Methodism, "as perhaps no other church among the Protestant denominations, is fitted, by its agressiveness, its inheritance, and its natural genius, to meet and resist Roman Catholicism." For *Zion's Herald* the solution lay in evangelizing to "foreigners ... to save them to a pure Biblical Christianity."[119]

While it is true that Catholic immigrants, particularly the Irish, made their way into the political sphere in cities such as New York and Boston,[120] the fears of Catholic domination most often expressed stemmed from continued immigration and family size among those immigrants. According to *Literary Digest* in 1912, there were more Catholics in the United States than there were members of any other single denomination, with 12.6 million. Next were Methodists (6.8 million), Baptists (5.6 million), Lutherans (2.3 million), Presbyterians (1.9 million), Episcopalians (950,000), Christian Reformed (450,000), Latter Day Saints (400,650), United Brethren (312,000), Dunkard Brethren (123,677), Friends (122,796); and Adventists (95,764).[121] Within months a subsequent article stated that the Catholic population was even higher than previously reported, with 2.8 million in New York alone, 1.6 million in Pennsylvania, 1.5 million in Illinois, and 1.4 million in Massachusetts.[122]

According to New York Baptist minister Dr. Charles F. Aked, of the twenty-five million who immigrated to the United States between 1890 and 1910, between twelve million and fifteen million were Catholic. Aked described them as "a class of people who are the most prolific in this country, among whom the birth rate is immensely higher than in some other sections of the community," and for this reason he feared the "spiritual tyranny of Rome."[123] The Presbyterian Ministers' Association of New York, which fought for "cordiality of Catholics and Protestants toward each other," attempted to calm fears, reminding Americans that "our nation was born a Protestant nation, several of the original thirteen colonies exclusively Protestant, and has attained its present high place as a Protestant nation."[124] But even Father Bernard Vaughan, who helped to celebrate the consecration of New York's St. Patrick's Cathedral (viewed as an opulent symbol of Catholic strength in America), boasted of the growing number of Catholics: "Try to restrain the growth of the Church. You may do it when you have held up the falls of Niagra; when, with an extinguisher you have quenched the forest fire; when, my brethren, with a little shovel you have flung back the mountain avalanches."[125]

Even if birth control advocates did not directly call for family limitation among the nation's Catholics, this constant reminder of numbers helped to fuel the fire of the birth control debate. Criticism of the anti-modern, authoritative, hierarchical, and political nature of the Church would portray Catholics as standing in the way of the movement. The perception that Catholics would soon outnumber Protestants, real or imagined, suggested they were procreating more rapidly for that very reason. But the qualitative judgments against immigrants who happened to be Catholic shaped the debate into one that would incorporate eugenics, social reform, and religion. Take into account, for example, the description of immigrant neighborhoods by the Reverend Edward Judson, pastor of New York's Memorial Baptist Church: "Children swarm in the streets like rabbits in a warren. Night and day one is confronted by the hideous spectres of prostitution, pauperism, drunkenness and crime ... [and] alien races jostle each other, Latin, Celt, Slavic, Semitic."[126] Even though no denominations condoned the use of contraceptives or the use of birth control at this time, this kind of description from the religious community eventually helped to divide the religious camps in the debate that was to unfold.

On one level, the relationship between religion and birth control remained devoted to the morality of personal behavior. However, the political struggle that was rooted in demographic change in the United States by 1920 forced participants into a debate on a broader political level. The population shift from one that had forged a nation with a clear Protestant majority to one that appeared increasingly culturally chaotic with an inflow of immigrants who traditionally had large families would undeniably play a role in the religious birth control debate. According to some Protestants, those who actively prevented pregnancy would not only suffer personal consequences but would also contribute to political consequences.

The fear of a growing Catholic population, not only in the United

States but worldwide, was further exhibited in a *Current Opinion* article in 1915. According to the report, Protestant churches should become aware of population trends, noting that, according to Dr. Meyrick Booth, "Present-day Protestantism, which in practice stands for a declining birth-rate, is ... being driven back in all the great centers of civilization." The report blames the "influx of large masses of European Catholics who cling tenaciously to their religion, and to the much greater prolificity of these stocks as compared with the native population" for the population trend in the United States:

> The New England States, the original home of American Puritanism, are now important centers of Catholicism (Massachusetts shows 1,100,000 members of the Roman Catholic Church and 450,000 members of all Protestant Churches combined!). In Illinois there are about a million Roman Catholics, while the strongest Protestant body (the Methodists) cannot show more than 300,000 adherents. In New York state we find 2,300,000 Catholics and about 300,000 Methodists, while no other Protestant body numbers more than 200,000.[127]

This article, presented in this widely read, mainstream publication, serves as another powerful indicator of the fear of changing demographics. In any decade of American history the arrival of immigrants in large numbers would cause concern among those desiring to maintain the status quo in the United States. But this period marked the beginning of an even stronger era of nativism.[128] Fears of challenges to the culture because of newcomers were very visible, and what appeared to be ever-increasing numbers of Catholics posed a threat to those who wished to maintain a "Protestant" America. The nation faced political challenges as well, for in this democratic society, election results, from the local level to the national level, might be swayed by a strongly Catholic voting base.

Even though Jews were the objects of fear and scorn in the United States, the *Current Opinion* article demonstrates just how much greater the threat of Catholicism was than the threat of Judaism. A rare mention of Judaism appears in a researched report comparing family size among various religions. The investigation was conducted by the New York religious paper *Federation* and concluded that in New York City, Jews had the highest number of children per marriage, Roman Catholics the second highest, with orthodox Protestants, liberal Protestants and agnostics following.[129] The author appeared less concerned about Jews ranking highest in family size than about the overall increase in the number of Catholics. Prevailing fears were based in an awareness that real numbers of Catholics far outweighed the real numbers of Jews. There was concern that Jews now numbered one million in New York, but as it was primarily a matter of race,[130] there was no real fear that Jews were attempting to convert others, "unlike the religious training of Catholics."[131] Furthermore, Jews did not tend to migrate from New York to "other parts of the country."[132]

Though this article is valuable in that it clearly demonstrates the religious bigotry that abounded in the nation and the way in which contraception played a role in that bigotry, there is something problematic in the premise of the author's argument. It gives the impression that because "Protestantism ... stands for a declining birth rate," that Protestant religious doctrine must have approved of contraception. Indeed, the author concludes with a quote by a Protestant Dr. Booth: "If Protestant thinkers are alive to the gravity of the situation, is it not time that they should ask themselves very seriously the question: Are we prepared to accept this extreme Malthusianism, this anxious and drastic restriction of the family, as the true ideal of Christian marriage?"[133] The suggestion that Protestants condoned birth control was misleading because contraception was not officially sanctioned by any church. However, for those who understood "Protestantism" as more of a social concept, the connection became clear. Whether or not individuals were actively practicing birth control, Protestants had smaller families. Booth accurately recognized that acceptance of Malthusian ideals and the belief that smaller family size assured various benefits had permeated the Protestant segment of society. Nations that were industrialized, progressive, "civilized," and Protestant had experienced declining birthrates since the early nineteenth century, and Protestant attitudes had evolved.

Though leaders of various denominations had demonstrated their concern that members of their own congregations might be using contraceptives, it was impossible to determine just who was practicing contraception, which methods they were using, and what their religious affiliations were. Sanger and directors of other birth control clinics would eventually keep records of religious affiliation among their clients in an effort to prove to authorities that women would demand contraceptives regardless of official religious teaching. But at this point, the debate over legalization had not developed a religious focus. Sociologists addressed it more in terms of class. Middle- and upper-class women had greater access to contraceptive information, even when illegal, and they happened to be Protestant. In addition, the British roots of Malthusian philosophy would influence Anglo and northern and western European society more than others, helping to advance the practice of limiting births among the upper classes, who happened to be Protestant.

The growing fear of having too many Catholics in the United States is obvious from the *Literary Digest* and *Current Opinion* articles, making the religious/political concern clear. But it is important to recognize the emphasis placed on birthrates among non–Protestants. If the fear simply came down to numbers, more of an emphasis might be placed on evangelism or conversion of immigrants to Protestantism. Catholic clergy expressed their concern during these years that immigrants were often met by non–Catholic social workers and settlement-house workers on their entrance into the United States, and these clergy worked diligently to provide a "Catholic welcome" into their new homeland in order to prevent imigrants from losing their faith. Catholic universities worked to develop programs for sociology and social work majors that would compete with those provided in non-Catholic institutions. Still the element of "family size" drew a significant amount of attention. The article does not suggest the implementation of a program to limit the number of Catholics through birth control; rather it suggests that Protestants stop limiting the sizes of their families and start having more children. More important, however, is the article's reference to "these stocks," for the immigrants coming into the United States in large numbers from southern and eastern Europe were not only largely Catholic but considered of "lower stock."

Class played an increasingly prominent role in examinations of American society after the turn of the century and is reflected in U.S. census results. The classifications determined by the government in each census are some of the best indicators of national concerns, and the 1910 census was the first to use economic class as a category. Formerly designating "occupation," respondents were now required to note themselves as "employer," "self-employed," or "wage earner," as well as "native," "foreign," or "colored."[134] The concerns emphasized not only quantity but also quality and indicate the most basic standards by which mainstream America was judging quality. It is here where we see more of a link between Protestantism and eugenics.[135]

# Notes

1. Martin E. Marty, *Modern American Religion, Volume 2, The Noise of Conflict, 1919–1941* (Chicago: University of Chicago, Press, 1991), pp. 1–10. Also see Marty, *Modern American Religion, Volume 1, The Irony of It All, 1893–1919* (Chicago: University of Chicago Press, 1997); William R. Hutchison, ed., *Between the Times: The Travail of the Protestant Establishment in America, 1900–1960* (New York: Cambridge University Press, 1989); Robert Moats Miller, *American Protestantism and Social Issues: 1919–1939* (Chapel Hill: University of North Carolina Press, 1958); Donald B. Meyer, *The Protestant Search for American Realism: 1919–1941* (Berkeley: University of California Press, 1960); and Ferenc Morton Szasz, *The Divided Mind of Protestant America: 1880–1930* (Tuscaloosa: University of Alabama Press, 1982).

2. John M. Riddle, *Contraception and Abortion from the Ancient World to the Renaissance* (Cambridge, Mass.: Harvard University Press, 1992), p. 5; John M. Riddle, *Eve's Herbs: A History of Contraception and Abortion in the West* (Cambridge, Mass.: Harvard University Press, 1997), p. 89.

3. William H. Robertson, *An Illustrated History of Contraception: A Concise Account of the Quest for Fertility Control* (Park Ridge, N.J.: Parthenon Publishing Group, 1990), pp. 112–116.

4. Ellen Chesler, *Woman of Valor: Margaret Sanger and the Birth Control Movement in America* (New York: Simon and Schuster, 1992), pp. 35–37. For more on contraceptive methods available by the nineteenth century, see chapter 7 "The 'Most Fashionable' Contraceptive Devices" in Janet Farrell Brodie, *Contraception and Abortion in Nineteenth Century America* (Ithaca, N.Y.: Cornell University Press, 1994), pp. 204–252; Linda Gordon, *Woman's Body, Woman's Right: A Social History of Birth Control in America* (New York: Penguin, 1976); James Reed, *From Private Vice to Public Virtue: The Birth Control Movement in American Society* (New York: Basic Books, 1978); and Richard W. and Dorothy C. Wertz, *Lying-In: A History of Childbirth in America* (New Haven: Yale University Press, 1989). For primary sources on the subject, see Charles Rosenberg and Carroll Smith-Rosenberg, *Birth Control and Family Planning in Nineteenth Century America* (New York: Arno Press, 1974). For an extensive study of more general history, which became available later in the Sanger years, see Norman E. Himes, *Medical History of Contraception* (New York: Gamut Press, 1963 [1936]).

5. The primary research was conducted by French zoologist F. A. Pouchet in 1847 and American physician R. T. Trall in 1867.

6. For the first findings in spermicide research, see John R. Baker, "The Spermicidal Powers of Chemical Contraceptives I; Introduction, and Experiments on Guinea-Pig Sperms," *Journal of Hygiene* 29 (1929-1930), pp. 323–329. Also see Norman Himes, *Practical Birth Control Methods* (New York: n.p., 1938), pp. 69, 74–75.

7. For more on Victorian moralism in this matter, see Carroll Smith-Rosenberg, *Disorderly Conduct: Visions of Gender in Victorian America* (New York: Oxford University Press, 1985); S. Chandrasekhar, *"A Dirty, Filthy Book": The Writings of Charles Knowlton and Annie Basant on Reproductive Physiology and Birth Control and an Account of the Bradlaugh-Besant Trial* (Berkeley: University of California Press, 1981); David Pivar, *Purity Crusade: Sexual Morality and Social Control, 1868–1900* (Westport, Conn.: Greenwood Press, 1973); and David J. Rothman and Sheila M. Rothman, eds., *Birth Control and Morality in Nineteenth Century America: Two Discussions* (New York: Arno Press, 1972).

8. "Act of Incorporation," *First Annual Report of the New York Society for the Suppression of Vice, Feb. 11, 1875*. The annual reports laud their own efforts and describe the extent to which members would go to conduct raids and "aid police." For another laudatory perspective, see Charles Trumbull, *Anthony Comstock, Fighter* (New York: Fleming H. Revel, 1913). For criticsm see William Lee Curry, "Comstockery: A Study in the Rise and Decline of a Watchdog Censorship," Ph.D. dissertation, Columbia University, 1957; Brodie, pp. 253–266.

9. Reed, p. 391; *Congressional Globe*, 1873, p. 297.

10. Edward Bristow, *Purity Movements in Britain Since 1700* (London: Gillard MacMillan, 1977), pp. 100–104, 136–140; Pivar, pp. 111–114.

11. Madeline Gray, *Margaret Sanger: A Biography of the Champion of Birth Control* (New York: Richard Marek, 1979), pp. 62–63, 77–78; Chesler, pp. 97–98, 102–103.

12. Lawrence Lader, *The Margaret Sanger Story and the Fight for Birth Control* (Westport, Conn.: Greenwood Press, 1955), p. 67.

13. Barbara J. Harris, *Beyond Her Sphere: Women and the Professions in American History* (Westport, Conn.: Greenwood Press, 1978), pp. 98–104; Mabel Newcomer, *A Century of Higher Education for Women* (New York: Harper & Brothers, 1959), pp. 22–32.

14. Rosalind Rosenberg, *Beyond Separate Spheres: Intellectual Roots of Modern Feminism* (New Haven, Conn.: Yale University Press, 1982), p. 54. Also see Sarah Grand, "The New Aspect of the Woman Question," *North American Review* 158 (March 1894), pp. 270–276.

15. Rosenberg, pp. 179–182.

16. Sara M. Evans, *Born for Liberty: A History of Women in America* (New York: Free Press, 1989), pp. 177–178; Mari Jo Buhle, *Women and American Socialism, 1870–1920* (Urbana: University of Illinois Press, 1981), pp. 257–265.

17. Robert Wiebe, *The Search for Order, 1877–1920* (New York: Hill and Wang, 1967),

pp. 137–145, 153–154. Also see Sean Dennis Cashman, *America in the Gilded Age: From the Death of Lincoln to the Rise of Theodore Roosevelt* (New York: New York University Press, 1988), pp. 351–363; Richard Hofstadter, *The Age of Reform: From Bryan to FDR* (New York: Alfred A. Knopf, 1955), pp. 216–223.

18. Cited in Robertson, pp. 90–91.

19. Constance M. Chen, *"The Sex Side of Life": Mary Ware Dennett's Pioneering Battle for Birth Control and Sex Education* (New York: New Press, 1996), pp. 205–222; Chesler, p. 63.

20. Reed, pp. 162, 220, 222. For the Chicago story see Kathleen Tobin-Schlesinger, "The Changing American City: Chicago Catholics and the Birth Control Movement, 1915–1935," *U.S. Catholic Historian* (spring 1997), pp. 67–85.

21. Chesler, pp. 143–145; 232–233.

22. For an account of her intentions, see Sanger's autobiography, *My Fight for Birth Control* (New York: Farrar & Rinehart, 1931). In addition, see Sanger papers available at the Library of Congress, Washington, D.C., and in the Sophia Smith Collection at Smith College in North-hampton, Massachusetts. For similar disagreements and ultimate cooperation between birth control advocates and eugenicists in Britain, see Richard A. Soloway, *Demography and Degeneration: Eugenics and the Declining Birth Rate in Twentieth Century Britain* (Chapel Hill: University of North Carolina Press, 1990).

23. For more on Malthus see Allan Chase, *The Legacy of Malthus* (New York: Knopf, 1977).

24. See Warren S. Thompson, *Population: A Study In Malthusianism*, Ph.D. dissertation, Columbia University, 1915.

25. Scott Nearing, "'Race Suicide' vs. Overpopulation," *Popular Science Monthly*, January 1911, pp. 81–83.

26. Norman St. John-Stevas, *The Agonising Choice; Birth Control, Religion and the Law* (Bloomington: Indiana University Press, 1971), p. 15.

27. V. Drysdale, *The Small Family System: Is It Injurious or Immoral?* (New York: B. W. Huebsch, 1917), pp. 174–176. Also see Adelyne More's chapter "Militarism and the Birth Rate," in *Uncontrolled Breeding, or Fecundity versus Civilization, a Contribution to the Study of Over-Population as the Cause of War and the Chief Obstacle to the Emancipation of Women* (New York: Critic and Guide Company, 1917), pp. 64–71.

28. Eric B. Ross, *The Malthus Factor: Population, Poverty and Politics in Capitalist Development* (New York: Zed Books, 1998), pp. 58–60.

29. William Petersen, *Malthus: Founder of Modern Demography* (New Brunswick, N.J.: Transaction Publishers, 1999), pp. 197–201; David M. Kennedy, *Birth Control in America: The Career of Margaret Sanger* (New Haven, Conn.: Yale University Press, 1970), pp. 21–22.

30. Eric B. Ross, p. 60.

31. Gordon, pp. 81–90.

32. Kenan Malik, *The Meaning of Race: Race, History and Culture in Western Society* (Washington Square, N.Y.: New York University Press, 1996), p. 101.

33. H. G. Wells, *The Outline of History, Volume I* (New York: Doubleday, 1971 [1920]), pp. 112–123.

34. Daniel Pick, *Faces of Degeneration: A European Disorder, c. 1848–c. 1918* (New York: Cambridge University Press, 1989), pp. 11–15; Lothrop Stoddard, *The Revolt Against Civilization: The Menace of the Under Man* (New York: Charles Scribner's Sons, 1923), pp. 17–19.

35. Chesler, pp. 186–199.

36. Margaret Sanger, *The Pivot of Civilization* (New York: Brentano's, 1922), p. 22, 220–242.

37. See chapter 6, "Toward Racism: The History of an Idea," in John Higham's *Strangers in the Land: Patterns of American Nativism, 1860–1925* (New Brunswick, N.J.: Rutgers University Press, 1994), pp. 131–157.

38. David Starr Jordan, *The Blood of the Nation: A Study of the Decay of Races Through the Survival of the Unfit* (Boston: American Unitarian Association, 1903), pp. 9–10, 27–29.

39. William Z. Ripley, "Races in the United States," *Atlantic Monthly*, December 1908, pp. 745–759.

40. Gunnar Myrdal, *American Dilemma: The Negro Problem and Modern Democracy* (New York: Pantheon, 1975 [1944]), p. 114, cited in Robert Singerman, "The Jew as Racial Alien: The Genetic Component of American Anti-Semitism," in David A. Gerber, ed., *Anti-Semitism in American History* (Urbana: University of Illinois Press, 1986), p. 114.

41. Lothrop Stoddard, *The Rising Tide of Color Against White World-Supremacy* (New York: Blue Ribbon Books, 1920), pp. xxx–xxxi.

42. *Ibid*, pp. 253–263.

43. Henry F. Suksdorf, *Our Race Problems* (New York: Shakespeare Press, 1911), p. 333.

44. Stuart Creighton Miller, *The Unwelcome Immigrant: The American Image of the Chinese, 1785–1882* (Berkeley: University of California Press, 1974), pp. 191–204.

45. Arna Bontemps and Jack Conroy, *Anyplace But Here* (New York: Hill and Wang, 1966), pp. 159–161.

46. Higham, *Strangers*, pp. 155–157.

47. Thomas M. Shapiro, *Population Control Politics: Women, Sterilization, and Reproductive Choice* (Philadelphia: Temple University Press, 1985), p. 33.

48. Carole R. McCann, *Birth Control Politics in the United States, 1916–1945* (Ithaca, N.Y.: Cornell University Press, 1994), pp. 99–100.

49. *Ibid.*, pp. 102–104. Also see *Eugenics Record Office, Bulletin No. 8, Some Problems in the Study of Heredity in Mental Diseases* (Cold Spring Harbor, N.Y.: 1912), reprinted from *America Journal of Insanity*, vol. 69, no. 1, pp. 31–89; and Harry H. Laughlin, *Eugenics Record Office, Bulletin No. 10A, Report of the Committee to Study and to Report on the Best Practical Means of Cutting Off the Defective Germ-Plasm in the American Population — The Scope of the Committee's Work* (Cold Spring Harbor, N.Y.: 1914).

50. Kennedy, pp. 114–115; Amy B. Eaton, "Eugenics in America," *Survey*, June 3, 1911, pp. 352–354.

51. Dr. C. B. Davenport, "Euthenics and Eugenics," *Popular Science Monthly*, January 1911, pp. 16–20.

52. For more on the eugenics movement, see Shapiro, pp. 32–40; Daniel J. Kevles, *In the Name of Eugenics: Genetics and the Uses of Human Heredity* (Cambridge: Harvard University Press, 1995); Mark H. Haller, *Eugenics: Hereditarian Attitudes in American Thought* (New Brunswick, N.J.: Rutgers University Press, 1963); and Kenneth Ludmerer, *Genetics and American Society* (Baltimore: Johns Hopkins University Press, 1972).

53. "Eugenics and Social Welfare," *Survey*, September 21, 1912, pp. 753–754.

54. *American Journal of Sociology*, March 1907, pp. 607–632, 695–716.

55. Richard Hofstadter, *Social Darwinism in American Thought* (New York: George Braziller, 1959).

56. Henry James Forman, "Eugenics in England," *Independent*, June 20, 1912, pp. 1373–1376. For more on the British story, see Pauline M. H. Mazumdar, *Eugenics, Human Genetics and Human Failings: The Eugenics Society, Its Sources and Its Critics in Britain* (New York: Routledge, 1992), and Soloway, *Demography and Degeneration.*

57. Marouf Arif Hasian, Jr. *The Rhetoric of Eugenics in Anglo-American Thought* (Athens: University of Georgia Press, 1996), pp. 90–94

58. Montague Crackanthorpe, "The Friends and Foes of Eugenics," *Fortnightly Review*, October 1912, pp. 740–748. Also see Crackanthorpe's *Population and Progress* (London: Chapman and Hall, 1907).

59. Sidney Low, "Is Our Civilization Dying?" *Fortnightly Review*, April 1, 1913, pp. 627–639.

60. Herbert, "Eugenics in Relation to Social Reform," *Westminster Review*, October 1913, pp. 377–386.

61. Malik, p. 102

62. McCann, pp. 99, 107.

63. *Eugenics Records Office, Bulletin No. 10A*, p. 56.

64. *Ibid.*, pp. 46–57.

65. Philip R. Reilly, M.D., J.D., *The Surgical Solution: A History of Involuntary Sterilization in the U.S.* (Baltimore: Johns Hopkins University Press, 1991), pp. xiii, 41–45.

66. Malcolm Evan MacGregor, "A Plea for the Reduction of the Birth Rate," *Westminster Review*, March 1912, pp. 348–352.

67. Theodore Roosevelt, "Race Decadence," *Outlook*, April 8, 1911. See "On Race Decay and Wilful Sterility," in Andrea Tone, ed., *Controlling Reproduction: An American History* (Wilmington, Del: Scholarly Resources, 1997), pp. 159–162; Reilly, p. 43.

68. A. Chase, *The Legacy of Malthus: The Social Costs of the New Scientific Racism*, p. 127.

69. Charlotte Perkins Gilman, "Race Improvement," *Independent*, March 25, 1909, pp. 629–632. For more on feminist views of motherhood and race suicide, see Gordon, pp. 139–145.

70. Gilman, pp. 629–632. For what was considered the "antifeminist" view of birth control, see William Hill, "A Healthy Race: Woman's Vocation," *Westminster Review*, January 1910, pp. 11–19.

71. *The Child in the City: A Series of Papers Presented at the Conferences Held During the Chicago Welfare Exhibit, May 11–25, 1911* (Chicago: Department of Social Investigation, Chicago School of Civics and Philanthropy, 1912), pp. 133–152.

72. Charles R. Henderson, *Education with Reference to Sex* (Chicago: University of Chicago Press, 1909).

73. "The Chief End of Man," *Current Literature*, May 1910, pp. 528–531.

74. American Social Hygiene Association, *First Annual Report, 1913–1914* (New York: American Social Hygiene Association, 1914), pp. 39–44.

75. *Report of the Sex Education Sessions of the Fourth International Congress on School Hygiene and of the Annual Meeting of the American Federation for Sex Hygiene, Buffalo, New York, August, 1913* (New York: American Federation for Sex Hygiene, 1913), pp. 64–71.

76. Nellie M. L. Nearing and Scott Nearing, "When a Girl Is Asked to Marry: Why It Is the Most Important Moment in Her Life," *Ladies' Home Journal*, March 1912, p. 7; "What Is Meant By Eugenics," *Ladies' Home Journal*, September, 1912, p. 14.

77. John Harris, "Unfit for Parenthood," *Westminster Review*, May 1912, pp. 578–581; John Harris, "Our Defectives," *Westminster Review*, July 1912, pp. 25–27.

78. Havelock Ellis, "Eugenics and St. Valentine," *Nineteenth Century*, Ma, 1906, pp. 779–787.

79. Margaret Sanger, "The Question of Conception," *Woman Rebel*, March 1914, p. 8.

80. Emma Goldman, "Love and Marriage," *Woman Rebel*, March 1914, p. 3.

81. "The Unfit," *Woman Rebel*, April, 1914, p. 10.

82. "Into the Valley of Death — For What?" *Woman Rebel*, April 1914, p. 12.

83. Shapiro, p. 42; Kennedy, p. 112.

84. Gordon, pp. 228–229; Margaret Sanger, *My Fight for Birth Control*, p. 145; Planned Parenthood Association of the Chicago Area, History, Chicago Historical Association Archives.

85. June Rose, *Marie Stopes and the Sexual Revolution* (Boston: Faber and Faber, 1992), pp. 90–92, 134–135.

86. Rose, p. 134.

87. Marie Stopes, *Radiant Motherhood* (G. P. Putnam: London, 1920), quoted in Rose, p. 135.

88. Rose, p. 219. For an additional negative portrayal of Stopes, see C. Blacker, *Birth Control and the State* (New York: E. P. Dutton, 1926).

89. Charles Howard Hopkins, *The Rise of the Social Gospel in American Protestantism, 1865–1915* (New Haven: Yale University Press, 1940), p. 3. Also see Harlan Beckley, *Passion for Justice: Retrieving the Legacies of Walter Rauschenbusch, John A. Ryan, and Reinhold Niebuhr* (Louisville, KY: Westminster/John Knox Press, 1992), pp. 34–56.

90. Hopkins., pp. 5–7, 99–103.

91. *Ibid.*, pp. 123–125, 203.

92. Hutchison, pp. 4–5.

93. *Ibid.*, pp. 13–16.

94. Frederick A. Bode, "Religion and Class Hegemony: A Populist Critique in North Carolina," in Martin E. Marty, ed., *Protestantism and Social Christianity* (New York: K. G. Saur, 1992), pp. 61–62.

95. Ronald C. White, Jr., and C. Howard Hopkins, *The Social Gospel: Religion and Reform in Changing America* (Philadelphia: Temple University Press, 1976), pp. 80–83.

96. See Chapter 5, "Premillennial Christian Views of God's Justice and American Injustice," pp. 128–149, and chapter 6, "The Protestant Majority as a Lost Generation, a Look at Fundamentalism," pp. 150–172, in R. Laurence Moore, *Religious Outsiders and the Making of Americans* (New York: Oxford University Press, 1986); George Marsden, *Fundamentalism in American Culture: The Shaping of Twentieth Century Evangelicalism, 1870–1925* (New York: Oxford University Press, 1980).

97. *Annual of the Southern Baptist Convention, 1911*, pp. 43–44; *Annual of the Southern Bap-

*tist Convention, 1912*, pp. 29–31; John Lee Eighmy, *Churches in Cultural Conflict: A History of the Social Attitudes of Southern Baptists* (Knoxville: University of Tennessee Press, 1972), pp. 72–73.

98. Szasz, pp. 96–99.

99. Clifford Nelson, ed., *The Lutherans in North America* (Philadelphia: Fortress Press, 1975), pp. 354–356. Also see Abdel Ross Wentz, *A Basic History of Lutheranism in America* (Philadelphia: Fortress Press, 1964).

100. Marsden, "Reformed and American," in David F. Wells, *Reformed Theology in America: A History of Its Modern Development* (Grand Rapids, Mich.: William B. Eerdmans, 1985), p. 8. For more on the overall complexity, see chapter 9, "Denomination as a Canopy," in Marty, *The Irony of It All*, pp. 150–190.

101. John M. Glenn, "Social Service in the Episcopal Church," *Survey*, November 5, 1910, pp. 175–177.

102. For a general history, see Alan M. G. Stephenson, *Anglicanism and the Lambeth Conferences* (London: SPCK, 1978).

103. Egal Feldman, *Dual Destinies: The Jewish Encounter with Protestant America* (Urbana: University of Illinois Press, 1990), pp. 60–73; Lloyd P. Gartner, "Immigration and the Formation of American Jewry, 1840–1925," in Marshall Sklare, ed., *The Jew in American Society* (New York: Behrman House, 1974), pp. 33–40; Jonathan D. Sarna and David G. Dalin, *Religion and State in the American Jewish Experience* (Notre Dame, Ind.: University of Notre Dame Press, 1997), pp. 139–154.

104. Nathan Glazer, *American Judaism* (Chicago: University of Chicago Press, 1989), p. 60.

105. *Ibid.*, pp. 62–64.

106. Max I. Dimont, *The Jews in America: The Roots, History, and Destiny of American Jews* (New York: Simon and Schuster, 1978), pp. 173–178.

107. Egal Feldman, pp. 132–138.

108. Dimont, p. 200; Glazer, pp. 3–5.

109. Gerald Sorin, *Tradition Transformed: The Jewish Experience in America* (Baltimore: Johns Hopkins University Press, 1997), p. 32.

110. John Higham, *Send These to Me: Immigrants in Urban America* (Baltimore: Johns Hopkins University Press, 1984), p. 150.

111. R. Scott Appleby, *"Church and Age Unite!": The Modernist Impulse in American Catholicism* (Notre Dame, Ind.: University of Notre Dame Press, 1992), pp. 7–8.

112. "The National Catholic Welfare Council," *Catholic World* 109 (July 1919), p. 436, reprinted in Robert D. Cross, *The Emergence of Liberal Catholicism in America* (Cambridge, Mass.: Harvard University Press, 1958), p. 206.

113. Higham, *Strangers in This Land*, pp. 3–11, 28–31. Also see Ray Allen Billington, *The Origins of Nativism in the United States, 1800–1844* (New York: Ayer, 1974).

114. Moore, *Religious Outsiders*, p. 51.

115. The rise of the Know-Nothing Party is explored in Carleton Beals, *Brass-Knuckles Crusade: The Great Know-Nothing Conspiracy, 1820–1860* (New York: Hastings House, 1960).

116. "A Question Answered," *Independent*, June 12, 1913, pp. 1321–1322.

117. "The Vatican's Cure for the American Church," *Independent*, November 9, 1911, pp. 1047–1048.

118. "Catholic Success a Spur to Protestantism," *Literary Digest*, February 10, 1912, pp. 271–272.

119. *Ibid.*, p. 271.

120. For studies of Catholics in American and New York politics, see James S. Olson, *Catholic Immigrants in America* (Chicago: Nelson-Hall, 1987); Carl Wittke, *The Irish in America* (Baton Rouge: Louisiana State University Press, 1956); and Steven P. Erie, *Rainbow's End: Irish-Americans and the Dilemma of Urban Machine Politics, 1840–1985* (Berkeley: University of California Press, 1988).

121. "Faint Hopes Over Church Statistics," *Literary Digest*, February 10, 1912, p. 272.

122. "Official Catholic Statistics," *Literary Digest*, April 13, 1912, pp. 757–758.

123. "Will Roman Catholicism Ever Conquer North America?" *Current Literature*, November 1910, pp. 525–528.

124. *Ibid.*, p. 527.

125. *Ibid.*, pp. 526–527.

126. Rev. Edward Judson, "The Church in Its Social Aspect," *Annals of the American Academy of Political and Social Science*, November 1907, p. 3.

127. "Protestantism Falling Behind Through Unproductive Marriages," *Current Opinion* 58 (January 1915), p. 40.

128. Diane Ravitch, ed., *The American Reader: Words That Motivated a Nation* (New York: HarperCollins, 1991), p. 182; Higham, *Strangers in This Land*.

129. "Protestantism Falling," p. 41.

130. For more on the race perspective, see I. Zangwill, "Jewish Race," *Independent*, August 10, 1911, pp. 288–295; M. Fishberg, "Jews: A Study of Race and Environment," *Nature*, June 29, 1911, pp. 578–579; "Will the Jews Ever Lose Their Racial Identity?" *Current Literature*, March 1911, pp. 292–294; G. F. Abbott, "The Jewish Problem," *Fortnightly Review*, April 1910, pp. 742–754.

131. "The Jews in Council," *Independent*, January 26, 1911, pp. 208–209.

132. "The Hebrew Council," *Outlook*, January 28, 1911, pp. 138–139.

133. *Ibid.*

134. Isaac A. Hourwich, "The Social-Economic Classes of the Population of the United States," *Journal of Political Economy*, March 1911, p. 188, and April 1911, pp. 325–326.

135. Shapiro, p. 37.

# Chapter Two

# Religion and the Roots
# of Birth Control

## *Religion and Contraception Through the Ages*

Religious questions regarding marriage, procreation, sexuality, and life itself were very much shaped by the numerous issues prevalent in early-twentieth-century America. Religion's participation in proposing solutions to society's ills, and whether the solutions included birth control, was determined by varying doctrine shaped to answer the questions posed in this period. Very little had been written or stated publicly by church spokespersons regarding birth control between the passage in 1873 of the Comstock laws and 1916, when Sanger gained the attention of the press with the opening of her first clinic, a clear indication that this was a contemporary issue. But when the subject of controlling conception became public, churches were called on to provide answers based on centuries of teaching. The fact that differences of opinion erupted among the churches only in the early twentieth century demonstrates just how contemporary this debate was, based in cultural and political differences among the churches in America during this period. Throughout the centuries there was essentially a religious consensus among those denominations that were rooted in Judeo-Christian foundations and Western thought.

Very little evidence exists that would shed light on Judeo-Christian opinion regarding the control of reproduction before 1900. However, when the specific condemnation of contraceptives does appear, it suggests that sex without the purpose of procreation equals sex for pleasure, and sex for pleasure equals vice. Modern feminists attribute much of the general condemnation of sex for pleasure to early Christian and pre–Christian teachings considered "antiwoman." For example, Aristotle considered women morally inferior and subordinate to men, while his contemporaries, both philosophers and physicians, recommended abstinence as a way to conserve energy — which, according to them, was expelled by ejaculation.[1]

Judaic teaching presented sexuality largely as utilitarian — a means to produce, an insurance of heirs, God's blessing on a people to survive and to thrive.[2] The Book of Genesis exemplifies this in the often quoted passage: "Male and female he created them. Then God blessed them, saying, 'Increase and multiply; fill the earth and subdue it.'"[3] This ideal provided the foundation for Jewish and Christian teaching, though many have disagreed on whether the phrase was a blessing or a command. No Old Testament text referred directly to contraception. The closest was the story of Onan, an account that debaters cited throughout the Sanger movement. That passage stated: "And Judah said unto Onan, go in unto thy brother's wife and perform the duty of a husband's brother unto her, and raise up seed to thy brother. And Onan knew that the seed should not be his; and it came to pass, when he went in unto his brother's wife, that he spilled it on the ground, lest he should give seed to his brother. And the thing which he did was evil in the sight of the Lord: and he slew him also."[4] Still, the biblical position was not clear, as theologians disagreed on whether God punished Onan for uncompleted coitus, referred to as onanism, or for disobeying him.[5]

An examination of Christian teaching of the second and third centuries finds much direct condemnation of abortion. For example, Athengoras equated it with homicide, adding, "for the fetus in the womb is not an animal, and it is God's providence that he exist."[6] And Clement condemned women "who, in order to hide their immorality, use abortive drugs which expel the matter completely dead, abort at the same time their human feelings."[7] Religious critics generally equated abortion with contraception, making specific references to contraception more difficult to uncover. In Galatians 5:20, however, St. Paul includes in his list of sins of the flesh *pharmakeia*, often translated as "sorcery" or "magic," but which is the same word the ancient Greeks had used in reference to birth control.[8]

The evolution of any definitive Christian stand on reproductive control came from the teachings of St. Augustine in the fourth and fifth centuries. Augustine reportedly lived a lustful life until a mystical experience at the age of thirty-three resulted in his conversion to Christianity, and as Bishop Hippo he wrote extensively on sex and marriage. In *De bono conjugali* he wrote that since "procreation is the reason for marriage, it is the sole excuse for the conjugal act," and in *Contra Faustum* he stated that "the external law which requires respect for the natural order permits only those sexual relations which are necessary to procreation."[9] Essentially, St.

Augustine taught that procreation was the purpose of marriage: "Intercourse even with one's own legitimate wife is unlawful and wicked where the conception of the offspring is prevented. Onan, the son of Judah, did this and the Lord killed him for it." [10] Twelfth- and thirteenth-century theologians reiterated Augustine's position, and between 1227 and 1234 Pope Gregory declared marriages of those intending not to have children null and void.[11]

Martin Luther and John Calvin, prominent founders of Protestantism, both had strongly objected to contraception, though in discussions of procreation and marriage, they stressed the additional importance of marital companionship.[12] Early Protestants differed from Catholics in that the Catholic Church still held a very high regard for virginity and demanded celibacy from members of religious orders. In this respect Protestants appeared to take procreation even more seriously than did Catholics. Furthermore, their diminished focus on the Virgin Mary was viewed as increasing the power of patriarchy even further. In this period in history, when women were given a clear separate status in both Protestant and Catholic faiths, the worship of Mary granted women a particularly high place in Catholicism that they did not experience in Protestantism. In addition, Mary was not married, allowing for women a status besides that bestowed in marriage. On the other hand, Protestants glorified marriage and the home, and maintained women should be subject to their husbands and honored for their childbearing.[13]

In 1522 Luther stated that for women procreation was "the purpose for which they exist," and he subsequently condemned those "who seem to detest giving birth lest the bearing and rearing of children disturb their leisure."[14] Both Luther and Calvin condemned Onanism; however, Calvin accepted some degree of "joy" in the sexuality of marriage. He professed that although procreation remained an important function of marriage, more importance should be placed on "mutual help."[15] Their teachings ultimately proved significant to the twentieth-century debate, for it was on this point that religious teaching regarding birth control pivoted in 1930. The idea of companionate marriage was drawing tremendous attention from psychologists and sociologists by the 1920s. The notion that marriage should serve as something more than a vehicle for procreation, that it should exist as a satisfying relationship, was becoming widely accepted. As such teachings of social scientists were promoted among modernists as sound and rational, nonmodernists resisted adopting them.

In the nineteenth century, however, the churches remained in opposition to birth control. However, religious statements regarding such were all but nonexistent. Perhaps because of the strength of this condemnation coming from Victorian society at large, the churches found it unnecessary to make frequent statements. For whatever the reason, very few clerical statements appeared before and during the nineteenth century, and when they did, they were largely in response to scientific or political developments.

In 1827 scientists discovered the existence of eggs in mammals and by the 1840s had developed the theory that female ovaries periodically released eggs. Until this time it was believed that eggs were discharged in response to sexual stimulation.[16] In 1853, in response to these new findings, the Roman Penitentiary ruled that it was permissible for couples to abstain from sex during the time the wife was believed to be fertile.[17] The use of this "rhythm" method became widespread among Catholics during the 1930s as the only accepted form of birth control, with official Vatican sanction by 1951.

Though clerical acceptance of preventing conception appeared to be developing by the mid-nineteenth century, opposition to birth control intensified during the latter part of the century in Europe as French birthrates plummeted.[18] Nationalism of the late nineteenth century, and with it pronatalism, aided in this response. For example, the Swiss cardinal Gaspar Mermillod blamed France's defeat in the Franco-Prussian War on a declining birthrate: "You have rejected God, and God has struck you. You have, by hideous calculations, made tombs instead of filling cradles with children; therefore, you have wanted for soldiers."[19] In 1886 the Vatican proclaimed a confessor had a duty to inquire "prudently and discreetly" if he had a "well-founded suspicion" that a penitent practiced contraception.[20]

As strong as the Victorian moralist sentiment was in the United States condemning contraceptives, there was little heard from the churches. Orthodox Congregationalist spokesman Rev. John Todd referred to contraception and family limitation as "the cloud with a dark lining." He advertised his 1867 book, *Serpents in the Dove's Nest* (one of fifteen encouraging chastity, temperance, and morality for America's youth) as calling necessary attention to the recent development of "measures to *prevent* having children."[21] Aside from Todd few clergy spoke publicly about contraception. Some did remind their congregations of the evils of contraceptive use, parroting lay moralists who warned that contraception would eliminate the primary check on illicit sex, that is, pregnancy. Others warned that separating sexual intercourse would alter the roles of, and relations between, men and women. By and large, however, the clergy was silent.[22] Only after 1900, as the eugenics movement took hold and birth control activists forced the issue into the public sphere, were churches forced to take a stand.

Much of the way in which various denominations reacted to developments in population theory and contraception stemmed from their particular beliefs regarding society, a church's role in society, and the possibilities for reform here on earth. An examination of this reaction becomes quite complicated, if only because of the number of denominations in the United States that were competing for public recognition. The Catholic Church, perceived as a single force with a powerful voice, was complex in itself, with varying birth control statements coming from bishops, priests, lay publications, and finally the pope. American Jews, who would not take on an extremely prominent role in the debate, nonetheless were worth watching as well, and equally valuable views of religion and society would arise from Orthodox, Conservative, and Reform Jews, complicating the Jewish position.

Ultimately, however, American Protestants were perhaps the most important, and the most difficult, to watch in the entire birth control debate. While it was true that this was traditionally a Protestant nation, and politically Protestants were reacting to an influx of non–Protestants in this period, Protestants themselves made up anything but a unified force. This lack of unity was very important to the evolution of the birth control debate. As discussed in the previous chapter, denominations that adhered to traditionalist teaching would resist changing their positions on contraception, while moderate to liberal Protestants embraced scientific developments, social reform, and modernism. But the divisions were far more complex than that. For example, the more liberal Unitarians and Universalists would have comparatively little problem eventually adapting their doctrine to accept the use of contraceptives. However, they were far from public in their position and generally did not condemn denominations that did not take the same position. On the other hand, Northern Baptists and Northern Methodists took very public positions and took very active roles in social reform, including eugenics and eventually birth control, as they saw improving society as a primary responsibility. In retrospect, their positions appeared generally moderate and reflective of changes in society at large, yet in comparison to Southern Baptists and Methodists, they seemed almost radical.

At the same time, Methodists and Baptists, both Northern and Southern, portrayed the Catholic Church as politically manipulative, corrupt, and not truly Christian at all, helping to shape the birth control debate into one that appeared Catholic and non–Catholic. Lutherans were criticized by non–Lutherans for not taking a more active role in society, but Lutherans traditionally had placed more value on faith over good works, limiting their responsibilities to their own congregations. Yet, the conservative

Missouri Synod Lutherans would ultimately differ strongly from United Lutherans on the issue of contraception, ironically taking the same side as Southern Baptists and Catholics. The subtle differences were endless, but the more serious ones became more evident as the birth control debate unfolded. The nature of each denomination's doctrine would determine a particular role in the birth control debate, and the very nature of contraception as an issue of life, and as an important element of marriage in which religion would have a stake.

## Religion and Twentieth-Century Social Concerns

Some of the development of doctrine stemmed from the religious challenge to address issues of marriage, children and women's roles as the divorce rate climbed, as family size among the dominant culture decreased, and as women questioned traditional roles for themselves. From the beginning of this new public debate, churches were placed on the defensive. Feminists in particular quoted early Christian teachings, either official or from the pulpit, in their efforts to portray religion as antiwoman. Perhaps the most prominent was Matilda Joslyn Gage, who in *Woman, Church & State* summed up her sentiments: "All the evils that have resulted from dignifying one sex and degrading the other may be traced to one central error, a belief in a trinity of masculine gods, in one from which the feminine element is wholly eliminated."[23]

Gage's emphasis on the trinity may appear to be aimed at the Catholic Church, but she condemned all religion. Regarding reproduction, Gage and other feminists claimed Judeo-Christian religious leaders in general considered childbearing itself—not just the pain associated with childbearing—as the woman's curse for original sin as outlined in the fall of Eve in the Book of Genesis. In her 1907 examination of race suicide concerns, entitled *The American Idea*, Lydia Kingsmill Commander expounds on the writings of Gage, commenting on contemporary religious teachings. In addition, she insists that centuries-old teaching must be reconsidered in light of modern society. Commander wrote: "Probably the expression of Martin Luther—'If a woman becomes weary or at last dead from bearing, that matters not; let her only die from bearing, she is there to do it,' was not extreme in his day," but modern developments demand re-examination.[24]

Religious teachings on birth control at this point in time were ambiguous not only because denominations had not been forced to take a stand but also because religious figures generally considered the subject matter too delicate for discussion. In a time when mainline denominations criticized the depiction of kissing in motion pictures, many would not find it easy to address the topic directly. This is evident, for example, in a *Christian Workers* magazine article of 1917. The conservative Moody Bible Institute publication reprinted a report from the *Chicago Daily Tribune* with the following preface: "The topic is not one admitting of general discussion in the press, but its grave importance justifies this reference to it. It is not only the world's people who are to blame in the premises, but we fear some professing Christians are not free from it. May the Lord use the testimony of this fearless woman to warn any who are guilty of this crime against humanity and sin against God."[25]

The *Tribune* story reported on a speech by former public welfare commissioner Leonora Z. Meder to the Evanston Woman's Club, in which she rebuked women who used contraception stating: "God in his wisdom is wiser than these women of fads and whims. His plans, not theirs, are the ones to follow. He would hardly despise children when He said: 'Suffer little children and forbid them not, for of such is the kingdom of heaven.'" She added: "You have only to visit the insane asylums at Elgin, Kankakee, or Dunning to see the appalling ruin to both mind and body brought on by this heinous practice."[26]

This comparatively early religious commentary on contraception is important for a number of reasons. First, it notes that the delicateness of this subject would be outweighed by the demands to make this discussion public (a practice which was further encouraged by fashionable conversations about Freud and sexuality during the 1920s). Second, it clearly indicates that Catholic authorities were not the only religious figures decrying contraceptive use. And finally, it brings to light the recognition among clergy that their followers were using birth control. If some did not see the need to take a public stance concluding what this would do to society, they were at least pressured to define their positions among their own congregations. Furthermore, in the modernist debate, traditionalists would publicly hold onto traditional doctrine, or what they maintained was traditional doctrine, while more liberal Protestant and Jewish denominations might be swayed to change their positions to meet social and congregational appeals.

The editors of *Christian Workers* accurately recognized that even "professing Christians" were practicing birth control. Much of the literature published early in the birth control debate consisted of denominational leaders reminding their congregations that they did not approve of birth control. This fact indicates that church spokespersons understood that, even though contraceptives were still considered illegal,[27] their use was becoming more widespread, even among their own followers.

By 1917 advocate and physician William J. Robinson recognized the significance of religious opinion on the matter, when the debate was made public. He had already published three books, *Sexual Problems of Today, Eugenics and Marriage,* and *Sex Morality — Past, Present and Future,* and claimed he had spoken to a minister who could not think of any place in the Bible that condemned the use of preventives. Robinson maintained that if there were, those who guided their behavior according to biblical teachings should refrain from using prohibited means of contraception but not attempt to force their morals and conduct on others who were guided by different standards of morality. He added: "I do not sneer at religion … but I simply say that this is a question which we cannot discuss. Religion is a matter of faith and not reason; you believe so and so and that is all there is to it. Another man believes differently. Let him get his salvation in his own way as long as he does not injure you."[28]

But the religious debate over birth control did not begin with the legalization of contraceptives; it began with eugenics. As the eugenics movement took hold, voices from both inside and outside the churches declared that the quality of the human race should be of religious concern. It is here that we see those preaching the Social Gospel, those wishing to build a "Kingdom of God," those who would accept modernist notions to improve society, begin to take eugenics seriously. By 1885 the newly founded American Economic Association had already recognized that the nation was suffering from "a vast number of social problems, whose solution requires the united efforts, each in its own sphere, of the church, of the state, and of science."[29] The widely accepted notion in America at the turn of the century, that religion, government, and the scientific community could and should work together toward social reform helped pave the way for a new kind of religious discussion about population.

The most prominent "social gospellers," Walter Rauschenbush, Washington Gladden, Lyman Abbott, Henry Emerson Fosdick, and Charles W. Potter, for example, saw the nation's cities in desperate need of physical improvement and spiritual improvement through Christ.[30] According to Rauschenbush, professor of church history at Rochester Theological Seminary, it was necessary "to set Christendom praying on our new social problems."[31] He praised Presbyterians, Episcopalians, Baptists, Methodists, Congregationalists, Unitarians, Universalists, Disciples of Christ, and even Catholics for their social action but criticized Lutherans for not doing more.[32]

More specifically, according to J. Herman Randall, pastor of the

Mount Morris Baptist Church in New York City, the human ideal could be achieved through social betterment, and that it was "time for truth," not dogma, but "scientific and spiritual truth." To Randall the Kingdom of God was the attainable perfect social order, and the supreme ideal was the perfection of human life.[33] According to Walter Laidlaw, secretary of the Federation of Churches in New York City, Protestants should respond to the swell of population in the cities. He likened poor, "basement-born" children to the stable-born Jesus and urged each church to develop a committee to address the special needs of childhood, old age, prisoners, dependents, defectives, and "the strangers within our gates." Laidlaw claimed that it was the job of Christianity to perfect the human race and concern itself with the "evolution of humankind."[34] There was a growing understanding among many mainline to liberal Protestants that religion would inevitably become involved in the ethics of eugenics, that it had an obligation to address race betterment, and that social reform might be doomed if religion concerned itself only with environment and not with heredity.[35]

In *The Challenge of the City* Josiah Strong displayed some prejudice against immigrants but disputed eugenics claims that the heritage of these people would aid in the deterioration of the dominant race in America. Strong argued that the essence of the Kingdom of God lay in environment, not heredity. According to Strong, "We know of Americans, cultivated, educated, scholarly, occupying high positions in the educational or literary world, whose parents were humble, European peasants, in some cases unable to read. ... A foreign heredity is overcome by an American environment." He added that there was little evidence that heredity played any significant part in establishing the physical degeneracy of the poorer population.[36]

Dr. G. Stanley Hall, president of Clark University and a leading supporter of eugenics, in a speech to the American Society of Sanitary and Moral Prophylaxis in New York, urged religious leaders to fulfill their obligation to "transmit the sacred torch of life undimmed, and if possible a little brightened," as this was part of Abraham's covenant with God. However, he criticized the use of contraception among the upper classes, saying that "preventives," abortion, prostitution, venereal disease, and divorce, especially in the "native-born population," were contributing to race degeneration.[37] Similarly, Harvard University president Charles Eliot noted that religious figures had not only a right but a responsibility to take stands on issues of sex and procreation. Eliot maintained that scientific knowledge had made tremendous strides in recent years, and "with this knowledge goes the responsibility and duty of applying it in defense of society and civilization."[38] John M. Coulter, professor of botany at the

University of Chicago, went so far as to describe eugenics as more of a religion than a science because of its "concern for human welfare."[39] Paul Popenoe, one of the most influential population theorists of the twentieth century wrote in 1915, "The faith of the social worker, the legislator, the physician, the sanitarian in his method of improving the race is very literally the kind of faith that St. Paul described as the substance of things hoped for, the evidence of things not seen. ... We eugenists have a stronger faith, because it is based on things that are seen, and that can even be measured. We think that we can prove that it is, on the whole, man who makes the environment, not the environment that makes man."[40] Edwin L. Earp, professor of Christian sociology at Drew Theological Seminary, agreed that it was the responsibility of the Christian in building the Kingdom of God to control social forces, and he called for a rational program of eugenics.[41] Samuel Zane Batten, professor of social science at Des Moines College and chairman of the Social Service Commission of the Northern Baptist Convention, supported eugenics, maintaining that the current system of charity was contributing to degeneracy. According to Batten:

> Christian man must now learn how to appraise all the factors that enter into the life of man, heredity, environment, personal will and divine grace, and must so use these factors that together they should work for man's whole progress and perfection; he must know how to manage all the forces of the universe for the advantage and the superiority of the race; he must begin to subsidize and use the mighty agencies of the Church, the Family, the State and the School in behalf of these great ends.[42]

*Christian Century*, a voice of moderate to liberal Protestantism, is an important publication to watch during this era for mainstream statement on birth control and before 1920 reflected the general lack of clarity in the Protestant stance. The publication did not address the issue of contraception directly; when the subject was addressed indirectly, the position appears more anti–Catholic than anti–birth control. In an article of 1917 the publication emphasized the importance of religious upbringing, simply stating: "RELIGION'S FUTURE IS WITH THE CHILD," and "It is a sorry home that has no ritual for the expression of its respect for its own history and its reverence for Almighty God." But although the article focused on the spiritual well-being of the child once it arrived, it also briefly mentioned eugenics: "We are just now passing through a period in which much interest is taken in the bodies of our children. The science of eugenics declares that they must be well born. Nursing manuals set forth how they should be fed. All this is well, but when we go only so far we have failed."[43] Though this is hardly a sanctioned approval of birth control, it does not denounce the principles of eugenics and opens the discussion further.

## Secular Examination of Religious Teaching

Throughout the debate over birth control, arguments for and against ultimately appeared in a variety of forms from a variety of sources, and a religious theme would prevail in many of them. Before 1920 they were limited mainly to religious opponents who were beginning to outline their theses and to lay opponents using historical religious teachings to support their own positions. Most significant, however, were those of birth control advocates who were attempting to find flaws in what might be considered standard religious doctrine. As leaders of the movement, they understood that religion could not be detached from the issue of preventing conception in many peoples' minds; therefore they could not ignore it. Instead, they chose to face religion in a head-on battle. If religion was going to stand in their way, they needed to take action to weaken arguments in theological teaching, and they began to do so quite successfully.

By 1921 *Christian Century* had begun to clarify a liberal Protestant position somewhat in "The Glory of Fatherhood" when it stressed the importance of procreation. According to author Ira L. Parvin, "There is a dignity, an honor and a glory about fatherhood that is unsurpassed in any other relation of life." Parvin added that it was important not only to become a parent but to bear a number of children. The real father lives a multiplied life, double life, quadruple and so on, according to the number of his children. He lives not only in the present but in the future also. The man who is not a father lives only in his own time. But, added Parvin, "fatherhood may be a man's loftiest glory or his profoundest shame; it may be his highest honor or his lowest disgrace. It may be surrounded with a halo of majesty and dignity that is almost Godlike, or it may be attended by a vulgarity and a coarseness that is bestial. When fatherhood is the accident of unlawful lustful passion, it puts man on a level that is lower than that of a beast. Such a man is not a father; he is less than a sire; he is only an irresponsible progenitor."[44] Parvin condemned the act of engaging in intercourse when pregnancy was not welcomed. His comments might be construed to imply that this "beastliness" pertained only to sexual relations outside marriage. However, Parvin noted that although such "lustful passion" was worse out of wedlock, it was almost as bad in wedlock.

In addition, to have relations with one's wife after his passion had "spent its novel force" was equally contemptible.[45]

In examining attitudes toward birth control, this article was valuable because it touched on the most important aspects of the birth control debate for the next twenty years. First, this was a matter concerning married couples and would continue as such throughout the debate; and second, the primary reason for intercourse was procreation with the idea of marital love playing a secondary role. The topic of procreation was where the arguments focused their attention. With tremendous concern over the state of the American family and rising divorce rates, theologians followed the lead of psychologists, sociologists, and social scientists and began to examine what marriage was intended to be.[46] In an effort to solidify existing marriages, some church leaders began to wonder if conjugal love should rank first in importance.

Throughout the struggle arguments for and against legalizing contraception appeared in a variety of forms from a variety of sources, and a religious theme prevailed in many of them. Before 1920 they were limited mainly to religious opponents outlining doctrine in order to clarify their stands to lay opponents using religious teachings to explain or support theirs. However, there did exist some birth control advocates who attempted to find flaws in standard religious doctrine that would weaken arguments in some theological teaching. In 1916 a publication entitled *Christianity and Sex Problems* directly addressed the issue of religious attitudes toward birth control. Originally published in London, it reflected the situation in the United States. It is valuable to examine British statements early in the debate on birth control, because they were among the first to make more direct connections between religion and contraception. Even though contraceptives were legal in Britain, the two nations shared similar views on class, social purity, and reform. The movement was, of course, international in scope, and the British sentiment regarding race and social theory had laid the groundwork for Anglo-Saxon philosophies in the United States.

This book's dedication, "To all my fellowmen and women, however much tempted and however far fallen, whose faces are still turned toward the ideals of love and holiness and truth," gave the impression that author Hugh Northcote would elaborate within a conservative religious framework. Instead, he attempted to convince the reader that clerical criticism of birth control was minimal: "Christianity has ever been suspicious of, but has never unreservedly condemned non-procreative marriage." He added: "The early Church did not discourage the syneisactic, i.e., non-procreative state of marriage *per se*, but only on account of its general impracticability and the dangers and abuses attendant on it."[47] This argument is supported by Noonan in *Contraception: A History of Its Treatment by the Catholic Theologians and Canonists*, the most thorough examination of Catholic birth control doctrine. According to Noonan, the early Church developed teachings opposing contraception only in response to Gnostics and pagans who held hostile attitudes toward procreation.[48] The issue, added Northcote, needed to be examined once again, in modern light.

Northcote's work was not unique in its effort to portray religious attitudes as less than condemning. Others dissected doctrinal arguments in much the same way. More important, Northcote's work exemplifies the general way in which even those who condoned the use of contraceptives did so within clear limitations. They opposed the "rash and general adoption" by a society of the practice of prevention. A widespread disinclination to accept the responsibilities of parenthood constituted a "formidable menace to the progress and future prosperity of a nation."[49] Religious shifts toward acceptance that took hold by 1930 reflected similar hesitation to opening the floodgates to unlimited use.

Once the issue resurfaced after 1900, denominations were called on for their opinions. The morality of contraception was only one of several areas in question during an era of rapid change, and many realized they would benefit from knowing just where the churches stood. Following a survey, the "official" denominational positions were spelled out by James Marchant in *Birth Rate and Empire*. Published in London, it emphasized the views of British churches; nevertheless, it served as a good indicator of American views. American birth control advocates, most notably Sanger, educated themselves on the subject in Britain before initiating action in the United States, patterning their work on that of Marie Stopes. Much of the reaction to the movement in Britain was similar to that in the United States. Marchant was not a neutral participant in the debate as secretary of the National Birth-Rate Commission in England and member of National Council for the Promotion of Race Regeneration; his and the commission's sentiments clearly lay with those in opposition to legalization. He praised the Roman Catholic Church for its consistent and direct teaching, which was based in uncompromising opposition to any interference with the natural birth of children. He considered the Anglican Church's teaching less authoritative than that of the Roman Catholic Church, but the Lambeth Conference of Anglican bishops in 1908 also voiced that denomination's opposition. Anglican and Episcopalian churches worldwide were represented at the conferences, and their discussions and decisions had global effects. The 1930 conference marked profound changes in official religious teaching regarding birth control that would influence other denominations as well. But the 1908 conference marks the real beginning of denominational discussion. Until that time, and for years since, religious arguments on both sides were heard from individuals, both lay and clerical, but did not serve as any official denominational teaching. The 1908 Lambeth proclamation was the first of an official stature: "The Conference regards with alarm the growing practice of the artificial restriction of the family, and earnestly calls upon all Christian people to discountenance the use of all artificial means of restriction as demoralising to character and hostile to national welfare. The Conference affirms that deliberate tampering with nascent life is repugnant to Christian morality."[50]

In Jewish tradition motherhood and family life were held in high esteem, and according to one rabbi's report to the Birth-rate Commission, the "use of preventives is strongly condemned as unclean and demoralising." The official position of Nonconformists was more elusive because of the very nature of nonconformity, in which there was no formal authoritative voice for churches as church members behaved according to enlightened consciences. However, a statement drawn up by several leaders stated: "The attitude on Christian morals commonly held does warrant the conclusion that the great majority of Nonconformists, if confronted with the problem, would unhesitatingly condemn the use of all mechanical or chemical means of prevention, and would strongly insist on the voluntary moral control of all natural functions."[51]

"Voluntary moral control" eventually became the objective for many of those who had been called on to clarify their stands, and many found that if they had to draw a line, they would do so at artificial means of contraception. To some it might seem that the religious birth control debate limited itself to the most conservative and fundamentalist of believers who were reacting to the presence of technological methods of prevention. However, as mentioned before, those methods were widely available in the mid-nineteenth century. Instead, the more liberal affiliations were the ones who brought this point of contention to the forefront of the debate. As a result, they complicated the argument rather than simplifying it. Those who would later criticize the Catholic Church for holding that "natural law" dictated propagation of the race and that nothing should interfere with it were at this time condemning artificial contraception as "against nature," and they therefore were forced to answer to questions of the "naturalness" of abstinence.

Marchant edited a second book entitled *The Control of Parenthood*, which was published and distributed in the United States, as well as in Great Britain. In this publication Dr. Mary Scharlieb restated the positions of denominations outlined in the previous work, elaborating somewhat on the various positions. According to Scharlieb, Catholic doctrine dictated that married couples should come together only with the intention of procreation; and even though one could not pretend that all Catholics abode by this teaching, it did have some effect; Catholic families averaged 6.6 children while the general population averaged 3.13. She also noted that Anglican bishops had recognized the limited use of periodic abstinence in severe cases where health and financial reasons might warrant family limitation but that "recourse to drugs and to appliances is dangerous, demoralizing and sinful."[52]

## The Lambeth Discussions

The Lambeth Conference of 1908 had condemned contraceptive use, citing moral and family decay, material greed, and health risks connected with them. Furthermore, the bishops considered the global race issue of serious importance. According to conference chairman G. F. Bristol, there was cause for concern for the world at large because of recent birth rate trends: "There is the danger of deterioration whenever the race is recruited from the inferior and not from the superior stocks. There is the world-danger that the great English-speaking peoples, diminished in number and weakened in moral force, should commit the crowning infamy of race-suicide, and so fail to fulfil that high destiny to which in the Providence of God they have been manifestly called."[53] Evidence such as this demonstrated time and again that there was more to the religious birth control dispute than simply variations in canon. The years from 1908 to 1910 are important to watch in the development of the Anglican position. It is impossible at this point to make a detailed prediction regarding the entire Lambeth communion of churches and whether it would place continued importance on procreation of the better stock or go so far as to suggest limiting the procreation of lesser stock, but the general concern about the future of the race was evident. As early as 1910 the Anglican Church was being urged to incorporate eugenics measures into marriage doctrine, teaching couples that marriage should be entered into only under conditions of "soundness of mind and body." Furthermore, restrictions should be put in place based on "known laws of health and human progress."[54]

In the United States Episcopalians were praised by eugenicists as being among the first to put the practical measure of marriage regulation into action. In his 1911 publication *Christ's Social Remedies* Harry Earl Montgomery had commended the American Society of Sanitary and Moral

Prophylaxis for its work and spoke for many eugenicists in his call for the prohibition of marriage of the unfit. According to Montgomery: "Nearly every case ... of criminal moral depravity ... is produced by ancestral influences. Good seed generates sound and healthy fruit, and imperfect parentage can yield only defective offspring."[55]

Two years earlier, Anglican Archdeacon Peile, in *Eugenics Review*, recognized a natural reluctance of the clergy to support eugenics but gave his own cautious approval. "These subjects must be approached for the sake of humanity and civilization," wrote Peile.[56] By 1912 an Episcopal cathedral in Chicago, the Cathedral of Saints Peter and Paul, was requiring a physician's clean bill of health before performing a wedding. Clergy there refused to marry a couple unless "both contracting parties produce certificates from reputable physicians that they are normal bodily and mentally and have no communicable or incurable diseases."[57]

The Lambeth Conferences were especially significant, in particular because the Conference of 1930 has been viewed by historians as the turning point in the debate over birth control. However, other denominations were beginning to struggle with the issue. When addressing the problems of marriage and the family early in this century, Catholic, Protestant, and Jewish denominations obliged themselves to spell out the purposes of marriage. Before 1920 all three ranked procreation as the first purpose of marriage. Catholics ranked "mutual assistance in life" and "the restraint of concupiscence" second and third. Protestants ranked "the avoidance of sin" and "the mutual help and comfort which husband and wife may render the one to the other" behind procreation, where Jews focused on "life-companionship" and "the education of children."[58]

The Lambeth Conference of 1908 reflected the value placed on procreation in marriage, without specifically ranking the purposes of marriage, but the bishops were already drawing a line between "artificial" means of contraception and "restraint." They recommended the following:[59] "(a) The prohibition of so-called Neo-Malthusian appliances, and of patent drugs, and corrupting advertisements. (b) The prosecution of all who publicly and professionally assist preventive methods. (c) A proper and efficient standard and status of those who practise [sic] midwifery. (d) The national recognition of the dignity of motherhood, evinced by the provision of adequate care, protection, and assistance for women before and after childbirth."[60] But they also stated, "Abstention from marriage is within a man's moral right; self-restraint in marriage is within his right; but to marry with the deliberate intention of defeating one of the chief ends of marriage is to deprave the ideal of marriage."[61]

Difficulties arose as a result of such discourse. Though clerics sought to clarify their positions, thereby satisfying church members in modern times of confusion, they actually complicated the issue. For instance, three major points in this brief statement alone opened the door to argument. First of all, by qualifying "restraint," birth control advocates demanded to know why there was any difference between that and any other methods. Were not the motivations behind using contraception and restraint the same? Second, birth control advocates contended they did not hope to "defeat" procreation within a marriage, only to limit it through the spacing of children. Finally, the bishops referred to procreation as "one of" the chief ends, implying there are other equally important purposes in marriage. In another passage the bishops' term "preventive abortion"[62] angered advocates, most of whom promoted preventive education as a way to limit the number of abortions.

In 1920 the bishops reaffirmed their condemnation, emphasizing the "grave physical, moral and spiritual perils incurred by the use of contraceptives," and condemned "the teaching which under the name of science and religion encouraged married people in the deliberate cultivation of sexual union as an end in itself."[63] They also reaffirmed their position against the use of condoms, even to prevent venereal disease, opening the discussion to debate even further. Resolution no. 69 stated: "The Conference must condemn the distribution or use, before exposure to infection, of so-called prophylactics, since these cannot but be regarded as an invitation to vice." And resolution no. 70 resembled statements of the Comstock crusade fifty years earlier: "The Conference urges the importance of enlisting the help of all high-principled men and women, whatever be their religious beliefs, in co-operation with or, if necessary, in bringing pressure to bear upon, authorities both national and local, for removing such incentives to vice as indecent literature, suggestive plays and films, the open or secret sale of contraceptives, and the continued existence of brothels."[64] In this conference the bishops devoted their discussion to the many problems facing the family in general and included increased use of contraception among the problems.

Recognizing the value of church support, Marie Stopes hoped to influence the bishops before the 1920 conference and sent a lengthy message to each of the 267 bishops who attended. She claimed the message was divinely inspired, calling it "A New Gospel to All Peoples: A revelation of God uniting physiology and the religions of man." Stopes wrote: "My Lords, I speak to you in the name of God. You are his priests. I am his prophet. I speak to you of the mysteries of the union of man and woman. ... No act of union fulfils the Law of God unless the two not only pulse together to the highest climax, but also remain thereafter in a long brooding embrace without severance from each other." According to Stopes, the Christian churches were mistaken in their notion that sexual union was designed solely for the purpose of creating children. Rather, God commanded that couples should use the best means of birth control "placed at man's service by science, and that the bishops must teach their flocks that "the pure and holy sacrament of marriage may no longer be debased and befouled by the archaic ignorance of the centuries."[65] There is no record of how the bishops reacted, except that they did not change their position that summer. Stopes gained the wrath of other clergy, however. The Catholic Fr. F. M. de Zulueta described the *New Gospel* as "a most profane compound of imaginary mysticism and pornography." Even friends and associates criticized her for writing it.[66]

## *Other Protestants Speak*

Though birth control historians mark the 1930 Lambeth Conference as a distinct event in which religious figures dramatically shifted their position on birth control, it was already clear in 1908 and 1920 that foundations of religious positions were not that solid. The scene among denominations in the United States was similar. Not all denominations addressed the contraception question in detail, but in detailing their views on the sanctity of marriage in reaction to the rising divorce rate, the values they held for procreation were apparent. For instance, in classifying marriage as an ordinance of God, and the family as a divine institution, Presbyterians declared in 1912:

1. God created the race male and female, that the relation of husband and wife might be possible.
2. He created Adam and Eve and related them to each other as husband and wife.
3. The Scriptures teach us that it was God who "set the solitary in families."
4. In His Word God has specifically legislated concerning marriage and the formation of the family.[67]

In finding no direct reference to contraception among published proceedings, it should not be concluded that any denomination was evading or ignoring the issue. It must be remembered that at the time of the above statement, Margaret Sanger had not yet begun her work in the United States. Though many Protestants feared the discrepancy between birthrates among Catholics and old Protestant stock, there was not yet a social movement with which to contend. Even after Sanger began her struggle to make information available, law enforcement agencies succeeded in having her arrested and convicted. There was no need for American churches, as there had been for European churches, to participate in social or legislative action to see that the problem was addressed.

Another area which illustrates clerical concern for the rise in contraceptive use is found in available catechism literature. Religious education spoke to matters of the family, especially marriage, in its preparing of ministers for pastoral duties. Seminarians were reminded of the importance of urging couples to enter into marriage with proper understanding and intentions as they watched the divorce rate climb and the status of women change. Here one example of United Lutheran teaching indicates how clergy of various denominations were to approach the subject when counseling: "Let him know that marriage is honorable, well pleasing to God, ordained by Him, and is the natural and Christian mode of life. Let him show the sin, the danger and the sad individual consequences of the modern disparagement of marriage and motherhood; that home-life is the true life, and that it must come to ruin where marriage is despised."[68] Writing before the beginning of Sanger's movement, the author recognized the already changing structure of the family. He did not propose solutions for the difficulties in society at large; that was not the purpose of this work. However, it is unlikely that he or any other prominent Lutheran would do so. Doctrine varied among different Lutheran sects, but none of them encouraged reaching beyond their congregations to speak to the subject of marriage, the family, contraception, or any other topic.

Lutherans criticized the Lambeth Conference encyclical of 1920 for doing just that, inspiring movements outside the Church, and for representing Anglican bishops as the singular voice of Christianity. Regarding the bishops' "Home and Family" resolutions, United Lutheran spokesman Charles M. Jacobs[69] said only that they called for "no extended comment."[70] Though he saw no role for Lutherans in social or legislative matters, Jacobs expressed hope that in the future they could at least let their own voice be heard on subjects regarding marriage and the family, perhaps through the National Lutheran Council.

There would not be heard a common Lutheran voice on birth control; nevertheless, the subject was addressed. The conservative Missouri Synod decried contraception, no longer citing the story of Onan as much as it would the verses of Psalm 127: "Lo, sons are a heritage from the Lord, the fruit of the womb a reward. Like arrows in the hand of a warrior are the sons of one's youth. Happy is the man who has his quiver full of them!

He shall not be put to shame when he speaks with his enemies in the gate."[71] In addition to biblical explanations, clergy provided medical evidence as to the health risks of contraceptive use. According to the Lutheran opposition, eighty-five percent of all women in Chicago hospitals were there because of birth control. One cleric wrote: "All forms of contraceptives are more or less injurious to the health, both of husband and wife, but particularly of the latter, as every reputable physician will testify."[72]

On the larger political and social levels, the *Lutheran Quarterly* found little fault with eugenics when looking at the positive influence it could have on strengthening the "European race." A review in 1914 of a *Hibbert Journal* article entitled "Eugenics and Politics" never mentioned contraception specifically but implied that its use among the upper class should, at the least, be discouraged:

> The decline of the birth rate in the upper-classes from four and one-half to one per marriage means that society sheds one-half of its best people in every generation, and supplies the vacancy with the offspring of inferior classes whose families still average more than seven. Moreover, the evil is aggravated by the postponement of marriage in the middle-classes, thus reducing the number of children. The result will be the elimination of the middle-class, and the survival of the unfit and the defective.[73]

The author indicated no recommendation to encourage contraceptive use among the lower classes, only to urge others to have more children. Actually, his objectives mirror those of birth control advocates. Those who promoted contraceptive use pledged to strengthen the family by limiting the number of children, while he maintained that middle- and upper-class families would become stronger with more children: "We must look to the family for the supply of capable men. … The family is the only mechanism which human wit has ever contrived that has attractiveness enough to bind the individual's caprice to travel in regular orbits, and to build up an orderly society out of the gravitation of social units. The family lies at the roots both of the school and of the factory and of the Church. If the State wants good citizens it must keep the family in good condition."[74]

American Episcopalians raised the issue directly, though briefly, in their discussion of modern problems affecting the family at its General Convention in 1916. There the Joint Commission on Legislation on Matters Relating to Holy Matrimony reported on its New York meeting of the previous year in which it outlined the purposes of marriage as follows: "Marriage is intended for the mutual companionship and support of husband and wife in good and evil estate; for the procreation of children; and for their nurture and training. To ignore or defeat any of these purposes is a sinful violation of God's institution."[75] From this the message was clear. Even though procreation did not appear first on the list, it weighed equally among the other aims. However, when it came to the specific topic of contraception, the convention had only this to say: "The subject of Eugenics in reference to marriage is beset with so many difficulties, legal, medical, moral and religious, that the Commission is not prepared to recommend any legislation by the Church on the subject."[76]

Mainstream Methodists and Northern Baptists, as well as the more conservative Southern Baptists, approached issues of marriage and the family in the same way many denominations did, expressing their concern for the decline of the family and the rising divorce rate. They said little, if anything, about contraception in particular. Instead they focused nearly all their attention on temperance. A panacea for them, temperance was discussed, preached, and praised in every pulpit, conference, and convention before 1920, and they felt that once enacted, problems in American families would largely dissipate. After passage of the Volstead Act committees on temperance and social service redirected their efforts to reporting on the status of the family. After some amount of research their primary goal became lowering the divorce rate by calling for uniform divorce and marriage laws among the states. Their eugenic concerns were apparent in those appeals, as they recommended that couples be required to obtain physicians' certificates of health when applying for marriage licenses. According to Methodists, couples should show "freedom from vicious diseases" before entering into marriage.[77]

The Baptist *Standard* supported a eugenics law proposed in Michigan,[78] and the Southern Baptist Convention proposed uniform legislation that would require medical examinations and that "those afflicted with infectious disease or other maladies disqualifying them for marriage and threatening the health, happiness and usefulness of offspring shall be prohibited from marrying."[79] In addition to blood tests, Baptists and Methodists proposed a substantial waiting period between obtaining a license and the ceremony itself and enforced publication of impending marriages. They had no intention of limiting numbers of burdensome children by promoting contraception; they wanted to ensure that "bad" marriages not take place at all.

Even after Sanger's movement was well underway, there was very little mention of birth control. If anything, Baptists wanted to preserve the traditional role of women and disregarded any attempts to encourage freedom of the modern woman, which meant limiting the number of her children. In response to the notion that poor women might be having more children than they could afford, Northern Baptists supported some form of public relief. In 1920 they maintained it was "a life and death matter to women and babies" to see enactment of the Sheppard-Towner Act for the protection of maternity and infancy.[80]

Feminists of the period contended that the Sheppard-Towner Act, passed in 1921 and renewed until 1924, was a ploy to gain female votes while portraying all women as mothers. Proponents viewed it as a way to lend much-needed relief to lower-class pregnant women and infants, providing pregnancy and "well baby" checkups. Religious leaders who had demonstrated concern for the plight of poor mothers who had difficulty providing for their families publicly supported the measure. Advocates of birth control, however, viewed it as undermining their cause. Sheppard-Towner did not support birth control, and Sanger argued that the measure's benevolence was "superficial," near-sighted, and "dysgenic." She maintained that women wanted to have fewer children, but Sheppard-Towner centers "would teach them to have more."[81]

Regarding marriages in general, Southern Baptists felt that to some degree the "burden" of many children actually kept more marriages together. In an article published in 1920 in the *Review and Expositor*, Rev. E. W. Stone wrote, "Another thing that helps to swell the number of divorces is the decreasing number of children in modern families. Where there are none at all, no bond exists to hold the pair together except respect for the marriage vow, and the romantic passion. If there are but one or two, either party feels capable of assuming the burden of their care."[82]

Members of the Christian Reformed Church held the same regard for temperance that Baptists and Methodists did but placed an even higher value on eugenics than they had expressed. In 1915 Charles P. Stahr wrote in the *Reformed Church Review*, "Laws preventing the marriage and reproduction of those mentally defective and physically unfit are not only justifiable, but wise and necessary." That statement alone represented nothing different from other assertions, but Stahr went on to recommend comparatively severe eugenic measures:

> We must, however, have laws not only controlling the marriage of the feeble-minded, using the term as indicating a broad class, but preventing their reproduction. Laws with this object in view can take two forms, a law permitting the sterilization of the class by a surgical operation, or laws requiring the segregation and proper isolation of the class according to sex.
>
> The first form has not met with favor up to the present time. It has been applied chiefly to certain classes of the criminal and

insane. The states of Indiana and Connecticut and Oregon, to our knowledge, have such laws in force at present.

The second form of law is a most commendable one.[83]

Though this position appears to contradict the more general one resting in opposition to contraception, in fact, it does not. The fact that religious conservatives could accept eugenics and not condone contraceptive use was not problematic, at least not in their eyes. The dichotomy lay in the attitudes toward reproductive control among two groups of people who were perceived as very different: the physically ill or "feeble-minded," and the general population. When Sanger gained the nation's attention in 1916 promoting "voluntary motherhood" within the mainstream, clerics formulated their variety of responses.

## *Catholics Speak Out*

By 1920 the position of Roman Catholics in the birth control debate was becoming clearer and more public, but it was still centered primarily on eugenics. In the discussion of eugenics in general, Catholic pronouncements essentially lay in opposition, but the were by no means unified or simple. Rather, the severe antagonism between eugenicists and Catholic stemmed from the anti–Catholicism inherent in the eugenics movement in England, as Catholics found themselves described in science journals and other publications as primary contributors to the decline of the race.[84] This sentiment naturally crossed the Atlantic, where demographics were changing rapidly.[85]

Catholics did not condemn all aspects of the eugenics movement. They engaged in complex discussions and publicly supported much of its intentions. And again, much of the discussion began in England. One of the most prominent Catholics in England's eugenics arguments was Rev. Thomas Gerrard, who eventually carried the debate into the area of contraception. In his response to the English Majority and Minority Reports of the Poor Law Commission in 1911 Rev. Thomas Gerrard claimed:

> We must move warily and scientifically. In the first place, it must be granted as a principle that the government of a country has a right to have recourse to compulsory segregation and surgery if such action is necessary for the good of the community. The State hangs people, shuts them up in the gaol, in lunatic asylums and in inebriate homes. On the same principle, it can, if necessary, carry out the eugenic reforms proposed.

The question is whether all such drastic measures are necessary.[86]

With regard to the regulation of marriage, Gerrard maintained that the Church had no authority to prohibit marriage between "degenerates" and that medical examinations before marriage addressed only the physical being. On the other hand, moral fitness and spirituality were already addressed by the Church, according to Gerrard, when it prohibited marriage between Catholics and non–Catholics, and between blood relatives. Still, he hinted that the Church might consider reinstituting other regulations that it had practiced in past centuries, though he did not detail what those regulations were.[87]

Gerrard subsequently condemned divorce as being antieugenic because it created an environment in which children suffer, but more important, he indirectly condemned the use of contraceptives: "Since the sexual appetite has for its proper object the procreation of children, any perversion of it, even within the marriage state is forbidden. It is the perversion of the appetite within the marriage state which is so largely responsible for the deplorable 'race suicide' so prevalent in this time."[88] Gerrard's argument about the difficult environment resulting from divorce was an important one because it helped to define the Church's unchanging stance against divorce. But it also aided in obscuring the division between nurture and nature. Social Darwinists had claimed nature was the most dominant factor in determining human quality and at the same time attacked Catholics for preventing nature from taking its course through their aid to the poor.

One Catholic who argued otherwise when the debate reached America was John Lapp, a regular columnist in *Catholic Charities Review*, who asked, "Is a person who is sick from overwork or contagion unfit to survive? Is the man whose morale has been broken by fruitless searches for work or for a living wage unfit for survival? Is he who has been crippled by an accident unfit? Is the individual who loses everything in the failure of a bank or a business or a corporation thereby unfit to survive?"[89] Much of the American Catholic examination of eugenics took place in the pages of the *Ecclesiastical Review*, beginning around 1910. In response to a presentation on eugenics at the sixtieth annual session of the American Medical Association in Indianapolis, the *Ecclesiastical Review* published a series of complex discussions with differing Catholic arguments. In "The Morality and Lawfulness of Vasectomy" for instance, Rev. P. A. Schmitt, S.J., concluded that performing vasectomies "cannot be said to be wrong in all cases"—in this case for the prevention of reproduction among convicted criminals. Still, he maintained that proponents of vasectomy assume that heredity is the chief, if not the sole, cause of degeneracy. Schmitt argued, "Whereas evil has many sources, such as a false method of education, mistaken or insufficient nutrition, especially the use of alcoholic stimulants, social and labor conditions which overtax the capacity of the individual, the strenuosity and nervous anxiety incident to the striving after material success, artificial living and the pursuit of enervating pleasures, — all of which contribute to the growth of insanity or mental and physical degeneracy."[90] The *Ecclesiastical Review* existed as a forum for clerics and Catholic theologians to examine, discuss, and analyze difficult religious questions of the day in an effort to help develop consistent doctrine for clergy to put into practice. The results were far from simplistic or dogmatic, as can be seen in the questions over reproductive control. Adding to the complexity was the publication of some articles in English and some in Latin, posing some problems in translating difficult arguments. The discussions, of course, branched from those begun in England and responded to developments in the United States. Yet they drew comments from Europe and the United States, which attempted to draw universal conclusions regarding questions of reproduction. These complicating forces caused a particularly interesting problem in the vasectomy series in 1910 and 1911.

The Rev. Theodore Laboure, of the Theological Seminary in San Antonio, Texas, took part in the discussion, presenting his analysis in Latin, based on his interpretation of Rev. Schmitt's early arguments, in their original German. By May of 1911 the discussion over the morality of the intention of vasectomy had become a complex one in itself, examining all of the contemporary arguments regarding factors contributing to degeneracy. One of the factors— according to many eugenicists— was large numbers of children in a family. According to Laboure, he had unwittingly concluded, because of his problem with translation, that "vasectomy is unlawful as a means against onanism; but that it is lawful when used in order to prevent the excessive number of children, and to prevent feticide, because here the good of society has to be taken into consideration."[91] Laboure was, by no means, the ultimate voice of the Church, and historians may never know exactly what he intended in his argument before it was brought to his attention, but the Catholic debate over birth control might have taken a different direction if that line of argument had been allowed to continue.

Their position was exemplified in *Eugenics Review*, where the editors printed a letter criticizing a pamphlet distributed by the Eugenics Education Society entitled "A Word on Racial Responsibility." The writer responded: "Throughout, the argument is concentrated on what is physical without any mention of man's main purpose in life, the development and perfecting of his spiritual nature." He added, "The aims of the Society, as set forth here, are to eliminate from the race all mental and physical disease, and so far they are very commendable. But good ends are sometimes pursued by evil methods, and until the Society shows that it reckons moral 'fitness' as even more desirable than physical, and that it tolerates no such immoral methods as artificial sterility, its programme must remain suspect."[92] Though this Catholic attack on eugenics is somewhat harsher than the Protestant one, the similarities were clearly there. They both seemed to accept the basic aims of eugenics but condemned its focus on the physical rather than the spiritual, the Catholics emphasizing the spiritual "purpose" of humans, the Protestants the spiritual "nurturing" of humans.

In this case the Eugenics Education Society responded to the Catholic allegation that it tolerated artificial sterility. According to Society president Leonard Darwin, the fourth son of Charles Darwin, the organization promoted the voluntary limitation in the size of families but considered the methods used, either abstinence or other means, a "moral question to be decided by each couple."[93] This notion became increasingly significant as the debate unfolded. Once the groundwork was laid in the religious realm for the acceptance of birth control by married couples in limited instances, the argument opened up to the issue of various contraceptive methods. Certainly, by the 1960s and 1970s the debate over contraception and particularly abortion had become centered on issues of privacy and personal choice. Early on in the debate, eugenicists may have used the personal choice argument as they recognized that implementation would ultimately require very intimate decisions. But in the hearts of eugenicists, society and the human race were at stake, making this anything but a personal matter.

This was especially true with regard to sterilization. Terms such as "artificial sterility" might be used to refer to contraception, but in the case of Catholic arguments, it was generally actual sterilization to which they referred. The practice was urged by eugenicists and legalized in various states, beginning with Indiana, to eliminate the propagation of the unfit. Directed primarily toward convicted criminals, it constituted part of a program in which "the criminal and 'hereditarily-tainted' populations should be segregated and sterilized."[94] Catholic theologians had been among the first critics of sterilization. A few were able to justify it in terms of maintaining social order, as capital punishment was designed to do. One of the principal players in this argument was Joseph Mayer, who in his work *The Sterilization of the Mentally Diseased*, used the arguments of Thomas Aquinas, who condoned the castration of certain convicted criminals. However, the vast majority opposed it. Many of the arguments coincided with general opposition to birth control. When the practice of sterilization intensified after the First World War, at the same time as did directives based on the same logic, Catholic opposition grew. This church of immigrants and "defenders of the poor" attacked compulsory sterilization, eventually influencing civil action and changes in the laws.[95]

As with conservative and mainline Protestants, Catholics in the United States did not begin fully to attack the use of contraception until Sanger's movement was well underway. There were some earlier declarations, largely in response to general criticism of large families among Catholics. For example, Cardinal Gibbons, in a 1903 interview, was quoted as saying, "A large family is a blessing. To defeat Nature in marriage is as criminal as to commit murder. No excuse is possible — neither financial reasons nor any other. The question of economics has no place, should have none, in regulating the size of families. That Catholics are taught this explains why, as a rule, they have large families."[96] However, when the Catholic opposition literature did appear, much of it responded more directly to Sanger's work. Rather than present strictly theological or dogmatic discourse on the sinfulness of contraception, Catholic publications attempted to convince their readers of the social, physical, and mental risks associated with its use. It was no accident that initial criticism came from Catholic physicians, for they had been aware long before clergy that women were asking for, and often getting, contraceptive information. Catholic physician and educator Austin O'Malley[97] stated such in the weekly *America*, where he displayed less than restrained tactics by referring to Sanger as the editor of the "dead and buried *Woman Rebel*, who was indicted for sending *Woman Rebel* through the mails, by a Government which does not grow faint at the moral aroma of the *Menace*, that spiritual reading of the submerged or decadent." In addition, he called section 1142 of the Penal Code of New York a law that such a civilized society should find unnecessary. The law made it a misdemeanor, punishable with imprisonment of several years, in O'Malley's words, to "give information subversive of the end of marriage: the procreation of children for the greater glory of God and their own external happiness."[98]

O'Malley's rhetoric was not representative of all the early Catholic opposition. Most of the literature was presented with much more logical and rational arguments based on natural law. The effort of the Church was not devoted entirely to persuading Catholics through logic that birth control was wrong; rather it demonstrated the growing attempt by Catholics to present themselves as Americans first, rather than simply Catholics. These few years were crucial for Catholics. Keeping in mind that they wanted desperately to appear as law-abiding Americans during the rebirth of the Ku Klux Klan, and as patriotic when the United States entered the European war, it is easier to understand why they sometimes shied away from religious arguments, opting for legal arguments. More civil analysis of the status of birth control revealed how the Church wanted to appear American and antianarchical.[99] But the fact that Catholics saw this as an issue of natural law made their political position even more difficult. For natural law could not be questioned or denied, and it applied to every human being, not just Catholics. As much as they wanted to appear similar to all Americans who were participating in the political process, when arguing against legalizing contraception on the basis of natural law, they were perceived as authoritarian and attempting to dictate their morality on others. At the same time, Catholics defended themselves by arguing that they were simply protecting a law that was already in place, while Baptists and Methodists were attempting to legislate their religious teaching through the prohibition of liquor.

In 1916, the year in which Sanger opened her first clinic in New York, *America* published an editorial criticizing Sanger for breaking a law "expressive of the moral sense of the community," thereby violating the rights of other citizens. The editorial effectively alluded to international strife in this decade of revolutions in China, Ireland, Mexico, and finally Russia, warning that this "spirit of revolt" and "new social anarchy" were threatening American society. According to the author, during the federal court proceedings in which Sanger was tried for violating postal laws, friends of the accused "left little undone or unsaid to show their contempt both for the law and for the Court."[100]

Another way Catholics could demonstrate their Americanism, while at the same time opposing birth control, was to proclaim that the greatness of America prohibited any realistic applications of Malthusianism here. Whereas neo–Malthusians argued that devastation in Europe before, during, and after World War I should be blamed on overpopulation, the opposition argued that there still existed large sections of the world that were uncultivated and uninhabited. In addition, they perceived the United States as one place in which both an abundance of land and economic prosperity would guarantee that subsistence increase faster than population. Indeed, scientific developments, according to Edmund E. Sinclair, could and did make the quality of life improve even more quickly.

A Bostonian concerned with recent publicity given to the subject of birth control, Sinclair submitted a commentary to *America*, which refuted

Malthusian arguments. If, as demographers had claimed, the United States was doubling its population every twenty-nine years, it must also be recognized that it was doubling its wealth even more quickly. Sinclair maintained that in 1880 the United States wealth amounted to $43,642,000,000, which in 1904 had increased to $107,104,192,410; two and a half times in only twenty-four years. "This example of our own land should surely satisfy Malthusians that *our* population, at least, is not out-running subsistence," wrote Sinclair.[101] He only briefly reminded readers that his was a Catholic argument when noting that American Catholics, "in Christian simplicity, preserve the ideals of matrimony, presenting numerous souls to God and sons to the State," portraying them more as Christians than Catholics, and as more obedient to the United States government than to the pope. Calling on Catholics to be the "dialecticians" in this matter, he firmly placed importance on secular reasoning, in this case economic argument, rather than on theology, doctrine, or dogma.[102]

## John A. Ryan Takes a Stand

In the case of social argument Monsignor John A. Ryan was the prominent dialectician. Ryan, a theologian who spoke more often as a social activist, headed the newly created social action department of the National Catholic Welfare Conference and taught moral theology and industrial ethics at Catholic University.[103] In this position he very clearly outlined church doctrine regarding social issues and public policy. On the subject of birth control he cited "natural law" arguments within the Church's stand, and often presented logical social arguments against it much in the same way the nonclerical opposition was doing. However, he was not just another opponent, nor was he acting as a spokesman for just another group taking the popular stance. It was because of Ryan that Catholic opposition was set apart from all the rest. In fact, it was because of Ryan that Church officials first gave the subject attention.

The timing, as well as the foundations, of his arguments illustrates the fact that they were not based in centuries-old dogma but constituted a reaction to the situation at hand. Ryan was the one who encouraged the Church to recognize the importance of the issue in 1907. In an essay published in the *Catholic Encyclopedia*, Ryan decried neo–Malthusians, claiming small families caused, or were the result of, varying degrees of egotism, materialism, and self-indulgence.[104] In 1915 Ryan responded to an article that *Harper's Weekly* had included in a series on birth control. The editor prefaced the series by stating that "full and accurate information about the controversy, with the arguments on both sides and the important facts in the case, is due to its readers." In the article in question Mary Alden Hopkins reprinted much of a lengthy reply by Ryan to an invitation to join the Birth Control League. Ryan wrote:

> I regard the practice which your organization desires to promote as immoral, degrading and stupid. The so-called contraceptive devices are intrinsically immoral because they involve the unnatural use, the perversion of a human faculty.... Such conduct is quite immoral as self mutilation or the practice of solitary vice. Any person who rejects this fundamental moral principle concerning the wrongfulness of perverting a faculty, must logically hold that there is no such thing as intrinsic immorality, and that moral badness is always identical with individual disutility, and that anything is right which any individual thinks is useful.[105]

He closed his letter by saying:

> I am invited to send two dollars for membership in the Birth Control League. I must respectfully decline with the observation that I had much rather give the money to an organization for the training of prize fighters. I would aid in the development of at least some manly and human qualities.
>     Yours, "more in sorrow than in anger,"
>                                                 John A. Ryan[106]

Hopkins included Ryan's letter as the only evidence of the American Catholic stand on birth control, a stand that she believed contradicted earlier Church teachings. Hopkins understood those teachings to declare a woman free from sin if her husband took measures to prevent conception under her protest, thereby opening the door to approval in some instances. Ryan responded in a subsequent letter to the editor, which criticized the source of her information — an English translation of a German translation of a Roman decision. Ryan said: "The translation is crudely literal, gives a ludicrous version of certain technical terms, and in one or two matters is positively misleading."[107] According to Ryan, Hopkins overlooked the more important conclusion that the husband was guilty of a grave sin; therefore, the official teaching of the Church was that all forms of contraception are morally wrong and unlawful.[108]

Ryan again addressed the topic in 1916 in an important article entitled "Family Limitation, Church and Birth Control," published in the Catholic University of America's *Ecclesiastical Review.* In this article he elaborated on the sinfulness of contraception without identifying any particular church teaching:

That all positive methods of birth prevention (abortion and all the so-called contraceptives) are condemned by the Church as grievous sins, is evident from the long list of official declarations on the subject during the nineteenth century by the Roman Congregations.... What is the rational ground of this condemnation? The fact that all these devices constitute the immoral perversion of a human faculty. According to natural reason, the primary and fundamental criterion of good and bad is human nature adequately considered. Actions which are in harmony with nature are good; those which are not in harmony with nature are bad.[109]

Ryan was less concerned with discussing the matter of sin than he was with warning of the social consequences. He did note that if all Catholics would just recognize that devices for the prevention of birth were grievously sinful, the situation would be relatively simple. But the primary focus of his argument attacked those who encouraged limiting family size. Ryan criticized the claim by birth control advocates that the quality of children should take precedence over the quantity, stating that both the quantity and the quality of the human race would be adversely affected by contraceptive use, again citing egotism, materialism, and self-indulgence. He also responded to the social arguments of birth control advocates who suggested legalized contraceptives would alleviate social ills. He recognized the eugenic ideals in the birth control movement, questioning their broad categorization of "defectives" and their concern for the "welfare of the race," which he contended meant the "welfare of the fortunate majority who do not desire the inconvenience of helping to support any considerable number of defectives." Regarding the need for social reform, Ryan suggested other methods that included improvements in living and working conditions.[110]

His principal argument was important, but embedded in it were three subtle references, which proved equally as significant in the debate to come. First of all, Ryan acknowledged the prevalence of contraceptive practice among the middle and upper classes, but in his opening paragraph he maintained that the underlying purpose of recent treatises had been "to make known and recommend to the poorer classes devices for the limitation of their families." The Catholic Church represented much of the lower classes and was now speaking for them on the birth control issue. According to Monsignor William J. White, Diocesan Director of Charities in Brooklyn, "Today in the United States, the Catholic Church is the church of the working-man, the church of the common people, whom our Savior loved."[111] In 1916 Catholics saw the bigotry against them expressed in demographic rhetoric, which would culminate in immigration restriction a decade later. Although the position taken by the Catholic Church was essentially no different from official positions of any other denominations in 1916, it would react to birth control advocates differently.

Whereas old Protestant stock objected to contraception among "their own kind," they could accept eugenics as a means to limit not only the number of "weak" specimens among the race but the size of the entire lower class. On the other hand, Catholics opposed contraceptive use among any group. They argued that segments of the middle and upper classes that were promoting contraception should beware of the limiting effects it would have on their own numbers, and they additionally condemned eugenics because it was, in some regard, directed at themselves. According to Thomas J. Gerrard of the Catholic Social Guild, who did not object to moderate forms of eugenics in which man "doesn't play God," God's action and man's action were intended to remain distinct, as perfection in this life on earth is unattainable.[112]

When birth control was more clearly connected to social control, some other denominations hesitated in condoning it as well. Again, the reasons had little to do with official doctrine, traditional teaching, or Scripture. Rather, the reluctance to support birth control was rooted in a denomination's understanding of its role in society. One of the clearest examples can be seen in Lutheran teachings, which theologically and historically valued faith over good works. As other Protestant denominations in the United States considered a variety of possible solutions to social ills, Lutherans resisted and were criticized for their resistance.[113] The conservative Missouri Synod Lutherans resisted even more strongly and remained in opposition, along with the Catholic Church, as the birth control debate unfolded. Regarding social reform in general, the Missouri Synod's president F. Pfotenhauer maintained, "The real business of the Church is to preach the Gospel. It is not the mission of the Church to abolish physical misery or to help men to earthly happiness."[114]

Ryan's brief reference to the attempt at controlling births in the lower classes said much about the religious/political/social environment in the United States. Second, Ryan, too, equated contraception with abortion, using the term "birth prevention" rather than "prevention of conception." Sanger and others would challenge this, maintaining they were, above all, interested in preventing conception. It was in this movement that clearer lines were drawn between abortion and contraception, and it was this early cloudiness that initiated further clarification on this point. Third, Ryan brought to light the matter of abstinence, though at the time of this article, it went relatively unnoticed. Ryan wrote:

> Non-Catholics sometimes assume that the Church forbids fam-
> ily limitation by any means whatever. They seem to think that
> the main object of the Church in her legislation on this subject
> is the greatest possible increase in population. Apparently they
> are unaware that it is not the deliberate control of births but
> the positive and unnatural means to this end that falls under
> the Church's condemnation. Against parents who keep their
> families small by chaste abstention from marital intercourse
> the Church has not a word to say.[115]

However, the Catholic discussion of abstinence had not come to an
end. In fact, the debate was just beginning. The question of using periodic abstinence, or the "rhythm" method, eventually became a Catholic
point of contention. When other denominations granted approval of contraception after 1930, the Catholic Church officially allowed use of the
rhythm method. For the time being, promoters of contraception demanded
explanation from those, Catholic or non–Catholic, who did not disapprove of abstinence yet prohibited the use of other methods.

Within Ryan's statement there was something more important than
his defense of abstinence. His acknowledgment that non–Catholics feared
a deliberate increase in the Catholic population held far more weight. He
did not calm the fears of non–Catholics here. In fact, in later years he
intensified those fears. In the 1922 publication of *The State and the Church*
Ryan defended what he claimed was the pope's position that any government should recognize Catholicism as the official religion and that in a
true democracy a Catholic majority would rule.[116]

It was primarily because of Ryan that the Catholic Church in America developed such a vocal stance against birth control.[117] In 1919 American bishops formally adopted their position prohibiting all artificial means
of contraception, repeating much of Ryan's earlier rhetoric of selfishness
in a pastoral letter.[118] As the birth control movement gained support, Ryan
became even more outspoken in his opposition. In an article in 1920 Ryan
outlined the evil consequences of using contraception. First of all, wrote
Ryan, couples faced the "degradation of the marital relation itself since the
husband and wife who indulge in this practice ... cannot help coming to
regard each other to a great extent as mutual instruments of sensual
gratification, rather than cooperation with the Creator in bringing children into the world." The decay of the potential for self-control and population decline would also follow.[119]

Even though Ryan's opposition to birth control at this point was the
most vehement among notable Catholics and non–Catholics, his general
position, as well as the Jewish position, would support those of both liberal

and conservative Protestants. Though denominations disagreed on whether it was social evil, individual immorality, or mortal sin, which surrounded the notion of preventing conception, they all agreed it was wrong. Because Ryan's social views on contraception so clearly tied in with his objectives for society at large,[120] Ryan's aims as head of the Social Action Committee of the NCWC were essentially no different from the aims of similar Protestant or Jewish committees formed to address social issues. The Christian Reformed Church's Permanent Committee on Public Morals expressed many of the same objectives in 1920: "The purpose of which this Committee exists is a real and vital part of the Church's duty toward the communities around her. If the Church takes no active part in defending the people from their enemies of intemperance, Sabbath desecration, social vice, family irreligion and the like, the people soon cease to care what the Church does or says in regard to other things and her influence in the world wanes and perishes."[121] In fact, the stand against contraception by the Reformed Church, as well as by Southern Baptists and Missouri Synod Lutherans, would go unchanged after other denominations shifted toward approval, much in the same way the Catholic stand would. Nevertheless, Catholics would become singled out as the birth control opposition, a development which began with a single event in 1921.

# *Notes*

1. Maggie Hume, *Contraception in Catholic Doctrine: The Evolution of an Earthly Code* (Washington, D.C.: Catholics for a Free Choice, 1991), p. 2; Uta Ranke-Heinemann, *Eunuchs for the Kingdom of Heaven* (New York: Doubleday, 1990), pp. 9–10.

2. John T. Noonan, *Contraception: A History of Its Treatment by the Catholic Theologians and Canonists* (Cambridge, Mass.: Harvard University Press, 1966), pp. 30–31; Hume, p. 2.

3. Genesis 1:27–28; Noonan, p. 31.

4. Genesis 38: 8–10.

5. St. John-Stevas, p. 64. The theological argument was more complex than indicated here. St. John-Stevas discusses the argument more thoroughly, as does Noonan throughout his work.

6. Athengoras, *Embassy for the Christians*, in *Patrologiae Cursus Completus ... Series Graeca*, ed. J. P. Migne, 161 vols. (Paris: J. P. Migne, 1857–1889, 6:91), cited in Riddle, *Eve's Herbs*, p. 83.

7. Clement of Alexandria, *Pedagogus*, 2.10.96.1, cited in Riddle, *Eve's Herbs*, p. 84.

8. Plato, *Charmides*, 157b, cited in Riddle, *Eve's Herbs*, p. 82.

9. *De bono conjugali*, c. 10, n. II; and *Contra Faustum*, XII, c. 61, in Dorothy Dunbar Bromley, *Catholics and Birth Control: Contemporary Views on Doctrine* (New York: Devin-Adair, 1965), pp. 9–10.

10. Noonan, pp. 119–131; Hume, p. 4.

11. Angus McLaren, *A History of Contraception, from Antiquity to the Present Day* (Oxford: Basil Blackwell, 1990), p. 129; P. P. A. Biller, "Birth Control in the West in the Thirteenth and Early Fourteenth Centuries," *Past and Present* 44 (1982), p. 16.

12. Myron Gordon and Frederick R. Abrams, "Ethical Issues in Fertility Control," in *Fertility Control*, ed. Stephen L. Corson, Richard J. Derman, and Louise B. Tyrer (Boston: Little, Brown, 1985), p. 6.

13. McLaren, *History of Contraception*, p. 150.

14. Steven Ozment, *When Fathers Ruled: Family Life in Reformation Europe* (Cambridge: Harvard University Press, 1983), pp. 100, 216; McLaren, p. 151.

15. Rosemary Radford Ruethers, *Religion and Sexism: Images of Women in the Jewish and Christian Traditions* (New York: Simon and Schuster, 1974), p. 300; McLaren, pp. 150–151.

16. Brodie, p. 80.

17. Batzill Hartmann, ed. *Decisiones sanctae sedis de usu et abusu matrimonii*, (Torino: Marietti, 1944), p. 130; Noonan, p. 439; Hume, p. 8.

18. Hume, p. 9. Also see Angus McLaren, *Sexuality and Social Order: The Debate Over the Fertility of Women and Workers in France, 1770–1920* (New York: Holmes and Meier, 1983); Maurice Kirk, Massimo Livi Bacci, and Egon Szabady, eds., *Law and Fertility in Europe: A Study of Legislation Directly or Indirectly Affecting Fertility in Europe, vol. 1* (n.p.: Ordina Editions, n.d.).

19. Noonan, p. 414; B. Deppe, "*Theologie pastorale*," *Nouvelle revue theologique* 31 (1899), pp. 455–456.

20. Noonan, p. 17; Hume, p. 9.

21. Brodie, p. 153; John Todd, *Serpents in the Dove's Nest* (Boston: Lee and Shepard, 1867). Also see G. J. Barker-Benfield, *The Horrors of the Half-Known Life: Male Attitudes Toward Women and Sexuality in Nineteenth Century America* (New York: Harper and Row, 1976).

22. Brodie, 153–154.

23. Matilda Joslyn Gage, *Woman, Church & State: The Original Expose of Male Collaboration Against the Female Sex* (Watertown, Mass.: Persephone Press, 1980 [1893]), p. 234.

24. Lydia Kingsmill Commander, *The American Idea* (New York: Arno Press, 1972), pp. 79–80.

25. "Birth Control, Unnatural and Immoral," *Christian Workers Magazine*, March 1917, 539.

26. *Ibid.*

27. Laws varied widely from state to state by this time, and often physicians could prescribe contraceptives for medical reasons unrelated to preventing pregnancy.

28. William J. Robinson, *Birth Control; or, The Limitation of Offspring by the Prevention of Conception* (New York: Critic and Guide, 1917), pp. 76–78.

29. Stanley P. Caine, "The Origins of Progressivism," in Lewis L. Gould, ed., *The Progressive Era* (Syracuse, N.Y.: Syracuse University Press, 1974), p. 16.

30. For more on the perceived responsibility of churches in society during this period, see Vida D. Scudder, "The Kingdom of Righteousness in American Life," *Dial*, February 16, 1913, pp. 128–130; and *Survey*, March 4, 1911, which devotes much attention to the subject in articles such as "The Religious Basis of Social Work," pp. 893–894; "The Men Who Built a Church," pp. 901–902; "The Pulpit in Public Affairs," pp. 907–908; Simon N. Patten, "The Social Basis of Religion," pp. 909–915; and Graham Taylor, "The Church Preparing for Social Action," pp. 916–921.

31. From *For God and the People, Prayers of the Social Awakening* (New York: Pilgrims Press, 1910), in "Church Preparing for Social Action," *Survey*, March 4, 1911, p. 919.

32. Walter Rauschenbush, *Christianity and the Social Order* (New York: Macmillan, 1914 [1912]).

33. J. Herman Randall, D.D., "The Religion of the Future," in *The Unity of Religions: A Popular Discussion of Ancient and Modern Beliefs*, J. Herman Randall and J. Gardner Smith, eds. (New York: Thomas Crowell, 1910), pp. 351–352.

34. Walter Laidlaw, "The Church and the City Community," *American Journal of Sociology*, May 1911, pp. 798–804.

35. E. Lyttelton, "Eugenics, Ethics and Religion," *Nineteenth Century*, July 1913, pp. 158–159; C. T. Ewart, M.D., "Religion and Eugenics," *Westminster Review*, October 1912, pp. 381–389.

36. Josiah Strong, *The Challenge of the City* (New York: Young Peoples Missionary Movement, 1907), pp. 94, 142.

37. "The Chief End of Man," *Current Literature*, May 1910, pp. 528–531.

38. William Trufant Foster, ed., *The Social Emergency: Studies in Sex Hygiene and Morals* (Boston: Houghton Mifflin, 1914), pp. 1–4.

39. John M. Coulter, "What Biology Has Contributed to Religion," *Biblical World*, April 1913, p. 221.

40. "Nature or Nurture?" *Journal of Heredity* 6 (May 1915), p. 227, in Haller, p. 161.

41. Edwin L. Earp, *The Social Engineer* (New York: Eaton and Mains, 1911), pp. xi–xxiii, 155.

42. Samuel Zane Batten, *The Social Task of Christianity: A Summons to the New Crusade* (New York: Fleming H. Revell, 1911), pp. 34–42. Also see Batten, "The Redemption of the Unfit," *American Journal of Sociology*, September 1908.

43. "Bringing Up a Child," *Christian Century*, May 31, 1917, p. 5.

44. *Ibid.*

45. *Ibid.*

46. For more on the views of behavioral scientists, see the critical Christopher Lasch, *Haven in a Heartless World: The Family Besieged* (New York: Basic Books, 1977).

47. Hugh Northcote, *Christianity and Sex Problems* (Philadelphia: F. A. Davis, 1916), p. 107.

48. Noonan, p. 56. Noonan gives an extensive analysis of doctrinal development from this period to the twentieth century. Also see Norman St. John-Stevas, *The Agonising Choice: Birth Control, Religion and the Law* (Bloomington: Indiana University Press, 1971).

49. Northcote, pp. 110–111.

50. James Marchant, *Birth Rate and Empire* (London: Williams and Norgate, 1917), p. 168. For complete testimony see The Lambeth Conference, 1908 (Resolutions 41, 43); The Lambeth Conference, 1920 (Resolution 68), *The Lambeth Conferences* (1867–1948), edition of the Society for Promoting Christian Knowledge.

51. *Ibid.*, p. 176.

52. Marchant, ed., *The Control of Parenthood* (New York: G. P. Putnam's Sons, 1920), pp. 107–109.

53. Randall T. Davidson, comp., *The Five Lambeth Conferences* (New York: Macmillan, 1920), p. 402.

54. Crackanthorpe, "Marriage, Divorce and Eugenics," *Nineteenth Century*, October 1910, pp. 701–702.

55. Harry Earl Montgomery, *Christ's Social Remedies* (New York: G. Putnam's Sons, 1911), pp. 175–180, 244.

56. Crackanthorpe, "Friends and Foes," p. 746.

57. Graham Taylor, *Religion in Social Action* (New York: Dodd, Mead, 1913), pp. 126–130; "What Is Meant by Eugenics," p. 14.

58. Marchant, *Control of Parenthood*, pp. 146–147.

59. These recommendations reflect the status of legal and available contraception in Europe.

60. Davidson, p. 402.

61. *Ibid.*, p. 400.

62. *Ibid.*

63. Lambeth Conference of Anglican Bishops, *Report*, 1920.

64. *The Lambeth Conferences (1867–1930)* (London: SPCK, 1948), p. 51.

65. Marie Stopes, *A New Gospel to All Peoples* (London: A. L. Humphreys, 1922), quoted in Rose, pp. 135–136.

66. Rose, p. 137.

67. *A Digest of the Acts and Proceedings of the General Assembly of the Presbyterian Church in the United States, 1861–1944* (Richmond, Va: Presbyterian Committee of Publication, 1945), p. 12.

68. G. H. Gerberding, *The Lutheran Catechist* (Philadelphia: Lutheran Publication Society, 1910), p. 223.

69. At this time Jacobs was teaching church history at the Lutheran Theological Seminary in Philadelphia. He later wrote *The Way — A Little Book of Christian Truth* (1922) and *The Story of the Church — An Outline of Its History* (1925).

70. Charles M. Jacobs, "The Lambeth Encyclical," *Lutheran Church Review* 34 (1920), p. 486.

71. Psalm 127: 3–5. Cited in Alan Graebner, "Birth Control and the Lutherans: The Missouri Synod as a Case Study," *Journal of Social History* 2 (summer 1969), p. 311.

72. *Lutheran Witness* 28 (1917), p. 196; Luecke, *"Be Fruitful and Multiply": Earnest Words to Married People* (n.p., n.d. [1914]), p. 7; Graebner, p. 310.

73. *The Lutheran Quarterly* 44 (April 1914), p. 264. Though unclear, it is probable that the author is quoting statistics stated in the *Hibbert Journal* article. I must note that there is nothing provided by the *Lutheran Quarterly* to substantiate these statistics, and they appear exaggerated when compared to others cited during this time period.

74. *Ibid.*

75. *Journal of the General Convention of the Protestant Episcopal Church in the United States of America*, Oct. 11–Oct. 27, 1916 (n.p., 1917), p. 500.

76. *Ibid.*, p. 503.

77. Rev. Edwin Locke, ed., *Journal of the Twenty-Seventh Delegated General Conference of the Methodist Episcopal Church Held in Saratoga Springs, New York May 1–May 29, 1916* (New York: Methodist Book Concern, n.d.), p. 618.

78. *The Standard* 61 (September 2, 1916), p. 4.

79. *Annual of the Southern Baptist Convention, 1920* (Nashville, Tenn.: Marshall Bruce, n.d.), p. 126. See other Southern Baptist resolutions on divorce in the *Annual, 1918*, pp. 107–108. A similar resolution passed by the less conservative Northern Baptists is found in the *Annual of the Northern Baptist Convention, 1916* (n.p.: American Baptist Publication Society, n.d.), p. 216.

80. "Does Congress Want Babies to Die?" *The Baptist* 1 (July 17, 1920), p. 872.

81. Nancy Woloch, *Women and the American Experience* (New York: McGraw-Hill, 1994), pp. 386–387.

82. Rev. E. W. Stone, "Divorce and Law," *Review and Expositor* 17 (1920), p. 19.

83. Charles P. Stahr, "Eugenics," *Reformed Church Review* 19 (January 1915), pp. 222–223.

84. Hasian, p. 90.

85. Sidney Webb, "Physical Degeneracy or Race Suicide?" *London Times*, October 16, 1906, p. 7, col. 1.

86. Thomas Gerrard, "The Catholic Church and Race Culture," *Dublin Review* 149 (1911), pp. 49–68, esp. 58.

87. Rev. Thomas J. Gerrard, *The Church and Eugenics* (London: P. S. King & Sons, 1912), pp. 43–45.

88. *Ibid.*, pp. 43, 45–46.

89. John A. Lapp, "Justice First," *Catholic Charities Review* 11(127): pp. 201–209, 207, in Hasian, p. 103. For more on Catholicism and eugenics, see Lawrence F. Flick, M.D., *Eugenics: A Lecture Delivered in the Catholic Summer School Extension Course, Philadelphia, January 17, 1913* (Philadelphia: John Joseph McVey, 1913); and Henry Davis, S.J., *Eugenics and Its Methods* (New York: Benziger Brothers, 1930).

90. "Rev. P. A. Schmitt, S.J., "The Morality and Lawfulness of Vasectomy," *American Ecclesiastical Review*, May 1911, p. 570.

91. Rev. Theodore Laboure, "Is Vasectomy Then Unlawful?" *Ecclesiastical Review*, May 1911, p. 577. Also see Laboure, O.M.I., "*De Aliquibus Vasectomiae Liceitatem Consequentibus*," *Ecclesiastical Review*, November 1910, pp. 553–558.

92. "Roman Catholic Criticism of Eugenics, with Reply from the President," *Eugenics Review* 12 (April 1920), p. 48.

93. "Roman Catholic Criticism," p. 49.

94. S. Herbert, "Eugenics in Relation to Social Reform," *Westminster Review*, October 1913, pp. 377–386.

95. Reilly, pp. 118–119.

96. Commander, p. 80.

97. O'Malley taught bacteriology at Georgetown University and English literature at Notre Dame. He wrote *Essays in Pastoral Medicine* (1906, 1907) and *Ethics of Medical Homicide and Mutilation* (1919), among other works.

98. Austin O'Malley, "The Dog or the Baby," *America* 8 (June 12, 1915), p. 223.

99. See Joseph M. McShane, S. J., "*Sufficiently Radical*": *Catholicism, Progressivism, and the Bishops' Program of 1919* (Washington, D.C.: Catholic University of America, 1986); and Elizabeth McKeown, *War and Welfare: American Catholics and World War I* (New York: Garland Publishing, 1988).

100. *America* 14 (February 12, 1916), p. 431.

101. Edmund E. Sinclair, "Concerning Birth Control," *America* 15 (August 12, 1916), p. 419.

102. *Ibid.*, pp. 419–420.

103. He authored a number of books on related subjects, including *A Living Wage* (1906), *Distributive Justice* (1916), and *The Church and Labor* (1920). See Douglas J. Slawson, *The Foundation and First Decade of the National Catholic Welfare Council* (Washington, D.C.: Catholic University of America Press, 1992), pp. 59–69; Will Herberg, *Protestant, Catholic, Jew: An Essay in American Religious Sociology* (New York: Doubleday, 1960), pp. 152, 154.

104. *The Catholic Encyclopedia* 12 (1907), p. 279, in Chesler, p. 211.

105. Mary Alden Hopkins, "The Catholic Church and Birth Control," *Harper's Weekly*, June 26, 1915, p. 610.

106. *Ibid.*

107. John A. Ryan, "The Catholic Church and Birth Control," *Harper's Weekly*, August 7, 1915, p. 144.

108. *Ibid.*

109. John A. Ryan, "Family Limitation, Church and Birth Control," *American Ecclesiastical Review* 54 (June 1916), p. 687.

110. Ryan, *Social Reform on Catholic Lines* (New York: Paulist Press, 1914) and *A Program of Social Reform by Legislation* (New York: Paulist Press, 1919).

111. *Proceedings of the First Conference of Catholic Charities* (Washington, D.C.: Catholic University of America, 1910).

112. Thomas J. Gerrard, "Eugenics and Catholic Teaching," *Catholic World*, June 1912, p. 295.

113. Walter Rauschenbush, *Christianity and the Social Order*, pp. 7–29.

114. *Ibid.*, pp. 24–25, from President F. Pfotenhauer, *Der Lutheraner* (N.p.: n.p., 1911), p. 150.

115. Ryan, "Family Limitation," p. 685.

116. John A. Ryan and Moorehous F. X. Millar, *The State and the Church* (New York: Macmillan, 1922), pp. 32–37. In this book Ryan also justified the creation of the National Catholic Welfare Conference to insure the government protection of the common good.

117. For more on Ryan's role, see Noonan, pp. 414–424, and Alvah W. Sulloway, *Birth Control and Catholic Doctrine* (Boston: Beacon Press, 1959), pp. 37–43.

118. The letter was read at all masses on George Washington's birthday (February 22, 1920), once again an attempt to connect American Catholics and their birth control stance to patriotism. See "Pastoral Letter of the Archbishops and Bishops of the United States, September 26, 1919," in Guilday, ed., *The National Pastorals*, pp. 312–313, cited in Chesler, p. 211. See also Noonan, p. 424.

119. Chesler, p. 212. See Ryan, "The Attitude of the Church Toward Birth Control," *Catholic Charities Review* 4 (December 1920), pp. 299–301.

120. See John A. Ryan and M. F. X. Millar, *The State and the Church* (New York: Macmillan, 1930).

121. *The Acts and Proceedings of the General Synod of the Reformed Church in America, Embracing the Sessions of June, 1920, 1921, 1922* 26 (New York: Board of Publication and Bible School Work, n.d.), p. 214.

# Chapter Three

# 1921–1926: Doctrine in Question, Battle Lines Drawn

In just a few short months in late 1921 and early 1922 the direction of the birth control debate took a sharp turn. The modernist trend in society suggesting the limitation of reproduction among the inferior stock had been gaining momentum, and the nature of birth control arguments were beginning to draw a dividing line between Catholics and non–Catholics. Yet when it came to making official and direct statements on contraceptive use, particularly to their own congregations, clergy on both sides essentially agreed that procreation was the purpose of sex and a primary purpose of marriage. If the religious discussion had been one involving only denominational doctrine outlined for followers, it would have developed in a far different manner. But it was not.

Because the prominent players considered it a social question, the battle was being fought in public, and denominational competition was shaping the debate into a highly politicized one.[1] As various denominations vied for numbers and considered eugenicists' arguments about population quality, the political implications of the birth control debate were brought to light. First, the traditional Protestant mainstream was losing political strength through changing demographics. And second, it feared a kind of political action it claimed was inherent in the Catholic Church and unacceptable in a free society. The first helped to set the stage for religious division on the issue, while the second deepened the battle lines. But it was a single event, which took place in November of 1921, that offered proof to birth control advocates that the Catholic Church would take its political action too far. That incident is commonly referred to as the Town Hall raid.

On the evening of November 13 Margaret Sanger scheduled the First

American Birth Control Conference at New York City's Town Hall, which was to be followed by a public forum to discuss the topic, "Birth Control: Is It Moral?" Sanger was scheduled to speak, as was Harold Cox, editor of the *Edinburgh Review* and former member of Parliament, and Mary Winsor, actress and women's rights activist. There was no way to predict how many would attend the meeting. However, by this time the movement had gained momentum, and publication of the meeting attracted the attention of both supporters and critics. The most significant critic turned out to be New York archbishop Patrick J. Hayes.

Hundreds had gathered to hear the speakers who arrived at the hall to find New York city police surrounding locked doors. After allowing the speakers and audience to enter, police refused to allow Sanger to speak. Stating they had come at the request of Archbishop Hayes, police worked their way through the crowd and removed Cox from the stage. After the audience lifted her to the stage, Sanger proclaimed: "One would certainly suppose that this display of liberty and freedom of speech was in Germany, not in America."[2] To the crowd's chants of "Defy them! Defy them!" and a round of "My Country 'Tis of Thee," police carried off and arrested all three speakers. Hundreds followed, cheering them in the patrol wagon and in the courtroom.

Sanger called to her audience: "[Police] Captain [Thomas] Donohue informs me that this meeting has been stopped by telephone. I asked him who was at the other end of the wire and he couldn't tell me." After leaving the courtroom she announced, "We have reason to believe that this meeting was closed by the influence of the Catholic Church."[3] The *New York Times* reported that Ann Kennedy, officer of the Birth Control Conference, told reporters she had seen a man in the Town Hall claiming to be Monsignor Joseph P. Dineen, who was secretary to Archbishop Hayes. According to Kennedy, the man declared he had been sent by the archbishop to the meeting. The paper subsequently reported that Dineen went to the Town Hall to meet Donohue, who claimed he did not know why he was called down there. Dineen did admit being there, saying Sanger had invited Hayes and that he was sent as Hayes's representative.

## Reaction in the Press

Whatever the exact circumstances were, the *Times* initially expressed its approval of the police action. In recent years the mainstream press had been critical of militant protests by suffragists in their demand for the right to vote, and many saw this as a similar effort by radical women.[4] A

*Times* editorial of November 15 similarly criticized the behavior of the speakers. That column contended that the question was not whether voluntary parenthood was a proper subject for public discussion or whether it should be "condemned or commended as compatible or incompatible with morality, for or against public policy." Instead, the important question was what dutiful citizens should have done when police broke up the meeting. According to the *Times*, they should have promptly and quietly obeyed rather than act like anarchists, "starting a riot." Perhaps they were wronged, as they had claimed, but their recourse should have been to work within the law. The editorial concluded the police were justified in charging them with disorderly conduct.[5]

This editorial exemplifies mainstream attitudes toward the birth control movement at the time of the Town Hall raid. To the activists themselves, and to the general public in the following years, the police action seemed outrageous. But in the first few days following the incident, there was very little criticism of the police or of Archbishop Hayes, other than by Sanger. Observers maintained Sanger knew where the Catholic Church stood and should have expected interference. However, the fact that the church had significant influence within the police department, and perhaps the entire legal system of New York City, was not ignored for long.

The *Times* continued its coverage of the Sanger/Catholic Church conflict. In December the paper published the archbishop's pastoral letter to be read at masses the Sunday before Christmas. Though he had formerly denounced public discussion of the subject, Hayes wrote that he now condemned birth control from religious and moral standpoints and that the time had come for public discussion. He commanded Catholics to keep birth control information out of their homes as they would any "evil spirit":

> The Christ-Child did not stay His own entrance into this mortal life because His mother was poor, roofless and without provision for the morrow.... He knew that the Heavenly Father who cared for the lilies of the fields and the birds of the air loved the children of men more than these. Children troop down from Heaven because God wills it. He alone has the right to stay their coming while he blesses at will some homes with many, others with but a few or with none at all.... Heinous is the sin committed against the creative act of God who through the marriage contract invites man and woman to cooperate with him in the propagation of the human family.... To take life after its inception is a horrible crime but to prevent human life that the Creator is about to bring into being is satanic. In the first instance, the body is killed while the soul lives on. In the latter, not only a body but an immortal soul is denied existence

in time and in eternity. It has been reserved to our day to see advocated shamelessly the legacy of such a diabolical thing.[6]

Two days later the *Times* gave Sanger an opportunity to respond to the pastoral letter. She first expressed her appreciation that the Church finally had clarified its stand in discriminating between contraception and abortion. Then Sanger wrote:

> I do not care to answer the Archbishop's theological statement concerning the will of the Almighty. His arguments are purely those based on assumption. He knows no more about the fact of the immortality of the soul than the rest of us human beings. What he believes concerning the soul after life is based upon theory and he has a perfect right to that belief; but we who are trying to better humanity fundamentally believe that a healthy, happy human race is more in keeping with the laws of God than disease, misery and poverty perpetuating themselves generation after generation.... There is no objection to the Catholic Church inculcating its doctrines to its own people, but when it attempts to make these ideas legislative acts and enforce its opinions and code of morals upon the Protestant members of this country, then I do consider its attempt an interference with the principles of this democracy, and I have a right to protest.[7]

It was in this exchange that the nation saw the religious debate over birth control made public. No longer was doctrinal discourse confined to the pages of denominational publications, nor were secular publications free from theological arguments. By extensively covering the Town Hall incident, and by publishing Hayes's pastoral letter and Sanger's response, the *New York Times* helped initiate a public debate. Of course the *Times* was not solely responsible for the publicity surrounding the debate. Catholic clergy were also responsible. The doctrine of social action outlined by the National Catholic Welfare Conference urged bishops to speak out on issues they saw as affecting the community and society at large.

The Town Hall incident did not mark the first time Sanger had been arrested, and she knew what to expect from law enforcement authorities. She also knew what to expect from Catholic authorities and could be blamed for baiting them. In her study of and participation in socialist activities before the war, Sanger learned the importance of identifying an enemy when initiating a social movement.[8] After she had rejected socialism in her effort to gain mainstream support of her cause, she could benefit in identifying the Catholic Church as her enemy, as Catholics had already been marginalized. Whereas Protestant and Jewish denominations held similar beliefs regarding contraception, it would have done her no good to create enemies out of either one of them. First, anti–Semitism in the United States was not strong enough to aid in making Jews the enemy in the birth control debate, and although Jews were considered of the inferior stock, particularly by race theorists, their numbers were not great enough to threaten the nation's demographics. And second, Jewish leaders were not taking an active role in blocking contraceptive legislation.

Protestants, on the other hand, represented much of the mainstream, which she needed to support her cause, and though they did not officially condone contraceptive use, many had already publicly considered population concerns as a primary responsibility. Furthermore, Sanger did not want to antagonize all traditional religious groups because she sincerely believed in the morality of her cause and wanted to convince them of that. At the same time, Catholic influence was viewed as a threat to American society and its political structure.[9] If she could convince the American public that the Catholic Church was now attempting to "enforce its opinions and code of morals upon the Protestant members of this country," she might gain even more support from the mainstream.

Archbishop Hayes recognized Sanger's tactics in creating an enemy of the Catholic Church and fought back. The battle became a two-sided one with both sides trying to appear as part of the mainstream. Sanger claimed Hayes had no regard for separation of church and state, and Hayes contended that Sanger had no respect for the law. The *Times* again made its pages available in the debate. On page 1 of the November 21 edition Hayes identified himself as a "citizen and a churchman, deeply concerned with the moral well-being of the city" when he wrote: "I feel it a public duty to protest against the use of the open forum for the propaganda of birth control. This I do in no sectarian spirit, but in the broader one of the common weal." He said he objected to the public discussion of a subject "that simple prudence and decency, if not the spirit of the law should keep within the walls of clinics, or only for the ears of the mature and experienced." He maintained that federal laws "reflect the will of the people ... for the benefit of the morals and health of the community" and said the Town Hall speech "made a mockery" of the law. He added, "The law of God and man, science, public policy, human experience are all condemnatory of birth control as preached by a few irresponsible individuals, without endorsement or approval, as far as I know, of a reputable body of physicians or medical society whose province it is to advise the public on such matters."[10]

Just two weeks before the Town Hall raid, an article in the Jesuit publication *America* referred to birth control as "race suicide." The article was written in response to a work supporting freedom of choice, which had been written by inventor and eugenicist Alexander Graham Bell and published in a recent edition of the *Journal of Heredity*. The *America* response criticized the practice of birth control in much the same way that Protestant doctrine had condemned it. The unnamed author demonstrated concern about suicide of the entire human race, not what was referred to as the superior stock, but spoke specifically to the sanctity of sex within marriage:

> The evil results of this practise [*sic*] are almost innumerable. One is that it degrades the conjugal love existing between husband and wife, for they naturally come to look upon their wedded state as a means of affording them sensual gratification, rather than as a means of serving God by bringing children into the world.... And then ... it increases the love of ease and luxury, and therefore weakens the will and the capacity for self-denial and mortification, which is a necessary condition for rendering faithful service to God. But the effect which strikes the State more potently than any, is that practises [*sic*] of this kind have led to the downfall of every great nation since the beginning of time.

The writer of this article did not predict the "Catholicizing" of the religious debate over contraception that unfolded following the Town Hall incident. In fact, he criticized the political action of "the bodies of reform in the country" who were "engaged in the uprooting of other great and tremendous perils" without doing the same against birth control:

> They have succeeded in enacting legislation against the use of any beverage that cheers and warms the spirit, and now they are even checking up the quantity of hair tonic, Florida water and other such toilet preparations on stock in drug stores, in order that no drink of undue alcoholic content may find its way to the bosom of the wayward human being. They are endeavoring to put the silencer, the clamp, the lid, and all other such air-tight appliances on the Lord's Day, that the tired workingman may get rested, will-nilly, for another week's slaving in the mills and factories. Another vicious vice which they have set their minds on suppressing is the execrable use of the noxious tobacco weed for smoking purposes— this habit, you know wastes I don't know how many millions of dollars and billions of calories of brain-power annually. And then those vicious sports, boxing, football, games of that ilk — ugh! No wonder they're trying to legislate those out of existence![11]

Even before the Town Hall incident, Catholics recognized that they were being criticized for any political action against birth control. At the same time, they watched as prominent Protestants worked actively to regulate tobacco, gambling, and sports, all of which the Catholic Church considered trivial when compared to birth control. Protestants had been even more active, and more successful, in the passage of "Sunday laws," which many Catholics contended were implemented more in the interest of Protestant Sabbath doctrine than in the interest of protecting workers. But prohibition was perhaps the greatest point of contention in this regard. Catholics had been outsiders on the prohibition issue, having refused to support it. They did not see their active political opposition to birth control as different from Protestant political opposition to liquor, but they would never convince the public that their intentions were just as noble, especially following the Town Hall incident.

## The National Press Responds

It would soon become apparent that the conflict over the Town Hall incident would not be confined to the *Times*, with Sanger and Hayes as the only players.[12] It soon reached the pages of other publications. The *Outlook* criticized the police action or, more important, the influence behind that action, which it said was taken on "the instigation of the Roman Catholic hierarchy of New York City." The editor pointed out that the *Outlook* article did not sympathize with Sanger's attempt publicly to discuss the subject of birth control. But, he contended, the police action "was clearly a dangerous and, we think, illegal violation by the police of the fundamental right of free speech guaranteed by the United States Constitution, and, moreover, it was carried out in a very brutal fashion."[13]

The *New Republic* was equally critical of Archbishop Hayes and for much of the same reason as the *Outlook* editorial. In late November, that publication, too, condemned the Church for "[using] the police as its puppets" and called the police action unconstitutional. The statement was not surprising since the publication had been one of the first in print, as early as 1915, to support legalizing birth control.[14]

The *New Republic* article following the Town Hall raid did not present a totally bleak picture for the birth control movement. In fact, the author contended that Hayes's action had actually helped the movement gain momentum, for insisting that the attempted denial of an open forum to birth control showed the fundamental weakness of the opposition. He added:

> To insist on "natural law" where there is no natural law is the first necessity of a doctrinaire institution. The best weapon that America possesses against such arbitrary enunciations is the weapon that Mrs. Sanger wields, the weapon of the open forum. To deprive her of that weapon would be to reinforce the unfortunate delusion that birth control can be boycotted as part of decent human conduct and that its practice, if indulged, must be surrounded by shame and hypocrisy.

As for the confrontation between Hayes and Sanger, the article concluded: "Setting Archbishop Hayes' opposition against the advocacy of Mrs. Sanger and her associates, at any rate, the outlook for the birth control movement is brighter than it ever was. He is not tackling a 'few irresponsible individuals,' but a people who, in the end, will accept birth control in principle as they have long since accepted divorce."[15]

The *New Republic* article made one brief but significant observation that could easily have gone unnoticed. The author noted: "We are glad, all things considered, that the hand of the Catholic Church should have been forced in this matter, and that opposition to birth control should now be voiced by one of its dignitaries."[16] This statement is important for two reasons. First, it reinforced the idea that the Church had not stood clearly against birth control until this time; second, it raised the possibility that Sanger had "forced" the Catholic Church to take a stand. Actually, the *New Republic* implied nothing more than that the incident itself had forced the Church formally to state a position. However, it was Sanger who had made the bold attempt to speak on the subject. She could predict how representatives of the local church[17] would react, especially after inviting Hayes to attend.

Although there were a few instances immediately following the Town Hall raid when people addressed the religious debate over birth control without singling out the Catholic Church, the public debate was becoming an overwhelmingly Catholic one. Sanger was succeeding in making the Church an enemy of non–Catholics on this issue. Not only was Hayes's behavior criticized, but so was what was perceived as the overall nature of the Church's doctrine and its birth control position.

The *New Republic* attacked authoritarianism in the Church as a whole in an article addressing the issue of contraception: "Those 'laws of nature' of which the Archbishop speaks so confidently and with such intimate knowledge, are the last resort of authoritarianism, and it is socially insane to give credence to them or to govern conduct by them or to involve one's religion with them as the Archbishop proposes." Regarding Hayes's contention that the "Heavenly Father, who cares for the lilies of the field and the birds of the air" would make provisions for the children of men, the article states: "To say that 'the Lord will provide' is to tell a pretty story. But behind such stories there is a real policy, the policy of holding men and women inside the Christian church — the Catholic church in particular — by correlating the chances of eternal salvation with a certain course of disciplined sexual behavior."[18]

An article published in *Current Opinion* illustrated how the nature of the debate had changed by February. An article discussing the work of Sanger stated: "It is true that Roman Catholic leaders are as hostile to birth control as they have always been."[19] This clearly was a misrepresentation as Catholic leaders had been no more hostile than other denominations in the past, and if they were now working more actively to block legislation, it was only a recent move. Rather the statement represents the general manner in which Catholics were being portrayed.

## *Sanger's* Birth Control Review

It is difficult to say whether Sanger fully understood at the time how much her movement would benefit from antagonizing the Catholic clergy. But, the opening paragraph in the December issue of her *Birth Control Review* demonstrated how quickly she worked to intensify the conflict: "[The Town Hall incident] has shown up the sinister control of the Roman Catholic Church, which attempts — and to a great extent succeeds — to control all questions of public and private morality in these United States. This accusation has been made against the church thousands of times — but not until the eventful night of November 13, 1921, have these sinister and unscrupulous powers been 'caught in the act.'" The article went on: "All who resent this sinister Church Control of life and conduct — this interference of the Roman Church in attempting to dictate the conduct and behavior of non–Catholics, must now choose between Church Control or Birth Control. You can no longer remain neutral. You must make a declaration of independence, of self-reliance, or submit to the dictatorship of the Roman Catholic hierarchy. This is a dictatorship of celibates who presume to decide on the morality of a question upon which they professedly have had and cannot have any basis of experience. The public of New York and of the whole country deeply resent this dictatorship, now exposed to the full light of day."[20]

Sanger's opening editorial in the *Birth Control Review* of January 1922 demonstrated her intention to continue her focus on the church as her enemy: "Efforts to suppress and to kill this great effort of civilization have had just the opposite effect…. The fight is now in the open. We know the source of the opposition to our movement. Our enemies have openly declared themselves." She added: "An even more desperate battle confronts us—not merely the fight against stupidity and prejudice and reaction, but the battle for free speech and honest expression. Already we are launched in that battle. Stand with us. Back up all of us who are on the fighting front!"[21] She called the investigation into the suppression of the Town Hall meeting "a ludicrous farce" and "an insult to every citizen of the United States." The investigating committee established by the mayor failed to link Hayes or the church to the incident.[22] Sanger wrote of the investigation: "What should have been a fair and impartial hearing was perverted into an inquisition…. The inspector and the Corporation Counsel did not even attempt to conceal their bitter malice, their prejudice being perfectly obvious from their conduct and their questions."[23]

John S. Sumner, secretary of the New York Society for the Suppression of Vice—and according to Mary Ware Dennett, Comstock's successor—had been given the opportunity to speak at the Town Hall meeting, which was rescheduled for November 18. His speech was reprinted in the *Birth Control Review*. Sumner's remarks reflected the sentiment of the mainstream. He insisted that there was no significant problem of overpopulation, at least not in Europe or the United States. Furthermore, an increase in knowledge about birth control had succeeded only in changing the moral attitude of men and women toward the marriage bond which was indicated by divorce statistics.

His remarks also reflected the attitudes of mainline denominations at the time. He reinforced the still widely held idea that the primary obligation of marriage was procreation: "The husband and wife are partners in an enterprise, and the crowning glory of that enterprise, the true consummation of marriage, is the child." He expressed the same concern churches had for strict marriage licensing but understood New York's laws to be adequate: "We believe that where there is the probability of *diseased or mentally defective progeny*, or where the *health or life of the mother* would be endangered by child-bearing, *parents* should be advised against further issue and should be informed *personally by a licensed physician* of any known harmless means toward such a result. This can be *legally done* at the present time. It requires no propaganda and no change in the State law."[24]

In that same edition of the *Birth Control Review* Sanger published an anonymous article by "a Catholic woman," a tactic she often used to convince her readers that the obstinate Catholic hierarchy did not speak for all Catholics. In this article the author wrote, "It must be remembered that the Catholic Church is a very old and conservative institution ... controlled absolutely by men, and that these men are vowed to celibacy.... Catholics are taught never to question a ruling of the Church, and even the wishes of local prelates are supposed to be accepted without question and yet it is plain to be seen that American Catholics are no longer being bound by these things."[25] These arguments were used again and again after the Catholic Church had been identified as the opposition. But Sanger went on to raise other arguments against Catholic teachings on contraception and the family that were rarely, if ever, used by others:

> They advocate an unrestricted birth rate, and yet they hold up as the model of motherhood, the Blessed Virgin Mary, *who had one child*. The Holy Family is offered as the perfect model of domestic life, and yet if we are to believe the teaching of the Church, St. Joseph was never the husband of the Virgin Mary in the real sense of the word, and I think it highly unlikely that even a Catholic husband would care to maintain such a relationship toward his own wife. ... Furthermore, we are taught that when the Angel Gabriel announced to the Virgin Mary that she had been chosen to be the Mother of the Messiah, he asked her consent, and answered her objections, as we find in the New Testament. Yet the Church does not give their Catholic women this same right of choice, but commands them "to be subject to your husband in all things."[26]

American Catholics who had supported the suffrage movement had already been offended by what they perceived as archaic attitudes of the church on the subject of women's rights. Both William Cardinal O'Connell of Boston and James Cardinal Gibbons of Baltimore vehemently condemned the suffrage movement, working ardently to discourage the participation of Catholic women. Sanger repeatedly pointed out that even though the church did not approve, thousands of Catholic women supported suffrage for women. Likewise, said Sanger, the Church's attitudes toward birth control did not reflect the desires of its followers.[27]

Sanger was a master of publicity, and her *Birth Control Review* was only one attempt to keep her and her cause in the public's eye. Managing editor Annie G. Porritt described useful propaganda methods in a closed session of the Fifth International Neo-Malthusian and Birth Control Conference held in London in July of 1922. In opening her presentation Porritt remarked, "Every movement which aims at a change in public opinion is necessarily dependent on publicity for its progress and success." She noted the benefit of the publicity following the Town Hall raid, maintaining that the opposition did a maximum of service to the movement with a minimum of trouble and inconvenience to the protagonists of birth control. Porritt stated, "Persecution furnishes perhaps the very best publicity. It touches people's sympathy and arouses their indignation as they cannot be aroused by cold reasoning, however marvelously presented. It forces the discussion of the questions involved and compels people to take a stand in regard to them."[28]

According to Porritt, the Catholic Church aided the movement by attacking it. Controversies were carried on in some of the most widely read newspapers in the country. Articles for and against birth control were solicited from anyone whose name was sufficiently known to attract attention, "thus accomplishing for the movement without expense to itself what would have cost the League hundreds of thousands of dollars if it had undertaken it on its own account."[29]

As for future publicity, Porritt explained that it must arouse emotion and be intelligent, well-based, accurate and capable of withstanding hostile criticism. Very important, the publicity must challenge "the indifference of the average man and woman engrossed in other interests. It must not be addressed to those who are already strongly for or against the propaganda. It must be a trumpet call to the unawakened, and must address them through any channel of interest that can lead to their attention."[30] One way that birth control advocates did this was by instilling public fear that the Catholic Church was attempting to infringe on freedom of choice.

## *Early Clerical Support*

In the aftermath of the Town Hall incident Sanger succeeded in pointing out faults in the religious opposition's arguments against her, but she still needed to gain some positive support from a legitimate religious source. Organizers of the Fifth International Neo-Malthusian and Birth Control Conference held in July were able to schedule presentations on the moral and religious aspects of birth control, but these were given primarily by laypersons. The only presentation by an American religious spokesperson was that of Rabbi Sidney E. Goldstein of New York City's Free Synagogue. Goldstein argued that birth control was indeed a scientific and legal problem, but it was also a moral one, and he addressed the various arguments against it. He refuted arguments that birth control would lead to race suicide and, regarding its illegality, contended that "no legal tradition can be allowed to curb or cripple a movement that means improvement and progress of the human race." As for contraceptive use leading to immorality and the desecration of marriage, Goldstein said there were no differences in moral standards between small families and large families: "The holiness of marriage does not depend upon conception; it does not depend upon contraception; it depends upon the sense of consecration that a man and woman feel who come together to live in the spirit of an exalted ideal of love. When this sense of consecration is present, no shadow of immorality can enter the temple of married life; when it is absent, nothing can save us from destruction."[31] He recognized the religious argument that birth control violated the commandments of God as one which was expected to silence all opposition. But, Goldstein contended, unlike those who had claimed to have received privileged Divine communication, he had never seen any sort of "authentic mandate from the Deity on the subject of Birth Control."[32] Goldstein did not name the Catholic Church as the religious opposition of which he spoke.

The most widely recognized individual from whom she obtained support at this time was William R. Inge, the dean of London's St. Paul's Cathedral, who had already blamed much of the world's problems on overpopulation among the inferior.[33] Three weeks after the Town Hall incident, an article written by Inge appeared in *The Nation*. The timing of the publication played well into the newly public religious debate. However, the article did not so much as mention the Town Hall incident or Margaret Sanger. Nor did Inge address the topic of birth control in terms of theology or religious doctrine. Instead, he presented a rational argument, maintaining that the small family had "come to stay." Recognizing the belief by both eugenicists and their opponents that their efforts were founded in morality, he insisted that the primary moral obligation in this matter was "to put away violent prejudices and to study the facts honestly." According to Inge, "It is rare indeed to find any discussion of the subject from the religious or moral side in which any attempt is made to consider in a rational spirit the economic and the medical facts on which a sound judgment must be based. Wilful ignorance is a moral fault."[34] He concluded that voluntary limitation of population had always been practiced and that any attempts to suppress the sale of the preventives resulted only in an increase in the number of abortions. Inge quoted a German birth control researcher who described the United States as "the classic land of abortion," claiming two million abortions took place in the nation each year, to which he responded: "I should be sorry to believe this; but it may be taken as proved that the Comstock legislation has achieved nothing except to substitute a crime for a practice which many good people regard as innocent."[35] According to Inge the Comstock laws should be repealed. In Inge Sanger found an internationally respected religious leader who declared a serious and immediate need for eugenics programs, and legalized contraceptives, as well.

## *Social Theory*

Ultimately, Inge proved far more than just a religious figure speaking in support of Sanger. He was one of the most outspoken social theorists of the time — one whose prescriptions included birth control when the fight for legalization began. Sanger took the opportunity to publish a subsequent article by Inge in her *Birth Control Review*, which supported the Neo-Malthusian warning of an overcrowded world. Inge said the world had reached the end of centuries of European expansion; that the "new countries [were] getting filled up," calling fears of race suicide absurd.[36]

Sanger biographers generally minimize her relationship with eugenicists, maintaining that she distanced herself from their bigotry. Still, the direction of her efforts toward the working class would ultimately bring eugenicists to her side, and for now, she welcomed any of their declarations which condoned limiting the birth rates among the poor and/or inferior. This was true of the work of University of Wisconsin sociologist and noted eugenicist Edward Alsworth Ross. In an article entitled "Controlled Fecundity," published in the *New Republic*, Ross, too, refuted claims of race suicide, citing population statistics to the contrary.[37] However, he claimed the high birthrate among the inferior class and the low birthrate among the upper class was disrupting natural selection. He encouraged births among the superior and promoted the distribution of birth control among the lower classes: "Curtailment of fecundity is most practiced by the capable and least by the inert and commonplace.... [T]here ought to be bigger families among the rising, and smaller families among the stagnating, more progeny left by the gifted, and fewer by the dull, less prudence in the good homes and less recklessness in the hovels and tenements."[38] By this time Ross had also become a popular supporter of immigration restriction, and his criticism of reproductive practices among the poor focused on the foreign born. By 1920 he accurately predicted the imminent passage of immigration legislation in his *Principles of Sociology*, when he wrote, "There is no doubt that barriers to immigration will be reared which will give notice to the backward peoples that enlightened humanity is not willing to cramp itself in order that these peoples may continue to indulge in thoughtless reproduction."[39]

Regarding religion, Ross noted, "the clergyman with few children or none at all has felt entitled to thunder like a Hebrew prophet at couples who stop at three or four children whereas their grandparents gave the world ten or a dozen."[40] Though he did not single out the Catholic Church, his description of clergy who have no children was often used in contemporary condemnations of Catholic clergy. Furthermore, in specifying the first fifteen hundred years of "the Christian Church" in the following quote, he is describing a Catholic Church that had not yet been challenged by Protestantism: "Through its first millennium and a half — during which its doctrines crystallized — the Christian Church was in the presence of a human mortality which must have been from two to four times that which we experience today. Naturally the Church became fixed in the idea that overpopulation is nothing to worry about and in her inspired wisdom she branded as a sin the deliberate curtailment of conjugal fecundity."[41] Even if Sanger did not enthusiastically embrace Ross's discourse in public yet, his suggestions for lowering birth rates among the urban poor accurately reflected the nature of her work. Furthermore, his brief mention of religion supported her position.

During this period, Sanger more thoroughly embraced the work of her friend, H. G. Wells. In his introduction to Sanger's 1922 *The Pivot of Civilization* Wells discussed the positions of traditional and modern factions, which he referred to as the New Civilization and the Old Civilization. Ironically, Wells attempted to minimize the deliberate isolation of Catholics, which Sanger was trying to accomplish. He maintained the ideas and practices of the Old Civilization were not identifiable with either Christian or Catholic culture, adding that it would be "a great misfortune if the issues between the Old Civilization and the New are allowed to slip into the deep ruts of religious controversies that are only accidentally and intermittently parallel."[42] To Wells the religious debate was between modernists and fundamentalists, or between those who apparently held onto dogma and those who were willing to use their religion to address the modern world. Still, in Sanger's chapter entitled "A Moral Necessity," she pointed continually to Catholics as the opposition.[43]

In general, Wells did not necessarily see the birth control issue as a religious one, or at least a denominational or doctrinal one, at this point. His commentaries on demographics illustrated more of a concern for the quality of population worldwide and in America in particular. Recognizing what he considered the intellectual and cultural superiority of the "Anglo races," he noted that the increase in numbers of "colored peoples" challenged British power throughout the world, and the numbers of "foreigners" in the United States were challenging America's British heritage.[44] In this sense his arguments were indirectly tied to religion or at least inherently to pro–Protestantism.

In many ways Wells's writings continued to be strikingly similar to those of Inge and Ross. By 1922 eugenicists, social theorists, neo–Malthusians, and Protestant leaders were weaving a complicated web of rhetoric that found a common ground in either direct anti–Catholicism or in the marginalization of Catholics. Even when they did not speak specifically of Catholics, it was becoming more and more clear in the public debate that Catholics were being labeled as breeders. Furthermore, Sanger successfully fueled the fire by accusing the Church of seeking undue political strength in attempting to crush her crusade. The fear of Catholic political and social action was inherent in the history of anti–Catholicism, and Catholic action on the issue of birth control simply provided evidence for those who suggested the Church might stand in the way.

## *Looking Back*

Ten years after the Town Hall incident Sanger recalled the event in her book, *My Fight for Birth Control*. In that work she discussed the movement up to the point of the book's publication in 1931, paying particular attention to the weeks surrounding November 13, 1921. She wrote that she had been reluctant to set up the American Birth Control League in the first place, preferring to work without the structure, mechanism, and dogmatism that she considered part of any social organization. Nonetheless, the league was formed on November 10 of that year out of necessity for building up public opinion.[45]

In detailing occurrences from the league's first meeting on November 13 until the February hearing, Sanger included various published reports from New York's *Times*, *Tribune*, and *Evening Post*, which she said proved that the public's opinion of her had changed: "The fight for the right to discuss the subject of birth control was an issue totally different from that of its practice. The right of citizens to decently discuss the question was to be fought for by the people themselves. It involved principles of democracy, liberty and education. It was no longer my lone fight. It was now a battle of a republic against the machinations of the hierarchy of the Roman Catholic Church."[46]

What had not necessarily begun or been intended as religious division in the contraceptive debate had nonetheless become one. Still, in 1922 the doctrine among various denominations remained unchanged. Eight years later birth control advocates claimed a remarkable shift had taken place toward support of their effort. Birth control historians mark that shift as taking place during the 1930 Lambeth Conference of Anglican

Bishops and in subsequent conventions of American Protestants and Jews who followed suit. However, the shift did not take place in just a few short months. The debate continued, and doctrinal statements between 1922 and 1926 documented how the groundwork was laid for religious acceptance.

## Seeds of Support

During the early to mid–1920s a more complex religious birth control debate began to unfold. An increasing number of individual liberal clerics publicly supported Sanger, maintaining that they had a moral responsibility to use scientific knowledge to better society by controlling the propagation of the unfit. The publicity surrounding these declarations forced denominations to begin to clarify their positions, and the modernist-fundamentalist debate was underway. Denomination after denomination began to address birth control — either directly noting the ongoing struggle to legalize contraceptives or through discussions of eugenics or the purpose of marriage. Although official positions on birth control had not yet changed, by 1931 religious leaders could look back on the mid–1920s and recognize that this was the time when the seeds were planted for the growth of liberalism in birth control doctrine.

Meanwhile, Sanger continued her condemnation of Catholics. The publicity surrounding the Town Hall incident had waned, and Catholic writers addressed the subject little more than anyone else did. However, birth control advocates succeeded in portraying the Church as the opposition. One of the reasons they were able to do so was that anti–Catholicism had gained a new kind of momentum. The recent wave of Ku Klux Klan fanaticism that had begun around 1915, and directed its attacks not only at blacks but at Catholics, Jews, and foreigners, was dying out, but the mainstream was taking legal action in its place. These years marked the height of the immigration scare, and Congress finally acted in severely restricting the entrance of immigrants from southern and eastern Europe, many of whom were Catholic.

The 1921 Immigration Act had been extensively criticized for failing to limit the number of southern and eastern Europeans coming into the United States. As a result, in 1924 Congress passed the Johnson-Reed Bill, which made changes in the quota system. The House Committee supporting the changes defended the Immigration Act of 1924 as "an effort to preserve, as nearly as possible, the racial status quo in the United States. It is hoped to guarantee, as best we can at this late date, racial homogeneity in the United States."[47] Even with immigration restriction their numbers continued to grow through births.

Congressional statements generally did not contain blatant anti–Catholic sentiment, even in the birth control debate, a condition critics attributed to political timidity.[48] However, conservatives outside Congress continued to voice their opinions.[49] Furthermore, liberals, and increasingly the mainstream, increased their criticism of Catholics. The perception of Catholic doctrine as part of the Old World and not well-suited for modern American society intensified as religious liberalism gained strength.

One of the most noted religious liberals in this period was Harry Emerson Fosdick, who described religious liberalism as "a spirit of free inquiry which wishes to face the new facts, accept whatever is true and state the abiding principles of Christian faith in cogent and contemporary terms." He subsequently condemned doctrine, which he said eventually becomes "petrified into dogma": "There is an ecclesiastical type of mind ready to use [doctrine], no longer as an inspiring elucidation of the convictions by which men really live, but as a mold into which men's thinking must be exactly run. Doctrine is then authoritative, a definition laid down in times past of the way in which men must always think."[50] Another outspoken liberal, Unitarian minister Charles Francis Potter, maintained that one sign of emerging changes in religion was the "great dissatisfaction with existing religious institutions. The churches founded on the old conception of religion are empty, or nearly so, and they are wondering what has happened."[51] The movement that had been referred to as the social gospel, in which religion was to play a prominent role in bettering society, had become more or less institutionalized in modernism by the mid–1920s, strengthening its criticism of traditionalists.

Fosdick and Potter did not include only the Catholic Church in the category of "old religion"; they were also critical of Lutherans and Calvinists who held onto what they considered to be centuries-old teaching. But as the birth control debate became Catholicized, it was the Catholic Church that gained a separate standing among the condemnatory statements of religious liberals. Speaking at the Sixth International Neo-Malthusian and Birth Control Conference in 1925, Potter denied singling out Catholics but said, "The Church — the very one which enshrines Mother and Child upon the outside of its convents — insists that to take practical measures to insure the happiness of the mother and child is what? Obscene and immoral."[52] At the same conference Episcopal minister William Garth went further: "So far as the Protestant Church is concerned and the Hebrew Communion, there is no organized opposition to Birth Control. So far as the Roman Catholic Church is concerned, they are against us." But he added what he considered a note of hope: "There was a time when [Catholic authorities] were perfectly willing to persecute men who maintained that the world was round. Now they certainly do not persecute people for that belief. Possibly on Birth Control they may so modify their position as to recognize the good work that it is doing."[53] Regarding hierarchy, ritual, and global denominational organization, Episcopalians were notably similar to Catholics, and they certainly were not considered part of America's liberal religious movement. So what could account for this statement? Garth was not representing any official doctrine, but he was beginning to echo some of what the Anglican Inge had previously voiced. He was nowhere near the racial theorist, but American Episcopalians were denominational cousins of the British Anglicans, naturally representing the upper crust and the elite in the racial superiority element of this debate.

## Liberal Supporters

One of the most apparent changes in the birth control movement from 1923 to 1926 was that Sanger and other birth control advocates were given more opportunities to speak publicly. In some instances clergymen themselves scheduled her to speak, demonstrating an increase, however small, in the number of her religious supporters. Still, the speaking engagements were often scheduled with hesitancy and sometimes surrounded with controversy. In addition, more individual clergy expressed their support of Sanger's efforts. However, the most important change — and one that was much less publicized — was in the way denominations officially addressed the issue.

The subject did not yet garner the attention that it would between 1927 and 1929, but several Protestant and Jewish groups recognized that the time had come to approach the subject of birth control directly. The more conservative churches reaffirmed their stands opposing contraceptive use. But some denominations ordered studies of the issue, declaring that societal forces demanded the topic be viewed in a new light. No denomination officially adopted changes in doctrine by 1926, but the stage was set for changes to come.

The movement was not gaining momentum as quickly as birth control advocates had predicted following the Town Hall incident — in particular because eugenicists still would not wholeheartedly embrace the legalization of contraceptives — nor was the Catholic Church the sole opposition. However, there was evidence that the religious opposition was wavering. Religious spokespersons debated Sanger but not with the intensity evident

in late 1921 and early 1922. In some instances clergymen themselves scheduled her to speak, demonstrating an increase — however small — in the
number of her religious supporters. These years marked a relatively quiet
period in the birth control debate. But changes in the atmosphere and in
some attitudes began to manifest themselves in the public arena.

Such was the case in 1923 when Rabbi Louis A. Mischkind of Tremont
Temple in the Bronx had scheduled Sanger to speak in an open forum
without permission of the board of trustees. When the trustees objected,
Dr. J. Max Weis of the Free Synagogue of Washington Heights granted
Mischkind permission to use his synagogue. Board president Seymour
Mork explained the action of the Tremont Temple board of trustees: "The
reason for our refusing the use of the Forum to Mrs. Sanger was simply
because we object to the auditorium of the synagogue being used for birth
control propaganda and that is, I think, a sufficient reason." He added,
"Our forum is made up mostly of boys and girls 14 and 15 years old and
so there was need to stop the affair at once."[54] Rabbi Mischkind resigned
as a result of the incident.

Though it appeared that Jews might be weakening in their opposition
to birth control, the attempt by Mischkind to grant Sanger a public forum
was not an indication that even he supported her views. He had previously
been reprimanded for scheduling other controversial speakers, including
Ku Klux Klan spokesman Oscar Haywood. Board president Mork also had
canceled that program. However, this time, members of the congregation
protested. At the Free Synagogue, where Sanger delivered her speech, "The
Need of Birth Control in America," members of Tremont Temple and its
allied organizations criticized their board of trustees' attitude toward free
speech. Free Synagogue's Rabbi Weis added: "To our forum, we invited
speakers who were considered enemies of society and which so many so-
called 100 per cent Americans denounce. I believe that no man who is
respectable, respected, honest and earnest should be barred from presenting his point of view."[55] Five days later the Men's Club of Tremont
Temple unanimously passed a resolution condemning the board's actions.[56]

News of Sanger's speaking engagements in the religious arena again
quieted down for a time. In December of 1924 Sanger addressed a meeting of two hundred Yale University divinity students with no notable negative reaction. This was undoubtedly due to the fact that the speech had
not been publicized ahead of time, causing "considerable surprise ... on
the Yale campus ... among students and professors when the announce-
ment was made" that Sanger had addressed the group.[57] Sanger's welcome
was overstated when she was mistakenly introduced as the mother of a
divinity school student. Her son Stuart was a student at Yale's medical

school.[58] Nonetheless, her remarks were well received, and reportedly steps were taken by graduate students to organize a special class for discussion of the subject of birth control. In addition, Sanger was invited to address the entire undergraduate student body at some unspecified time in the future.[59]

Three days later an audience filled Carnegie Hall to hear speakers address the subject at a meeting of the American Birth Control League, at which Sanger presided. The program featured Dr. James F. Cooper, clinical instructor of the Boston University School of Medicine and Medical College at Foo Chow, China, who told of China's population conditions. Also speaking were Dr. Dorothy Bocker, clinical director of the Birth Control League's research department, New York attorney I. N. Thurman, and Charles Francis Potter of the West Side Unitarian Church.[60] Police were present in the audience, but they did not interfere with the program.[61] The intensity of controversy over public speeches on birth control had clearly diminished. By 1925 the movement had succeeded in gaining substantial support from religious individuals. One conference on birth control that year marked a significant change in the way clergy were speaking to the issue. A growing number were now supporting the movement publicly.

Participants in the birth control conference adopted a resolution calling on churches to express their support as "a moral and religious force for the betterment of the human race and the establishment of the Kingdom of God among men."[62] Several ministers and rabbis spoke in support of the birth control movement, with Unitarians and liberal Jews taking the lead and empathizing primarily with the teachings of eugenicists. Rabbi Stephen S. Wise, founder of the Free Synagogue and activist in labor and antiwar issues, told the conference, "If the church and synagogue stand in the way of justice and the nobler order of human society realizable through birth control, so much the worse will it be for those religious organizations. The life of a child is a sacred thing and we ought to hold it so sacred as not to have life come into the world unless we are able to give it fair opportunity to find its highest service." Unitarian Charles Potter said he did not believe that widespread dissemination of information would increase immorality, as many religious figures had predicted. Potter said: "The lack of knowledge of birth control produces more immorality than would the open handling of pamphlets to the graduates of our high schools. Knowledge does not cause vice; it is ignorance that does it." He also contended that Christians should support the movement particularly because Christianity was chiefly responsible for the protection of the unfit, thereby increasing the number of feeble-minded in the world: "The Christian effort to save every child that is born in the world, together with the lowering of the death rate with the advance of science, means that more and more imbeciles are being saved to become a burden upon civilization. It is clearly the duty of Christianity, then, to prevent the birth of the unfit." Other religious spokesmen who declared their support of the movement included the following: The Rev. D. Karl Reliand, rector of St. George's Protestant Episcopal Church in New York City; the Rev. Dr. Frank S. C. Wicks, pastor of All Souls Unitarian Church in Indianapolis; the Rev. D. Nelson Springer, pastor of the Fourth Unitarian Church of Brooklyn; the Rev. Dr. A. Ray Petty, pastor of New York's Judson Memorial Baptist Church, and the Rev. William Garth.[63]

Nonreligious participants in the conference attacked Catholics, and this time also fundamentalist Protestants, for their position. Harry Elmer Barnes, controversial professor of history and sociology at Smith College, called for a new code of conduct to replace the existing religious code of morality, which he said was based on "myth, tradition and supernaturalism." Barnes said scientific experts and not clergymen should be consulted on drawing up such a code, adding, "It will probably be necessary to give up entirely the old concept of morals or morality and substitute the more accurate term descriptive of the new objective — namely morale." He defined "morale" as a code of superhygiene, designed to keep one always in tip-top condition, physically, socially, and industrially. He said that through such a system the ideals of William Jennings Bryan, John S. Sumner, the Ku Klux Klan and others "may really be replaced by those of Jesus Christ." Barnes added that "in light of the fact that all human process has been due primarily to the work of the few, probably will [sic] have to admit that it is better to sacrifice a thousand morons rather than handicap serious [sic] a single genius."[64]

Less biting was the statement by physician W. F. Robie of Baldwinville, Massachusetts, which addressed the problem of divorce.[65] Robie maintained that the giving of information about contraception was one of the "great necessities of modern civilization." He said that divorces and "wrecked homes" could be attributed in many cases to lack of information.[66] Though he did not mention any sort of religious teaching that supported his statement, this is a significant point on which denominations ultimately granted their approval of limited contraceptive use — in an attempt to prevent divorce.

Clarence Little, president of the University of Michigan and noted eugenicist,[67] specifically attacked the Catholic Church at that conference. Little urged participants to try to convince Catholic clergy and laity with whom they came in contact to see that the movement would help them share in a better civilization. However, later in the year, at the annual convention of the New York branch of the American Birth Control League, he focused his attack on Episcopalians. He declared he was "in a fog over the stand of the Protestant Episcopal ministers in their convention in New Orleans, in which they favored eugenics and adjured [*sic*] birth control." He held the two were "inseparably allied."[68]

## Mainline and Conservative Denominations

Episcopalians did not view their official positions on eugenics and birth control as contradictory. In 1925 they expressed their support of strict marriage licensing, as other denominations had, in order to prevent "the marriage of persons of low mentality and infected with communicable disease." However, they drew the line at preventing conception after marriage. For as concerned as they might have been about the inferior stock, condoning contraception was an entirely different matter, as such a declaration might well aid in lowering the birthrate among their own flocks. The Joint Commission on the Home and Family Life reported to the general assembly that birth restriction was a menace to family life, though it "is comforting to the self-indulgent to feel that their personal, selfish desires are in harmony with what passes for altruistic propaganda." It then quoted "with hearty approval" the declaration of the 1920 Lambeth Conference:

> We utter an emphatic warning against the use of unnatural means for the avoidance of conception, together with the grave dangers— physical, moral and religious— thereby incurred, and against the evils with which the extension of such use threatens the race. ... In opposition to the teaching which, under the name of science and religion, encourages married people to the deliberate cultivation of sexual union as an end in itself, we steadfastly urge what must always be regarded as the purpose for which marriage exists, namely, the continuation of the race through the gift and heritage of children. The other is the paramount importance in married life of deliberate and thoughtful self-control. We desire solemnly to commend what we have said to Christian people and to all who will hear.[69]

There were still relatively few congregations that granted permission for discussion of the topic. Even when they did, they did not necessarily condone the practice, only the right to speak about it. For instance, in January of 1926 the Judson Sunday Club of the Washington Square Methodist

Episcopal Church featured Sanger as a speaker. The audience listened as Sanger stated, "At present humanitarian work and racial improvements cannot be reconciled. By our laws and customs we are allowing the feeble-minded and insane to multiply and are taking care of their offspring." She added, "An eminent authority has said that of the 105,000,000 people in the United States only 20,000,000 are entitled to be called intelligent. The United States is spending eight billion dollars a year to meet the problems of infant and maternal mortality, disease, delinquency and crime, but the money is being spent entirely on palliative measures. Only by birth control can we get at the heart of the matter."[70] Methodists were very much interested in matters affecting society in these ways. For instance, they repeatedly addressed the cost to society, including the monetary cost, of liquor consumption in the form of burdens to hospitals, ambulance services, and law enforcement agencies. However, neither the twenty-ninth general conference in 1924 nor the thirtieth conference in 1928 even raised the issue of contraception. A search for at least an indirect reference during those conferences finds what could be considered a condemnation of distributing contraceptive information in the 1924 discussion of divorce. The episcopal address listed the following as causes of divorce:

> The frivolous temper of our times, the dissemination of loose views upon almost every subject, impatience of restraint, ridicule of the old-fashioned virtues, the quickened pace which keeps the nerves forever on edge, the passion for luxury, immodesty in dress, pernicious incitements of modern fiction, the unwholesome familiarities of the modern dance and the false pictures of life displayed in the modern playhouse, the passing of much of the sacred home life of yesterday, and, above all, the loss of the sense of God and of moral responsibility.[71]

The Methodists' episcopal address regarding amusements did not specifically mention contraception but did refer to the perceived moral decay of society that Anthony Comstock and others blamed on the availability of contraceptive information: "These recent years have brought us a depression of moral standards which must be the deep concern of every lover of mankind." It added:

> The integrity of manhood, the virtue of womanhood, the sanctity of the marriage relation, well-approved habits of clean living, of pure thinking, of high moral conduct in both sexes, have felt the withering touch of a wide-spread degeneracy. America, and other countries, should be reminded that many of the nations of the Old World came to their inglorious end as the

result of luxurious self-indulgence and excessive love of pleasure. It is imperative that those who direct the growing life of the Church be on guard against the blight of wasteful worldly standards of living and loose ethical practices.[72]

Not only was the address reminiscent of the Comstock crusade fifty years earlier; it also reflected the sentiment of those who opposed legalizing contraception during the 1920s. First, it appeared to Methodists, and to others, that too many couples were increasingly interested in the pleasure of marital sex over its purpose of procreation. Second, too many couples seemed to be limiting their family size to improve their economic status, allowing them to accumulate more worldly possessions.

These two fears were indicative of widespread fears during the decade of the 1920s in general. In that decade a fascination with psychology was gaining momentum, and the teachings of Freud had stimulated discussions regarding the pleasures of sex. In addition, Freud's contention that refusing to satisfy sexual urges might cause psychological damage confronted religious teachings that abstinence was an acceptable method of limiting family size. Regarding the perception of growing desires to raise personal economic status, religious leaders repeatedly decried the materialism they saw as pervading American society. They often criticized couples for having only two or three children with the intention of saving enough money for a fashionable automobile or a larger house.

Between 1923 and 1926 Baptists reported on the evil of divorce much in the same way Methodists did. However, there was one significant difference between the Baptist reports during these years and those of previous years. By this time prohibition was in effect, yet the divorce rate remained high. The Methodists' Committee on Temperance, Prohibition and Public Morals and the Northern and Southern Baptists' Social Service committees were forced to look elsewhere for causes of the breakdown of the American family. To different degrees they focused on race-track gambling, prize fighting, marathon dancing, motion pictures, and — important to the contraception issue — immoral literature.[73]

Continued attention was paid to marriage and divorce laws, though there was less emphasis on eugenics laws than there had been in the past. Methodists had turned their attention to limiting grounds for divorce to only that of adultery, while Southern Baptists expressed their desire to eliminate "child marriages" by working to raise the minimum age requirement for marriage. Northern Baptists worked for uniformity in marriage and divorce laws in general.[74]

Though Southern Baptists criticized the dissemination of immoral literature, they were reluctant to describe in detail what kinds of literature they considered immoral. However, they certainly included contraceptive information among what they referred to as obscene, vicious, and hurtful literature and expressed objections to publishers attempting to side-step postal laws in distributing such material. The confrontation between publishers and postal authorities developed as a major battle in which Sanger became involved. Before the 1926 convention of Southern Baptists the chairman of the convention's social service commission had met with the Post Office department solicitor concerning the mailing of objectionable literature. The social service commission reported to the convention that the solicitor seemed "entirely sympathetic with our purpose and point of view." He also suggested that those concerned take the matter up with local authorities. The committee urged "all of our people be vigilant and diligent. As far as possible we must protect our people ... against the evil and suggestive influences of every form of vicious product of the printing press."[75]

Those denominations did not allow their positions to waver easily, and they certainly would not do so in the case of contraception. An important article published in the *Reformed Church Review* in July of 1926 illustrated the way conservative Christians responded to changes in society by attempting to reinforce traditional family values. In "The Family as a Primary Social Unit" Albert G. Peters reminded readers that even though contemporary society placed importance on the individual, individuals could not thrive, nor perpetuate themselves, alone. According to Peters, though marriage had become "a contract into which most people desire to enter for their convenience and pleasure," the purpose of marriage remained essentially procreation: "The pairing of individuals for the purposes of reproduction and the perpetuation of the race is the biological function of the family. This was the design of God in creation and in race development. Though the function of sex may be to insure variation through the power of the potential, in this stage of the evolution of man and animals it is required to reproduce. God made man, male and female, in order that they might 'Be fruitful and replenish the earth.'"[76] This accurately represented the position of most conservatives in the mid–1920s. The conservative Missouri Synod Lutherans did not waver at all in their opposition during these years, stating that they had no desire to argue about "a movement [which] advocates the use of drugs and contrivances by which married people and others may 'cheat nature.'"[77]

## Modernists: Birth Control Warrants Study

The Northern Baptists made up one group that began to reconsider traditional stands against birth control in these years. In 1924 the Social

Service Committee reminded those attending the annual convention, "Jesus said to his disciples, 'Lift up your eyes; The field is the world,'" in suggesting there be more study of the world and the purpose of Christianity. The committee report stated: "As the facts become known the Christian principles which are pertinent to them must be recognized and applied.... [C]lasses for the study of good citizenship and a sane consideration of sex problems would seem just now to be timely and important. In some places the open forum for the discussion of vital human problems from the Christian point of view, is proving most helpful."[78] Though the report did not provide any solutions to problems concerning sex, it recognized the heated debate on issues regarding sex as needing "sane consideration." More important, it viewed the open forum as a vital tool in education.

Again, the committee did not mention the particular topic of birth control, but it did discuss "sex hygiene." Though "sex hygiene" encompassed a number of subjects, it referred in particular to methods of preventing the spread of venereal disease. It was a primary concern of eugenicists who vehemently warned that reproduction by people afflicted by venereal disease was one of the causes of race degeneration. But even though they might not condone the use of condoms, for example, to prevent pregnancy, they would for the prevention of the spread of venereal disease, opening up both the discussion and future access. The topic of sex hygiene was raised by the Northern Baptists' Social Service Committee in 1925, which noted that "sex hygiene and morals, eugenics and child welfare" were areas that needed "constructive and remedial social expression of Christianity." These were included among a wide array of other issues, including narcotics abuse, alcoholism, crime, industrial working conditions, education, athletics, and natural resource conservation. There was no proposal for solutions regarding these "areas of life and of living together," but the committee considered them areas "in which the most pressing moral problems of the present time arise."[79]

In raising the issue the committee demonstrated not only its awareness of the growing concern over the morality of sex and sexual behavior but also the value it placed on social action — a value very similar to the ones held by Methodists, the Christian Reformed Church and the Catholic Church. According to the report, "Spiritual regeneration and social redemption always go hand in hand. There can be no effective social progress that is not inspired and controlled by religious ideals and motives. There is no real religion that does not express itself in all the relations and activities of life." The report also expressed the comparatively liberal attitude Northern Baptists held toward adapting doctrine to changing social forces: "Social conditions change, and from time to time particular areas of social life are thrust into view as requiring special attention. Every such emergent social stress gives a special opportunity for the Christian spirit to express itself in human service, and sounds a call of duty as imperative as the Cross of Christ."[80] Such sentiments were not expressed by Southern Baptists, the Christian Reformed Churches, or the Catholic Church. Those denominations did not allow their positions to waver easily, and they certainly would not do so in the case of contraception.

During these years the Federal Council of the Churches of Christ in America also recognized the importance of studying sexuality when it raised the issues of sex and parenthood in its conventions. In 1925 the council's Committee on the Church and Social Service reported that arrangements had been made at the request of the American Social Hygiene Association to schedule discussions of training for parenthood and problems of the home. In addition, "systematic efforts [would] be made to inaugurate sex education and community prophylaxis under the guidance of field workers of the Association." Such candid discussion was common at Federal Council conventions, and it often offended some of the more conservative representatives in attendance. Nonetheless, such discussion paved the way for some of the first direct birth control statements made during religious conferences. Within two years the Federal Council took steps to study the specific issue of contraception. At the same time, Presbyterians proposed the study of issues related to the family. In 1925 the General Assembly's Committee on Christian Education briefly addressed the topics of prohibition, Sabbath-keeping, motion pictures, and divorce and urged that the Assembly "recognize the responsibility of the Church for the instruction of children and youth, concerning the more intimate experiences and relationships of life as these concern the individual, the family, the community, the state and the race."[81]

Many of the same issues were raised by Lutherans in 1926, including a specific reference to birth control. Delegates to the Universal Christian Conference on Life and Work held the previous year in Stockholm reported to the 1926 convention on "certain principles concerning the relation of the sexes." Regarding contraception, the report stated, "The Church ought to affirm more than ever at the present time that a chief aim of the married life is the birth of children, and that the blessing of God is often granted to a numerous family.... Apart from exceptional cases and those considerations of duty for which the individual rather than the Church is responsible before God, the Church should declare the limitation of birth by artificial means both anti-social and anti–Christian."[82] This statement appears clearly in opposition to birth control. However, by leaving even a little room for "exceptional cases," it opened the door to future argument.[83]

The *Lutheran Quarterly's* review in 1923 of the book *Men, Women, and God*, by the Scottish Rev. A. Herbert Gray, gave the impression that less-conservative Lutherans were heading toward approval of contraception. Reviewer Jacob A. Clutz described the book as "admirably written" noting that "two of the best chapters" were those entitled "The Art of Being Married" and "Unhappy Marriages." Clutz wrote, "Both of these are full of wise sayings and helpful device which, if heeded, would save many a married couple from making shipwreck of their happiness, and might even help many who have gone on the rocks to get off and to voyage safely and serenely to the end of their journey."[84] In "The Art of Being Married" Gray included a section on birth control, a subject he recognized as occupying a "very great place in the public attention" and one that raised "very important and very real questions for married persons."[85] In this address he condoned the use of contraception in some cases.

Gray did not present a sweeping acceptance of contraceptive use. His stand was one of limited approval. First, he considered a marriage between two healthy young people with the definite intention of having no children "unchristian." In addition, he described the artificial attempt to postpone the arrival of a first child as "a deplorable mistake." However, he added that "for most couples to have as many children as is possible is equally indefensible," regarding that practice as cruel to women, to children, and to society.[86]

Gray was considerably more radical in his approach to contraceptive method and the purpose not only of marriage but of sexual intercourse. He suggested that sexual intimacy may be "right and sacramental as an expression of mutual affection," not only "when the deliberate purpose of producing children enters into it." Gray wrote, "I am compelled to take my stand with those who believe that sexual intimacy is right and good in itself as an expression of affection. It has, as a matter of fact, a good many other consequences than the production of children. It constitutes a bond of very great worth between two persons. It is in many interesting ways beneficial to a woman's physical system; and it brings to men a general balance and repose of being which is of enormous value."[87]

Gray disagreed with other clerical teaching that abstinence was the only acceptable contraceptive. In fact, claimed Gray, the practice of abstinence by married couples living under the same roof created tremendous strain. It would be better to use some other form of "conception control," and he advised couples to consult a reputable doctor to assist in finding out "for themselves what [was] for them the right course to adopt."[88]

*Men, Women, and God* did not sway religious opinion. It attracted very little attention in the religious birth control debate. Its positive review by the *Lutheran Quarterly* was misleading because Lutherans did not grant approval of contraceptive use even when others did in 1931. However, publication of the book and the favorable review demonstrated further how some clerical opinion was opening up to change. During the shift in 1931, clergy addressed the subject much in the same way that Gray had in 1923. First, the affectionate expression of intimacy without the threat of pregnancy could help strengthen a marriage. Second, abstinence need not exist as the only approved method of preventing conception.

## Reform Jews

Even though Protestant denominations did not stray from their basic stand of opposition, by the mid–1920s it was clear that they began to enter into the discussion more seriously in order to clarify their positions. The same was true for Jews. In 1926 the Central Conference of American Rabbis described outside pressure put on that organization to take a stand. In this case it came directly from the Catholic Church. The National Catholic Welfare Conference had requested that the Central Conference protest a pending amendment to the Tariff Act that would make it "lawful to transmit through the United States mails, and to import into our country, information explaining and encouraging the practice of Contraception, and to place in the hands of the general public, instruction in the use of various methods and forms of instruments used in the indulgence of this practice." According to the Committee on Cooperation with National Organizations the Conference had yet to take a stand on contraception, and committee members could not agree on whether to support the NCWC. In voting, the division was clear: four in favor of cooperation and four against. In referring the matter to the Commission on Social Justice for further study, the chairman expressed satisfaction that the conference would finally "be in a position to declare itself on this all-important subject."[89]

The Commission on Social Justice subsequently reported:

> The question of birth control is one of growing insistence and of national moment, and should be considered from the standpoint of social health, of national welfare, of economic exigencies and, at the same time, of moral considerations as these latter bear on the individual, on family life and on human happiness generally. The traditional religious points of view ought

certainly to receive consideration but these should not, in the opinion of the Commission, constitute the determining factor.

Following a brief history of views on birth control beginning with the writings of Malthus, and a recognition that the practice was already widespread among various groups of people, the report appealed to the concerns of social welfare and eugenics:

> It is ... clear that as the result of an excessive birth rate, unnecessary hardships and misery are being visited upon thousands and thousands of mothers physically unable to bear the strain of frequent childbearing, and upon innumerable parents financially not in a position to take care of them; and that grave inroads are being made upon the well-being of our nation and other nations viewed as a whole, through the bringing in of a disproportionate number of children born within those classes of society where destitution, unhygienic conditions or irresponsibility prevail; these circumstances resulting in a comparatively poor progeny, to the detriment of the families concerned as well as of the nation. There is a growing and justified widespread opinion that the citizenship material ought to be more carefully and eugenically selected.[90]

While it was clear that Central Conference of American Rabbis could be the first formal organization of clergy to approve contraceptive use, it did not grant its approval at this time. In essence, the commission recommended only public discussion of the topic. However, that recommendation was not a restrained one. It urged that the topic "be brought out to the light of day from the secret places to which it has been, by old habit and an out-worn morality, consigned." It added: "The press and the forum [should] engage more energetically and courageously than they have been doing in bringing illumination to bear on this fundamental question."[91]

The report was a major step toward approving contraceptive use. But the commission refused to recommend an amendment to the Tariff Act. Its report stated that the mails should not be open to distribution of such information: "We are of the opinion that all information necessary for the guidance of parents can be fully and adequately imparted to them by their own family physicians. The information should be restricted to oral information. We oppose any change in the law which would permit the transmission of such information through the mails, as such transmission is destined to throw the door wide open to charlatans and exploiters and to encourage immoral practices."[92]

The rabbis' conclusion that both expertise and responsibility should lie with the medical community was an important one. When the federal courts finally ruled in favor of legalized distribution during the 1930s, the rulings addressed the concerns of physicians and protected them under the law.

## Anti-Catholicism and Xenophobia in the Popular Press

During the years between 1923 and 1926, a growing number of publications in the popular press added to the national religious debate by turning their attention to birth control, some specifically addressing the religious disputes surrounding the debate. Those that did not spoke to issues that had previously been raised by religious representatives. These included concerns regarding neo–Malthusian teaching, eugenics, materialism, and especially immigrant population statistics. Even when commentators of this period did not mention religion specifically, the element of fear surrounding demographic growth of Catholics and Jews was fundamental in their arguments.

Two separate articles published in *Ladies' Home Journal* discussed the growing trend toward smaller families, focusing on the fact that the immigrant population was growing at a faster pace than that of the native stock. In 1922 Royal S. Copeland, U.S. senator, physician, and New York health commissioner, wrote that

> 1921 statistics ... disclose the startling fact that during that year foreign-born mothers brought 76,084 babies into the world, at the rate of 78 per 1000 female foreign-born population. In striking contrast native-born mothers produced 58,157 babies, at the rate of 32 per 1000 female native-born population. The productivity of Italian-born mothers far exceeded that of any other race, their rate being 145 per 1000. The Russian-Poland [*sic*] mothers came next with 88 per 1000.[93]

The following year, physician S. Josephine Baker echoed Copeland's sentiments when she wrote, "If our good old Anglo-Saxon race is disappearing, it is a serious matter. It takes more than the fact that one is born in this country to make an American. We can console ourselves all we choose with the idea of Americanization, but if we continue having fewer babies born to native mothers and more born to foreign-born mothers, there is only one end in sight.... [I]t is a question of preserving racial integrity."[94] Baker also raised the question of a larger family lowering one's standard of living. She concluded that native-born women were more concerned about keeping up with "American standards," and because the foreign-born were less interested in worldly goods, they were less afraid of having more children.[95]

An article entitled "The Neo-Malthusians," published in the *Nation* in 1925, described the scientific arguments for and against birth control as bewildering, citing conflicting population projections. The author considered the trend toward research and distribution of contraceptive information "encouraging for the world at large." Remarking that throughout history people have learned what they could of birth control methods and applied them in their own lives, the author wrote: "Unless they are cowed by some special superstition or taboo, individual men and women have always snatched at knowledge and the chance of greater freedom for themselves."[96] One might rightly presume that although the author did not mention the Catholic Church in that statement, he might well have been referring to it. During this time Catholicism was commonly referred to as a religion preaching superstitions and taboos.

In 1924 *Harper's Magazine* editor Edward S. Martin wrote of the changing demographics and the American standard of living that others had addressed, but his commentary went a step further in targeting the religious aspect of the debate. In raising the possibility of taking the fashionable route of amending the constitution, he noted that forbidding or limiting propagation at the federal level, or framing "a regulation by the rules of which newcomers may be born only by permission of the constituted authorities" might be considered by some as a feasible solution to overpopulation. However, Martin explained, such an amendment would stir up trouble:

> The Catholics, for example, might not like it and might refuse to obey the law, and we might have discussion about the duty of citizens to obey the Constitution no matter what, and of the duty of other citizens to see that they did obey it, just as we have now about rum. ... And, of course, if the Catholics objected to the limitation of families, that would be the opportunity of the Klan, and political conventions and candidates for office would have to turn more flip-flops than they do now.[97]

Martin's article indicated how, three years following the Town Hall incident, the debate remained "Catholicized."

Another aspect that remained was the attention the American press was giving to statements by Dean Inge. An *Independent* article of 1926 reported Inge's statistics demonstrating how the birthrate among the lower class was four times that of the upper class in Great Britain. Though health commissioner Royal Copeland had not condoned contraceptive use in his *Ladies' Home Journal* article, the *Independent* compares the similarities between Copeland's statistics and those of Inge. Both sets of figures reflect the differences in birth rates among various sections of London and New York, but author R. le Clerc Phillips focused on the variances reflected in educational status. According to Phillips, because the most highly educated were having the fewest children, "intelligence extinction" was threatening. She referred to Inge as "that gloomy prelate whose dark forebodings have brought him such peculiar fame" but added that his statistics were being supported by others.[98]

In the years following the Town Hall raid Inge had continued to write not only of varying birthrates among different economic classes but also of the religious question regarding birth control. In 1923 he wrote a scathing article against Catholics entitled "Catholic Church and Anglo-Saxon Mind" for the *Atlantic Monthly*. He concluded that Protestantism was not a "spent force" as many had feared and that Catholicism was not the Christianity of the future, while making sweeping generalizations concerning the "backwardness" of Catholicism. Inge maintained that the "greater fecundity" of Roman Catholics had been exaggerated: "It is true that the priests condemn, and endeavor to prevent, the voluntary restriction of the family; but in these intimate relations of life men and women are apt to be refractory to priestly dictation."[99]

At the same time, he played into the fears of an already xenophobic America in his discussion of immigration from Ireland, Italy, and Poland. He predicted that the American government would "discourage immigration from the less advanced European nations." He added:

> A high birth-rate always indicates a low state of civilization: the law is exemplified in Ireland, in South Italy, in Poland, and in other Catholic countries. It is certainly no accident that Catholic countries have remained in a backward condition; and, where free immigration is allowed, the Catholic workman, with his low standard of living, may squeeze out the Protestant; and the same deficiency in education and in the industrial virtues, which keeps Catholic populations on a low level, also prevents them from being fully industrialized.[100]

In predicting the future of Catholicism, Inge wrote, "It is already conscious of standing in antagonism to modern civilization; and while this clearly defined hostility makes it the rallying-ground of those forces in modern life which resist the main currents of human thought, it is condemned, it seems to me, to fight a losing battle in the more advanced nations, and must content itself with the allegiance of peoples whom it can screen from contact with progress and enlightenment."[101] Throughout this article Inge was addressing more than the topic of Catholic doctrine regarding contraception. However, his arguments supported Sanger's attempt to make the argument a Catholic one.

The following year Sanger herself was given a similar vehicle through which she could voice her position when *American Mercury* published her article "The War Against Birth Control." She opened with a quotation by William Blake that immediately characterized the article as anti–Catholic. The quotation read: "…and priests in black gowns were walking their rounds, and binding with briars my joys and desires." The substance of her article centered on what Sanger referred to as the "counter movement," which she said had been "not so much an attempt to codify and ritualize sexual conduct among the population at large as an effort to control thought and speech upon the subject."[102]

Sanger again told her version of the Town Hall incident, which was growing farther from the truth. This time she wrote that the subsequent investigation "indicated that the police who broke up the meeting had received their orders, not from police headquarters, but from the clergy," when in fact the investigation had concluded the police acted on their own. More important than this relatively minor misrepresentation was her continuing criticism of the Roman Catholic clergy as waging warfare against birth control: "For at least fifteen hundred years the church has occupied itself with the problem of imposing abstinence upon its priesthood — an intelligent and trained body of men who have been taught to look upon complete asceticism as the highest ideal — and it is not surprising that such a class of professional celibates should be psychically sensitive to the implications of the idea of contraception."[103] She added, "We have conceded to Catholic and all other clergymen the full right to preach their own doctrines, both of theology and of morals. When, however, the Catholic clergy attempt to force their ideas upon non–Catholic sections of the American public and transform them into legislative acts, we believe we are well within our rights as American citizens when we voice our protest."[104] Once again she attempted to portray herself as a law-abiding citizen and Catholics as having little respect for the law. Sanger was clearly working hard to keep the confrontation alive. In addition, the Catholic clergy was not attempting to "transform [their ideas] into legislative acts." Contraceptives were already illegal. She was the one working toward changes through introducing new legislation.

Catholics were, however, developing more organized efforts to prevent legalization, and Sanger wasted no time in pointing out this fact whenever she had the opportunity. In the same article, she remarked on continued attempts by Catholic representatives to prevent birth control advocates from speaking in public, writing:

> Hotels have been boycotted by such organizations as the Knights of Columbus because the managers have purveyed luncheons to advocates of Birth Control. Halls contracted and paid for have been withdrawn at the last minute on account of pressure brought to bear upon their owners. Permits to hold meetings have been refused by mayors or other city officials in cities in which there was a powerful Catholic constituency. Few politicians, though they have sworn to uphold the Constitution, dare jeopardize their future as office holders by incurring the displeasure of clerical authorities who control the thoughts of their adherents.[105]

Sanger had already made similar, though more detailed, accusations in the *Birth Control Review*, blaming the Knights of Columbus for interfering with programs scheduled in Albany; Milwaukee; Hagerstown, Maryland; and Hartford, Connecticut. Furthermore, she warned the citizens of Connecticut that Catholics were demanding additional tax revenue allocations in addition to infringing on their freedom of choice: "Of the most sinister significance is this tacit confession of the Catholics that they need state aid to support the ever increasing numbers of unfortunate and unwanted children they are bringing into the world."[106]

## Catholic Commentary

Discourses written by Catholics on the subject of contraception between 1923 and 1926 generally did not reflect the vehement confrontation Sanger was describing during these years. However, a number of Catholic articles did appear in print. In "A Study in Numbers," published in *Catholic World*, author J. Elliot Ross illustrated the concern the Church had for keeping the Catholic population high.[107] The article verified the claim by critics that Catholics were intent on increasing their numbers. But its focus was no different from previous articles written by Protestants. Interestingly, Ross attempted to portray Catholics as martyrs in much the same way Sanger attempted to portray herself. He credited recent persecution for the increase in the number of Catholics in various cities: "For more than a year, now, a bitter campaign of vilification has been waged against us. Catholic teachers have been dropped from the public schools in some places, and a political and economic boycott has been declared against us…. [F]rom personal observation … this campaign is one of the best things for the Church in America that ever happened." He added, "Persecution brings out a latent faith, just as war brings out a latent patriotism. This anti–Catholic agitation has made thousands of lukewarm Catholics take a renewed interest in the Church."[108] Just as Sanger claimed persecution had ultimately proven to be good for her movement, Ross claimed persecution had ultimately proven to be good for the Catholic Church.

The most important Catholic work on the subject of contraception during these years was a pamphlet written by John M. Cooper, a sociology professor at Catholic University. In this work, published in 1923 and entitled *Birth Control*, he outlined an argument that became a key factor in the Catholic position. He argued that the physical relationship in a marriage was not an end in itself but a means to an end. That end was procreation. Catholics, as well as Protestants and Jews, were increasing their study of the marital relationship and the act of sexual intercourse in searching for causes of the high divorce rate. Cooper expressed a sentiment similar to those of the others, which concluded that increasingly there had been too much emphasis placed on pleasure. The way he expressed that sentiment was cited by others as setting Catholics apart. For the first time the "means and ends" argument was defined. Cooper wrote, "Physical sex pleasure and gratification is not an end in itself. It is biologically a means to an end. It is a sense gratification which nature and nature's Author has attached to procreation to induce mankind to carry on the task of bringing new human beings into the world and thereby to provide for the propagation and continuance of the race."[109] When various Protestant denominations eventually shifted their position toward approval, much of the ensuing discussion related to the "means and end" question. They eventually concluded that the sexual act was an end in itself, which helped establish closeness in a marriage. But it would be years before any official doctrine approached this line of teaching. At this point in time Cooper's writing reflected the teaching of various other denominations, and its substance was nearly identical to that of Albert Peters in the *Reformed Church Review* three years later.

According to Cooper, there were three elements important in a marriage:

> Passion, love, parenthood — all three go to the making of the
> domestic and marital relation. But the three are not of equal

worth judged by any wholesome human standard. Passion is
primarily self-seeking, self-centered, self-regarding, egoistic.
It may foster love no doubt; but it may also corrode or crowd
out love. Love and parenthood are primarily other-seeking,
other-centered, other-regarding, altruistic, and carry with them
a subtle atmosphere of the sacred and reverential.[110]

Again, this sentiment was essentially no different from those that had been
expressed by representatives of other denominations by this time. Regarding contraception, Cooper wrote, "Artificial birth control tends ... to
isolate sex passion from its natural controls and correctives, love and parenthood. It reaps the pleasures of sex while at the same time evading the
normally consequent sacrifices and responsibilities of sex." He added:

The evasion moreover of parenthood means as well the evasion
of the character-building and character-sustaining sacrifices
and responsibilities that parenthood entails. Contraceptive
practices in eliminating the parental element from the marital
relation, tend ... to eliminate from the marital relation the
sacredness that elevates sheer sex passion in marriage and at
the same time to eliminate from the lives of those who practice
them the stimuli to unselfish altruism that offset the stimulus
to selfish egoism given by physical sex gratification.[111]

Cooper's observations did not present anything very different from what
most non–Catholics were saying.

The National Catholic Welfare Conference, which published Cooper's
pamphlet, published a number of pamphlets containing statements supporting the Catholic position, many of them from non–Catholics. Included
in Leaflet No. 2 was a reprint of an editorial in the *New York Times* that
supported the Catholic contention that the so-called overpopulation problem was nonexistent. Catholics had decried neo–Malthusian warnings,
and the editorial cited statistics proving Malthus's population projections
were incorrect. The editorial cited a recent article in the *Geographical
Review* that calculated real population growth over the previous century,
and concluded that not only had Malthus overestimated growth, but he
underestimated the capacity for food production.[112]

In addition, the editorial writer commented on what he saw as a contradiction in the teachings of birth control advocates. He noted that it was
inconsistent for them to call themselves neo–Malthusians when Malthus
was concerned with a quantitative problem, and birth control advocates
were concerned with a qualitative problem. Here he recognized the theoretical difference between neo–Malthusianism and eugenics and also how
common it had become to link the two.

In her treatise on birth control Surgeon Reserve of the United States Public Health Service Lydia Allen DeVilbiss recognized religious opposition to birth control. However, she identified the Catholic Church as only one part of that opposition: "There is a school of thought as well as several groups of religionists who believe that it is woman's duty to bear all the children that she possibly can; and for her or her husband to adopt any method or resort to any act which might prevent a possible pregnancy from taking place is sinful, wicked, and opposed to the morals and the best interests of the race." However, she demonstrated her belief that the Catholic opposition demanded special attention when she added, "The one group who in particular advocate that women shall bear children regardless, and who would execrate anyone who dares suggest that there is possibly a way for a woman to bear her children with some reference to their health and welfare as well as for her own, is a body of religionists who have devoted their own lives to the principles and practice of celibacy!"[113]

Another later reference did not single out the Catholic Church among denominations. According to DeVilbiss, "The two great sources of the opposition to Birth Control are found in the purely selfish motives of the religionist who wishes his people kept in ignorance of Birth Control and its methods so that they will beget children and yet more children for the glory of God and the Church, and the capitalistic exploiter of labor who is afraid of a diminution in the cheap labor supply."[114] The first source of opposition she described could have been any conservative religionist, and the second source — the capitalistic exploiter of labor — was certainly not equated with Catholics.

In his foreword to DeVilbiss's book, Johns Hopkins University professor of psychiatry and early Sanger supporter Adolf Meyer stated that humankind was making progress in freedom while accepting responsibility. He wrote: "From being a dogmatically controlled being, spiritually and civically [*sic*], the man or woman of today is passing into the phase of undoubted personal responsibility to develop and use individual knowledge and individual judgment in eugenics."[115]

Meyer expressed the same sentiment in his own *Birth Control Facts and Responsibilities*, when he included a chapter on the religious and ethical aspects of birth control written by Rabbi C. A. Rubenstein. Rubenstein considered the growth of the birth control movement "a reaction against the unreasoning form of Puritanism." He urged individuals to act on the basis of individual reason, not according to dogma: "What most people believe is not what they have reasoned out for themselves, or what they themselves understand religion to be, but what men whom they regard as their superiors, or the systems they have been taught to regard as divine, tell them to believe or not to believe."[116]

In his preface Meyer presented what he considered the official Catholic view, which was taken from Ryan's *Family Limitation, the Church and Birth Control*, written in 1916. Following his summary, he pointed out that there was a common misconception in America regarding the Catholic Church and other religious opposition. That misconception related to abstinence. Meyer wrote, "There is no taboo even with the Catholic Church on the general question of family limitation. ... The differences lie only in the means of achieving the goal."[117] Although the Church did not officially sanction periodic abstinence as a method of preventing pregnancy until 1951, it was increasingly accepted by Catholic priests and bishops, and used by married couples, in the decades before. The debate among denominations over method heightened following doctrinal changes in 1930 and 1931.

## *Legislative Battles Begin*

Though questions over doctrine and means and ends would not disappear, neither would they consume the attention of everyone involved in the debate. Sanger would keep herself focused on the political aspect of religion as it pertained to her fight for legalization. Her warning to Connecticut citizens in 1924, for instance, that the Catholic Church was demanding a tax increase in order to support all of the "unfortunate and unwanted children they are bringing into the world," was a prime example. Her comment was made in response to a bill introduced in Connecticut's legislature that would have provided relief for dependent and delinquent children. Sanger contended that such a measure would be unnecessary if contraceptives were made legal. She had supported what she considered alternative legislation that would have permitted the distribution of contraceptives in Connecticut "under proper safeguards."[118]

Sanger spoke before the Judiciary Committee of Connecticut's lower house, requesting that poor women be allowed the information "which most any well-to-do woman can get now," after which, according to the *New York Times*, the auxiliary Bishop of Hartford "stood up and said his say against the bill, like any other citizen. The *Times* called the proceedings "tame" compared to the New York incident a little more than a year before. The editorial stated, "It does not appear that there was any rioting or violence, any giving of illegal information, or any other of the dread consequences fear of which leads New York authorities to put on the lid."[119]

Sanger saw no success in her legislative efforts in Connecticut or in New York, where she helped introduce legislation as well, and she continued to blame Catholics. For her, national legislation was years away. However, Mary Ware Dennett introduced a bill in Congress in 1926. Though an estranged participant in the Sanger movement, Dennett's accusations against the Catholic Church sounded much like those of Sanger. In her book *Birth Control Laws* Dennett published transcripts of the joint hearings by Senate and House Judiciary Sub-Committee on the Cummins-Vaile Bill, which challenged the Comstock Law. In her summary she included the testimony of only three people speaking against the bill, all of whom spoke as Catholics. They were John Ryan, Secretary of the National Council of Catholic Women Agnes G. Reagan, and Catholic social worker Sara Laughlin of Philadelphia.

Ryan, once again, argued under the authority of natural law: "We regard these practices about which information is proposed to be given as immoral — everlastingly, essentially, fundamentally immoral, quite as immoral as adultery, for instance, or rather a little more so, because adultery, whatever may be its vicious aspects, does not commit any outrage upon nature, nor pervert nature's functions." Reagan agreed, adding that the bill requested Congress "to open the gates that information ruinous to Christian standards of family life may stream through the mails and flood the land."[120]

Laughlin represented the International Federation of Catholic Alumnae and in a lengthy statement reported, "I can speak from personal knowledge of hundreds of mothers in whose homes I visit year after year in the course of work with their children. They do not want this information for their own use, and they do not want it circulated to be used as an insidious snare for their children when they have reached maturity." Dennett took exception to this statement in particular, contrasting her claim with statistics provided by birth control clinics in New York and Chicago that reported at least 30 percent of their requests for information came from Catholic women.

At the hearings, Dennett provided the following list of clergymen who endorsed the Cummins-Vaile bill:

Bishop Benjamin Brewster, of Portland, Me.

Bishop Frederick F. Reese, of Georgia.

Rev. Worth Tippy, secretary of the commission on church and social service of the Federal Council of Churches of Christ…

Rev. W. A. Longnecker, secretary of the Methodist Episcopal Conference, Iowa.

Dr. Felix Adler, president of the Ethical Culture Society of New York.

Rev. Stuart L Tyson, Princeton, N. J., formerly special preacher at the Cathedral of St. John the Divine, New York.

Rev. Arthur Ragnatz, Denver, western secretary of the American Bible Society.

Rev. Eliot White of Grace Church, New York City.

Rabbi Rudolph I. Coffee, of Oakland, Calif.

Rev. J. H. Melish, of Brooklyn, N.Y.

Dr. Frank Crane.

And the "unknown soldier," the Catholic priest who gave contraceptive instructions to his parishioner.[121]

Her list of religious supporters indicated the tide was changing, and it was true that the majority of religious opposition expressed at the hearings came from representatives of the Catholic Church. However, the summary of the hearings in her own *Birth Control Laws* omitted the testimony of others presenting religious opposition. One of those was the Rev. J. Frederic Wenchel, secretary of the Evangelical Lutheran Synodical Conference of North America. Insisting that he was speaking as a citizen and not as a churchman, Wenchel said he objected to the United States government's endorsing birth control by passing this bill. He stated: "It seems to me that the United States Government is approving birth control ... despite the fact there is a great portion of your citizenship which believes it immoral," and he added, "All the people who have spoken in favor of this bill have never yet spoken of man as a moral being. It has always been from the side of his physical nature, of a machine. Let us not degrade our humanity and think of him only in that light. As Dr. [John] Ryan has begun with a scripture quotation, let me end with one, that 'the devil is never so dangerous as when he appears in the garb of an angel of light.'"[122]

Mrs. Legare H. Obear denied representing any of the various "societies" to which she belonged but testified from a religious and moral position held by many Protestants: "I think we all approve of volunteer motherhood. But the sanction by law of the indulgence and abuse of the creative function by use of contraceptives fixes the age-long curse of indulgence on our Nation for coming generations. The body is a temple of God and must be kept holy, using the sex function for creation only. This is God's plan for emancipated and consecrated parenthood."[123]

The religious testimony, which Dennett left out of her interpretation of the hearings, should not be ignored. They represented a portion of the lobbying group, which succeeded against Dennett's efforts to repeal the Comstock laws. In addition, Obear's argument demonstrated the most important battle line developing in the debate. The difference between using artificial contraception and what clergy considered the more natural method of abstinence was clearly becoming a major point of contention. Even though a growing number of clergy were pledging their support, or at least studying the matter, the subject of birth control was still too controversial in the world of national politics. Critics blamed Catholic legislators, non–Catholic legislators with heavily Catholic constituencies, and the lobbying efforts of people like John A. Ryan for standing in their way. Even though Catholics did not constitute the only religious opposition to the movement, they were becoming increasingly visible in their opposition to birth control. Some actively opposed legislation while others let their voices be heard in Catholic and non–Catholic publications. Though family size among Catholics was declining in this period at an even more rapid pace than that among Protestants, visible opposition to birth control in one form or another became a symbol of loyalty to the Church.[124]

# *Notes*

1. For a basic outline of the 1920s religious discussion of birth control, see Leslie Woodcock Tentler, *Seasons of Grace: A History of the Catholic Archdiocese of Detroit* (Detroit: Wayne State University Press, 1990), pp. 478–480.

2. *New York Times*, November 14, 1921, p. 1.

3. *Ibid.*

4. Doris Stevens, *Jailed for Freedom* (New York: Schocken Books, 1976), p. 212. Also see Dorothy and Carl J. Schneider, *American Women in the Progressive Era, 1900–1920* (New York: Facts on File, 1993); Sherna Gluck, ed., *From Parlor to Prison: Five American Suffragists Talk About Their Lives* (New York: Vintage, 1976).

5. "Resistance Was Not the Remedy," *New York Times*, November 15, 1921, p. 18.

6. *New York Times*, December 18, 1921, p. 16.

7. *New York Times*, December 20, 1921.

8. For more on Sanger's socialist activities, see Kennedy, pp. 1–35; Chesler, pp. 56–175.

9. One attempt by liberal Protestants at this time to pacify critics by suggesting a more cooperative relationship with Catholics is demonstrated in a brief article entitled "Catholic Social Reformers Are Attacked," *Christian Century*, December 15, 1921, p. 25.

10. *New York Times*, November 21, 1921, p. 1.

11. Anthony Benedik, D.D., "Race-Suicide and Dr. Bell," *America*, October 29, 1921, p. 30.

12. See continued coverage in *New York Times*, November 17, p. 5, col. 3; November 18, p. 18, cols. 2–3; November 19, p. 1, col. 4; November 22, p. 16, col. 2; November 23, p. 9, cols. 1–2; and November 25, p. 7, col. 1.

13. "Birth Control and Free Speech," *Outlook*, November 30, 1921.

14. See "The Control of Births," *New Republic*, March 6, 1915, pp. 114–115; and responding letter to the editor, "Against 'The Control of Births,'" *New Republic*, March, 20, 1915, p. 184.

15. "Birth Control Taboo," *New Republic*, November 30, 1921, p. 9.

16. *Ibid.*

17. Hayes was affiliated with the nearby St. Patrick's Cathedral.

18. "The Sin of Birth Control," *New Republic*, December 28, 1921, p. 116.

19. "Birth Control as a Conquering Movement," *Current Opinion*, February 1922, p. 212.

20. "Church Control?" *Birth Control Review* 5 (December 1921), p. 3.

21. Margaret Sanger, "Notes for the New Year," *Birth Control Review* 6 (January 1922), p. 1.

22. See *New York Times*, January 18, 1922, p. 36, col. 3 January, 22, p. 5, col. 2; January 24, p. 1, col. 5; January 25, p. 14, col. 5; and January 25, p. 36, col. 3.

23. Sanger, "Notes," p. 1.

24. John S. Sumner, n.t., *Birth Control Review* 6 (January 1922), pp. 10–11. Sumner was referring to the attempt by the American Birth Control League to alter section 1142 of the Penal Law of the State of New York and sections 211 and 245 of the United States Criminal Law in order to decriminalize the dissemination of contraceptive information. In essence, the League wanted the subject of contraception deleted from the list of obscenities that the Comstock laws had prohibited from the mails.

25. "A Catholic Woman on Birth Control," *Birth Control Review* 6 (January 1922), p. 17.

26. *Ibid.*

27. See Sanger, *An Autobiography* (New York: Norton, 1938) and *My Fight for Birth Control* (New York: Farrar and Rinehart, 1931).

28. Raymond Pierpont, ed., *Report of the Fifth International Neo-Malthusian and Birth Control Conference* (London: William Heinemann, 1922), pp. 301–302.

29. *Ibid.*, pp. 304–305.

30. *Ibid.*, p. 307.

31. *Ibid.*, pp. 115–117.

32. *Ibid.*, p. 117.

33. For more on his pessimistic view of the human condition, see *Outspoken Essays* (1927), and *Christian Ethics and Modern Problems* (1930).

34. William R. Inge, "Control of Parenthood — Moral Aspects," *Nation*, December 7, 1921, p. 642.

35. *Ibid.*, p. 643.

36. William R. Inge, "Sex and Reproduction," *Birth Control Review*, January 1922, pp. 4–5.

37. The racist tone of his work suggests he understood that members of good, Caucasian stock were already limiting pregnancies, and the same should be encouraged among others. See *The Changing Chinese* (1911), *Changing America* (1912), and *The Old World in the New* (1914).

38. Edward Alsworth Ross, "Controlled Fecundity," *New Republic*, January 25, 1922, p. 246. Also see Robert Bierstedt, *American Sociological Theory: A Critical History* (New York: Academic Press, 1981), pp. 172–173.

39. Edward Alsworth Ross, *The Principles of Sociology* (New York: The Century Press, 1920), p. 37.

40. E. A. Ross, "Controlled Fecundity," *New Republic*, January 25, 1922, p. 243.

41. *Ibid.*, p. 244.

42. Sanger, *The Pivot of Civilization*, pp. xii–xiii.

43. *Ibid.*, pp. 190–219.

44. H. G. Wells, *Social Forces in England and America* (New York: Harper and Brothers, 1914), pp. 38–49, 321–382.

45. The League was incorporated under New York state law in April of 1922.

46. Sanger, *My Fight for Birth Control*, pp. 236–237.

47. *House Report 350 (68-1)*, p. 16, cited in E. P. Hutchinson, *Legislative History of American Immigration Policy, 1798–1956* (Philadelphia: University of Pennsylvania Press, 1981), p. 485. For more on the Immigration Act, see Hutchinson, pp. 185–195, 483–485; George M. Stephenson, *A History of American Immigration, 1820–1924* (New York: Ginn and Company, 1926), pp. 180–192; William E. Leuchtenburg, *The Perils of Prosperity, 1914–1932* (Chicago: University of Chicago Press, 1958), pp. 204–209; Robert A. Divine, *American Immigration Policy, 1924–1952* (New Haven: Yale University Press, 1952).

48. Chesler, p. 329.

49. The Klan voiced extremist anti–Catholicism. See Wyn Craig Wade, *The Fiery Cross* (New York: Simon and Schuster, 1987). For a description of general anti–Catholicism, see Lawrence H. Fuchs, "Election of 1928," in Arthur M. Schlesinger, Jr., and Fred L. Israel, eds., *History of American Presidential Elections, 1789–1968*, Vol. 3, 1971, pp. 2585–2590.

50. Harry Emerson Fosdick, *Adventurous Religion and Other Essays* (New York: Harper and Brothers, 1926), pp. 238, 245–246, 250.

51. Charles Francis Potter, *The Story of Religion* (New York: Simon and Schuster, 1929), p. 584.

52. Sanger, ed., *Sixth International Neo-Malthusian and Birth Control Conference, Vol. IV, Religious and Ethical Aspects of Birth Control* (New York: American Birth Control League, 1926), pp. 18–19.

53. *Ibid.*, p. 1.

54. "Synagogue Forbids Birth Control Talk," *New York Times*, April 22, 1923, p. 5, col. 7.

55. "Back Their Pastor on Free Speech," *New York Times*, April 23, 1923, p. 15, col. 2.

56. "Resent Birth Control Ban," *New York Times*, April 28, 1923, p. 4, col. 2.

57. "Mrs. Sanger Talks at Yale," *New York Times*, December 5, 1924, p. 21, col. 6.

58. Madeline Gray, *Margaret Sanger: A Biography of the Champion of Birth Control* (New York: Richard Marek Publishers, 1979), p. 237.

59. *Ibid.*

60. Potter acted as one of the most outspoken liberal members of the clergy. In addition to supporting the birth control movement in its early years, he helped define the modernist stance on evolution. He testified as a Bible expert for the defense during the Scopes Trial.

61. "Birth Control Meeting," *New York Times*, December 7, 1924, sec. 1, p. 2, col. 6.

62. "Ask Churches' Aid for a Better Race," *New York Times*, March 31, 1925, p. 7, col. 1.

63. *Ibid.*

64. *Ibid.*

65. An active member of the Voluntary Parenthood League, Robie lectured extensively on marital sex issues. By this time he had published *Rational Sex Ethics* (1916), *Sex and Life* (1920), *Art of Love* (1921), and *Sex Histories* (1922).

66. "Ask Churches' Aid," p. 7.

67. Educated in genetics research, he later concentrated his attention on eugenics. In 1925 Little became director of the American Birth Control League and president of the International Neo-Malthusian League.

68. "Fights for Birth Control," *New York Times*, November 29, 1925, sec. 1, p. 26, col. 2.

69. *Journal of the General Convention of the Protestant Episcopal Church*, Oct. 7–Oct. 24, 1925 (n.p., 1926), pp. 577–578.

70. "Hits Humanitarian Work," *New York Times*, January 11, 1926, p. 3, col. 5.

71. Raymond J. Wade, ed., *Journal of the Twenty-Ninth Delegated General Conference of the Methodist Episcopal Church* (New York: Methodist Book Concern, 1924), p. 182.

72. *Ibid.*, pp. 183–184.

73. There was similar focus by the Christian Reformed Church, though it limited its attention only to drinking and gambling during these years. See *Acts and Proceedings, Volume 27, 1923–1925*, pp. 262–265, 611–614, and 956–958; *Acts and Proceedings, Volume 28, 1926–1928*, pp. 182–185.

74. *Journal of the Twenty-Ninth Delegated General Conference of the Methodist Episcopal Church* (New York: Methodist Book Concern, 1924), pp. 463–464; *Annual of the Southern Baptist Convention, 1923*, p. 102; *Annual of the Southern Baptist Convention, 1925*, p. 120; *Annual of the Northern Baptist Convention, 1924*, p. 249.

75. *Annual of the Southern Baptist Convention, 1926*, pp. 109–110.

76. Albert G. Peters, "The Family as the Primary Social Unit," *Reformed Church Review* 5 (July 1926), pp. 300, 309.

77. *Lutheran Witness* 43 (May 20, 1924), p. 199.

78. *Annual of the Northern Baptist Convention, 1924*, p. 258.

79. *Annual of the Northern Baptist Convention, 1925*, p. 161.

80. *Ibid.*, p. 160.

81. *Minutes of the General Assembly of the Presbyterian Church in the U.S.A., Volume 4, 1925* (Philadelphia: Office of the General Assembly, 1925), pp. 50–51.

82. *Minutes of the Fifth Biennial Convention of the United Lutheran Church in America, October 19–27, 1926* (Philadelphia: United Lutheran Publication House, 1926), pp. 55–58.

83. For a more general presentation of the United Lutheran Church's view of the family as a social unit, see *The Family: A Study Book for Groups and Individuals* (Philadelphia: United Lutheran Publication House, 1925).

84. Jacob A. Clutz, "The Sex Problem," *Lutheran Quarterly Review* (October 1923), pp. 510–511.

85. A. Herbert Gray, *Men, Women, and God: A Discussion of Sex Questions from the Christian Point of View* (New York: George H. Doran, 1923), p. 149.

86. *Ibid.*, pp. 150–152.

87. *Ibid.*, p. 153.

88. *Ibid.*, pp. 153–154.

89. Isaac E. Marcuson, *Central Conference of American Rabbis, Thirty-Seventh Annual Convention,*vol. 36 (n.p.: 1926), p. 40.

90. *Ibid.*, pp. 102–103.

91. *Ibid.*, pp. 103–104.

92. *Ibid.*, p. 104.

93. Royal S. Copeland, "Alarming Decrease in American Babies," *Ladies' Home Journal,* July 1922, p. 37.

94. S. Josephine Baker, "The High Cost of Babies," *Ladies' Home Journal,* October 1923, p. 13.

95. *Ibid.*

96. "The Neo-Malthusians," *Nation,* April 15, 1925, p. 401.

97. Edward S. Martin, "The Population Problem," *Harper's Magazine,* November 1924, p. 802.

98. R. le Clerc Phillips, "Cracks in the Upper Crust," *Independent,* May 29, 1926, p. 633.

99. Inge, "Catholic Church and Anglo-Saxon Mind," *Atlantic Monthly,* April 1923, p. 440.

100. *Ibid.*, p. 441.

101. *Ibid.*, p. 448.

102. Sanger, "The War Against Birth Control," *American Mercury* 2 (June 1924), pp. 231–232.

103. *Ibid.*, pp. 233–234.

104. *Ibid.*, p. 234.

105. *Ibid.*, p. 235.

106. "A Calling of the Clan," *Birth Control Review,* March 1923, pp. 59–60.

107. Ross was teaching at the University of Texas and later taught at Catholic University and Columbia University. Among his publications were *Consumers and Wage Earners* (1912), *Christian Ethics* (1918), and *Sanctity and Social Service* (1921).

108. J. Elliot Ross, "A Study in Numbers," *Catholic World,* June 1923, p. 313.

109. John M. Cooper, *Birth Control* (Washington, D.C.: National Catholic Welfare Council, 1923), reprinted in Julia E. Johnsen, comp., *Selected Articles on Birth Control* (n.p.: H. W. Wilson, 1925), p. 342.

110. *Ibid.*, p. 344.

111. *Ibid.*, pp. 345–346.

112. "The Question of Birth Control," *Catholic World,* September 25, 1925, pp. 842–843.

113. Lydian Allen DeVilbiss, *Birth Control, What Is It?* (Boston: Smnall, Maynard, 1923), pp. 19–20.

114. *Ibid.*, p. 36.

115. *Ibid.*, p. vii.

116. Adolf Meyer, ed., *Birth Control Facts and Responsibilities: A Symposium Dealing with This Important Subject from a Number of Angles* (Baltimore: Williams and Wilkins, 1925), p. 95.

117. *Ibid.*, p. viii.

118. "The Hearing at Hartford," *Birth Control Review,* March 1923, p. 63.

119. "Backward Connecticut," *New York Times,* February 15, 1923, p. 18, col. 5.

120. Mary Ware Dennett, *Birth Control Laws: Shall We Keep Them, Change Them, or Abolish Them?* (New York: Grafton, 1926), pp. 130, 133.

121. *Cummins-Vaile Bill, Congress of the United States, Joint Subcommittee of the Judiciary Committees, of the Senate and House of Representatives,* April 8, 1924, p. 41.

122. *Ibid.*, pp. 19–20.

123. *Ibid.*, p. 24.

124. Tentler, p. 478.

# Chapter Four

# 1927–1929: Protestants Silent, Shift at Hand

The late 1920s mark an important period in the religious shift toward the acceptance of contraceptive use. Even though there developed little official religious support of the birth control movement, and the various examinations of doctrine grew increasingly complex, the battle lines between liberalism and conservatism were becoming more clearly drawn. On one side denominations were opening the door to acceptance that would take place within a few years. On the other there were those who increased their resistance to any modern secular trends that might influence their traditional teaching.

Published denominational addresses and discussions indicated that Catholics were not the only ones condemning the use of contraceptives. However, the public birth control debate made it appear that no one stood on the side of the Catholic Church. Catholic authorities were quite public in their statements and not only spoke to their congregations but fought legalization because they perceived this as a social issue. Still, even though doctrine remained unchanged, and the substance of conservative Protestant denominations echoed Catholic statements, the national press focused on the Catholic Church as the one with the most antiquated perception of birth control.

Successful immigration restriction and the demise of the Ku Klux Klan by the mid–1920s could have paved the way for a more tolerant attitude toward the Church in the latter part of the decade. However, there were those who worked to keep anti–Catholicism alive. One was eugenicist E. A. Ross, who in earlier years had focused on a need for immigration restriction. In his popular *Standing Room Only?* Ross pointed to high birthrates among the inferior that had already immigrated into the United States and suggested that, in opposing contraception, the Church had a specific agenda of eventual domination: "[Did] one not realize the stubborn resistance which venerable authoritative organizations always offer to adapting their position to changed conditions, one would suspect that ecclesiastics enjoy tormenting people with preposterous and non–Christian taboos, or else that they are scheming to rid themselves ultimately of Protestants and all other heretics, and schismatics by requiring their followers to outbreed and supplant them!"[1]

Such statements assisted in maintaining fear of the Catholic Church, but during the late 1920s most discussions about birth control focused far less on the perceived threat of an increasing Catholic population. Instead, they centered on the threat that Catholic authorities intended to force their beliefs on the rest of American society. An important event took place that proved to critics that this was true. New York's Catholic governor, Al Smith, decided to run for the office of president of the United States.[2]

Although Smith did not lose the election simply because he was Catholic, birth control advocates attempted to use his political ambitions to support their claims that the Catholic Church was scheming to take control of the United States. Furthermore, Catholic theologians who defended their position on contraceptive use during the late 1920s increasingly focused on its sinfulness for all humankind, not just Catholics. This provided additional evidence for critics that the Church was determined to dictate morality for the entire nation.

Catholics recognized this and presented counterattacks. In a 1927 lecture series at Saints Peter and Paul Jesuit Church in Detroit and Holy Family Church in Chicago, the Rev. John A. McClorey, S.J., of the University of Detroit argued that the Ku Klux Klan was lobbying the government to legislate discrimination on the basis of religion or race. In addition, according to the Rev. McClorey, "Prohibitionists, instead of allowing the liquor question to remain in the hands of individuals, or, at least, of the State, have burdened the already overloaded shoulders of the Federal Government with enforcement of a dry regime." Regarding birth control advocates, McClorey wrote, "These very people, who are insistent on others, especially foreigners, being patriotic, are themselves a crying example of disloyalty to the government.... They appeal to liberty of speech. But the State has a right to defend itself by legislation against moral corruption, against murder, theft, public indecency, Socialism, Bolshevism and birth control."[3]

McClorey was one of many Catholics who attempted to portray themselves as patriotic Americans, no different from native Protestants who participated in the public process for the betterment of society.

## Sanger Attack Continues

In 1928 Sanger intensified her attempt to stimulate fear of Catholics when the American Birth Control League was barred from participating in the New York Board of Education's Parents' Exposition at the Grand Central Palace in New York. Immediately following notification that her organization could not participate as had been promised, she implied that the action was instigated by the Church. At this time the momentum of anti–Catholicism was building as New York's Catholic governor, Al Smith, campaigned for president of the United States. Sanger forced the contraceptive debate into this arena. On April 20 she was quoted by the *New York Times* as saying, "Many people [are] attacking bigotry, ignorance and intolerance in the name of a New York candidate for the highest office in the land. But in my opinion it is from many of these same people that the present bigoted intolerance and prejudice against our organization arises."[4]

Five days later she attacked the Church directly for the ban and asserted that the election of Smith "as a representative of a church whose tyrannical intolerance is far worse than the lack of broad-mindedness which it criticizes in others would be a national calamity." She blamed Dr. William O'Shea, a member of the Board of Education, for denying the League participation in the exposition:

> The arbitrary action by [O'Shea] in bullying the Parents' Association into submission and acquiescence to his Catholic prejudices is a flagrant example of the bigotry and usurpation of power exercised by office holders born and bred in the Roman Catholic faith. This conflict brings into the open the menace of intolerant tyranny in the educational institutions of the United States. If such power is to be given national scope, through a Presidential aspirant, its disastrous effect on the future of American civilization will be incalculable.[5]

She added that Protestant and Jewish ministers and many social organizations in New York and throughout the country had praised the work of the birth control movement as "the most vital agency for the improvement of the human race."[6] To her accusations O'Shea responded, "We issued thousands of tickets to our school children and when they went there the exposition was to all intents and purposes a school house. I don't think that a school house is a fit place in which to teach birth control. I have no objections to Mrs. Sanger teaching it in other places.... Religion played no part in whatever action I took. Further, I can see no connection between this and the aspirations of any one for the Presidency."[7]

## *Debate in the National Press*

Many Catholics agreed with William O'Shea that they were not interested in denying the right to discuss birth control everywhere, but some national publications argued that the opposite was true. *The Nation*, for instance, continued its attack on the Church during these years, maintaining that Catholic authorities intended to extend their fight against contraception far beyond their own pulpits. In March of 1929 *The Nation* concluded that the only opposition to proposed legislative changes in New York state restrictions came from the Catholic Church.[8] According to that article, "Not content with preaching that contraception is a sin, [Catholics] are also unwilling that those who disagree with them shall be permitted even to learn about it." It added:

> The bill proposed in New York is purely permissive; if it becomes law no person in or out of the Catholic church need ever use measures of birth control or receive any information about them. But in spite of this a Catholic organization such as the New York Archdiocesan Union of the Holy Name Society, composed of 343 branches with a membership of more than 100,000 men, has protested to the legislature "against the adoption of the Remer bill in favor of the use of contraceptive methods."[9]

In addition, according to *The Nation*, similar misrepresentation was contained in a statement by Buffalo's Catholic bishop, who condemned the law as one backed by "the fanaticism of women whose philosophy of life is pagan, who are indolent in their habits, cowardly in their maternal duty to God and their country, and many of them sterile by the constant use of the practices which this bill would sanction."[10]

Claims of misrepresentation abounded on both sides. That same year, the *New Republic* provided an arena for both sides to clarify their respective positions, which each said had been misrepresented by the opposition. After P. J. Ward of the National Catholic Welfare Conference argued that Sanger had misquoted him in a *New Republic* letter to the editor, the publication allowed him to elaborate on the Church's stand. Ward described the stand as "reasonable and healthful" and "mindful of those elements that work for the best interests of society." Representing an organization committed to social welfare issues, he based his argument on the common good and state interests. As a Catholic, he argued the point on natural and moral law, stating that artificial prevention by mechanical, chemical, or other means was "intrinsically evil" and consequently, legislation regarding such applied "with equal force to Catholic and non–Catholic."[11]

This is precisely why non–Catholics objected to the Church's stand. The *Atlantic Monthly* addressed this sentiment the previous year in an article entitled "Mediaeval Thinking: The Catholic Church and the Modern Mind." As the title suggests, modernists criticized the Church not only for its contraceptive doctrine but in general for continuing to apply dogma, which had its roots in the Middle Ages. This article called the Church "a repressive system, without the constructive elements that appeal to enlightened minds." Without mentioning the issue of contraception specifically, this critique noted the most significant point of contention in the debate at this time: "By her own profession the Catholic Church assumes responsibility for the world's morality and the sanctification of mankind."[12]

In the *New Republic* Ward insisted that the Catholic position on contraception represented nothing different from the mainstream religious position at that time: "The Church does not forbid the limitation of families under all or any conditions.... It does not require child-bearing without regard to the health of the mother or to the family income. It simply teaches that if a limitation is placed on the number of children brought into the world it must be done through abstinence and continence."[13] Essentially that was where religious America, regardless of denomination, stood at that time. Only the Central Conference of American Rabbis appeared to be leaning toward allowing physicians to use their expertise in recommending methods of prevention, and an examination of both the popular press and the religious press suggests no one seemed to be paying attention.

During the late 1920s the press did recognize that not all religious opposition to legalizing contraceptive information was coming from the Catholics, but that recognition was reticent and certainly was overshadowed by the anti–Catholic argument. This was evident when the *New Republic* responded to Ward's article in an editorial in the same edition. The editorial claimed its objection was directed toward all religious groups who opposed birth control, not only Catholics. However, it continually pointed to the Catholic Church as the enemy:

> We do not see how anyone can agree with his position, except under the influence of a profound emotional bias which is beyond the reach of reason. ... The Catholic policy is in the first place an admission that the moral authority of the Church with its own communicants is not strong enough to ensure obedience, so that the admonitions of the priests have to be backed by the law; and in the second place, it is an attempt to improve people's morals by legislation, a policy to which prominent

> Catholics are bitterly opposed when the Protestants do it in the
> case of prohibition.[14]

This exchange in the popular press illustrated the way the birth control debate continually turned to the topic of Catholics, and from there to the issue of Catholic action, rather than to one of the Catholic position. The Catholic position was not a point of contention. In fact, if the popular press had examined more closely the Catholic position, it might have found more weaknesses in it.

Henry Pratt Fairchild of New York University pointed out such weaknesses in a letter to the editor of the *New Republic* following his criticism of Ward. Fairchild noted, among other discrepancies, that Ward's position on continence differed from that of Catholic theologian and social activist John Ryan:

> Throughout his article Mr. Ward emphasizes the position that
> the Catholic Church does not object to family limitation
> secured by continence, which it regards as both a possible and
> a practicable method. In an article in *The Survey*, for March 4,
> 1916, [Ryan], whose authority as a spokesman of the Church
> can hardly be inferior to Mr. Ward's says, "The Church does
> not positively and generally recommend this sort of restriction
> ... because she knows that the practice of conjugal abstinence
> will probably not be readily adopted nor chastely followed by
> the majority of married couples.

Fairchild assured readers that an examination of the evidence would show that "the Catholic attitude on birth control, far from being the uniform, definite, and inflexible doctrine that it is usually supposed to be, is vague, diffuse, and inconsistent."[15]

The greatest evidence of this was seen in the Jesuits' *Ecclesiastical Review*, where Catholic doctrinal debate was played out in the late 1920s. On examination of the *Review*, it became clear that Catholic theologians disagreed in their interpretations of doctrine. Furthermore, they strayed from describing or reinforcing basic tenets as they moved toward a more and more complicated debate concerning the reasons for the Church's position.

E. J. Mahoney was one who used the *Review* as a forum to defend the Church's teaching. In his article of August 1928 Mahoney admitted that the only adequate reason the Church could give that would insure that Catholics refrained from using birth control was that it was a grave sin against God. However, he added, it was often necessary to offer some reasons for this authoritative teaching. He suggested this was instrumental in convincing non–Catholics. It was an important measure since contraceptive use was "against the moral law binding all mankind."[16]

According to Mahoney, the most common argument against birth control, that of its "unnaturalness," should be abandoned. Pointing out that too many other modern tendencies—namely shaving, snuff-taking, and surgery—were also considered "unnatural," that argument had lost the strength of its foundation. He also criticized the argument that sexual intercourse for pleasure should always be considered sinful. That argument had also been weakened since Catholic teaching had concluded that eating for pleasure was not sinful; nor was enjoying the sensual pleasure of "bathing in a cool stream in summer, ... sitting before a glowing fire in winter."[17]

To him, only the "perverted faculty" argument held water. He insisted that any pleasure derived from pleasurable sexual intercourse should be considered within the larger idea of *bonum honestum*, or the good toward which rational human nature has a natural tendency. However, to follow this instinct toward sensitive pleasure, and at the same time obstruct the natural end of that behavior, was a sin. He added that it was fortunate that the "Christian conscience perceives without much difficulty the rather intangible thing which the philosopher describes as '*bonum honestum,*' and equally perceives the sinfulness of actions which secure sexual pleasure while frustrating the purpose of the faculty."[18]

John M. Cooper of Catholic University criticized Mahoney's analysis for a number of reasons. First, Cooper noted that if birth control were wrong because, as Mahoney indicated, it was "opposed to the good of rational nature," then contraception could be considered only venially sinful. This argument provided no grounds on which the Church could regard it as mortally sinful. Second, it was impossible to derive the "mortal sinfulness of contraception from the secondary unnaturalness of it as a perversion of faculty." For instance, lying was considered a perversion of the faculty of speech but was also considered only a venial sin.[19]

Third, Cooper asserted that it was difficult to ascertain what constituted a misuse or perversion in the case of sexual intercourse. Barring contraceptive practices as a perversion raised important questions regarding the natural function of the reproductive faculty after conception had already occurred and when one partner had already been diagnosed as sterile. Fourth, the question of sexual ethics that Mahoney raised only complicated the birth control position. According to Cooper, there should be no consideration of relative ethics because, he said, "were the Church to give in one inch on her adamantine stand against contraception, she would soon be impaled on one or other horn of the dilemma of stultifying and contradicting herself or of abandoning her ethics of sex all along the line." In fact, he formulated his conclusion by explaining the sinfulness of contraception along the same line. He claimed that it was "universally sinful, or, to use the synonymous term, intrinsically sinful, because if exceptions be admitted for particular circumstances, before long, by the familiar process of rationalization, the exceptions would become, if not the rule, at least so common and so numerous that the objective and subjective *bonum humanum* protected by chastity and marriage would be deeply and disastrously undermined and frustrated."[20] In reading Mahoney's discourse and Cooper's response, it becomes apparent that Fairchild was right; the Catholic position on contraception during the late 1920s was "vague, diffuse, and inconsistent." Critics still wondered exactly what the Church believed was sinful and why.

The *Ecclesiastical Review* did not exist only as an outlet for moral, ethical, and theological debate. Others used it to address the more realistic everyday concerns of individual priests and to focus on issues of pastoral care. For example, Joseph V. Nevins, S.S., of Washington, D.C., turned his attention toward the priest's role in preparing Catholics for marriage. In an effort to educate couples, whom he viewed as unaware of the demands of marriage, he elaborated on what the Church considered the primary duties in marriage. According to Nevins, first and foremost "marriage is *matris munium*, the function and burden of motherhood." He added, "It is this *first of all*, and anything else is negligible by comparison. Marriage cannot be rightly thought of as anything else and it is as such that it should occur to the mind of everyone.... As we think of the priesthood with the Mass in mind, and Sisterhoods as resting on renunciation and service, so marriage speaks of child-bearing."[21] In Nevins's interpretation procreation was undeniably the primary purpose of marriage.

When addressing the topic of birth control, Nevins said that the growth of the practice of birth control was "of distressing concern to every priest, and should be to every Catholic," referring to the availability of contraceptive information as "this evil." But he subsequently remarked on the situation in a way that could have been regarded as contrary to the usual Catholic insistence on dogma: "Birth-control ideas, under one form or another, or under one name or another, are in the air and in the minds of all. Some fight it more or less successfully; others are utterly demoralized by it.... And the net result is that, as Foster could say of Europe over a decade ago, 'We live in an age in which it is no longer possible merely to hand on generally accepted truths.' This is perhaps more true of the Catholic teaching and standards of marriage than of anything else."[22] Though Nevins did not go so far as to challenge the existing opposition to birth control, his suggestion that the Church could no longer depend on generally accepted truths reflected a similar attitude that existed among the most liberal Protestants of this time.

Where he did open the door was in the area of abstinence. Whereas Cooper had insisted that there be no exceptions to the sinfulness of birth control, Nevins accepted abstinence as a rational response to a wife's bitter complaints of her burden: "Reason forbids intercourse at times, just as reason allows refusal of it. Were this better understood by husbands, wives would be spared much distress and the interests and the duties of marriage would be better secured." He added: "An esteem for self-control, for modesty, even for continency and a tender regard and reverence for a wife are very much to be expected of the faithful."[23]

In a subsequent article Nevins asserted that if the Church were "to come to grips with the evil of birth control," it must "reckon with the host." According to him, the Church was tackling the subject in the wrong way by ignoring the significance of developments in society that encouraged couples to practice contraception. He blamed doctors for treating pregnancy as pathological and recommended that Catholics be warned to see only soundly Catholic physicians for maternity cases. He also blamed the contemporary lay mentality for encouraging smaller families: "One hears constantly from dutiful mothers that for their faithfulness to their marital obligation they are regarded by others as fools and are told to their faces that they ought to be ashamed, that a large family is vulgar, that they are doing an injustice to their other children, that they are throwing away their lives, and all the rest of the outrageous rot."[24] In addition, high rents and the cost of homes, as well as the growing trend toward materialism, encouraged women to have fewer children. Moreover, Nevins insisted that clergy and, even more, parishioners were responsible for miscommunication that created a misunderstanding of Catholic doctrine:

> Not infrequently one hears or hears of people quoting a priest, especially a confessor, something to the effect that this is no sin, that one has done his or her duty as regards childbearing, etc. Sometimes it is of rigoristic tenor: that a wife may not lawfully refuse a drunken husband, or that it is wrong to have intercourse when conception is no longer possible; etc. The point is, *not* that these things were or were not said to them, but that they say that they were said.... They are generally due to disingenuousness or to misunderstanding.[25]

Still, he did not provide any explanation of the facts regarding doctrine.

Though the years between 1927 and 1929 saw a great increase in the number of published articles reflecting the Catholic stand on birth control, the same was not true for Protestants. The topic had reached the status of full debate among Catholics, but such a debate was not reflected in Protestant convention papers or in the Protestant press. The lack of direct discussion, however, was significant. While Protestant churches intensified their study of the American family, especially with regard to the climbing divorce rate, there was little said of contraception. They could hardly have been unaware of the debate taking place; more likely, they were avoiding a stand.

The subject of eugenics was remarkably absent from Protestant discussion. The Episcopalians, who had been criticized in the past for supporting eugenics but not birth control, were the only ones to address it during a convention. Even then, they resolved only to urge federal and state authorities to restrict the marriage of "physically or mentally defective persons."[26] More important, however, was the manner in which Episcopalians and other Protestants addressed the ideals of marriage in their criticism of divorce.

The topic of divorce no longer was addressed within the larger subject of the family; clergy addressed the topic of the family within the pressing issue of divorce. This was not necessarily new. The trend had developed earlier in the decade. However, what was new was the shift toward a different emphasis on the purpose of marriage. Clearly, the emphasis was less and less on procreation and more and more on the function of the family as a social unit.

This change of emphasis was largely becuase of the growing value placed on the social sciences. The expertise of sociologists, social workers, and other social scientists weighed heavily in the direction taken in family values discussions. However, even though churches increasingly applied social issues and social science rhetoric to their discussions of the functions of the family and the purposes of marriage, they continued to hold tightly to what they had considered as the spiritual and Christian purposes.

It is difficult to determine exactly what role the cries of birth control advocates played in all this, but whatever the causes of the shift were, the result was clear. To Protestants the emphasis on marriage was shifting from childbearing to child rearing. Though having children remained an important part of marriage, the focus on guiding children into roles as conscientious Christians and productive citizens got increasing attention.

What churches did criticize was a trend they blamed on psychologists and psychiatrists: that of an increasing acceptance of marrying with the idea of happiness in mind. According to clergy from all denominations, couples who entered into marriage with the intention of being happy would become discouraged and frustrated once they were confronted with the difficult responsibilities of parenthood. In addition, they would seek divorce when they were no longer happy. One Episcopalian elaborated on this attitude in the book *Forthright Opinions Within the Church*, which devoted a chapter to "Christian Training for Marriage."

Episcopalian minister and headmaster of Groton School in Massachusetts Endicott Peabody wrote that one of the most common causes of the divorce evil was the "notion that a person has a right, a primary right it seems, to happiness. There is no thought of the great principle of Jesus of losing one's life for another and so finding it." He suggested that "married people would be much happier if they forgot their own happiness and worked together for the happiness of their children; they would then have their thoughts centered in the same direction and would not have time to brood over any small arguments that they must have anyway."[27]

Though the happiness of one's children was an admirable goal in Peabody's eyes, it was not so according to the dean of Barnard College, Virginia C. Gildersleeve.[28] To Gildersleeve the goal of making one's children happy helped contribute to the breakdown of the family. She condemned the claim by parents that the comfort of their children was essential: "They want their children to be comfortable and amused *all* the time. American parents love their children dearly, and intensely desire their happiness. They are also often afraid of them. For these reasons, being very shortsighted, they do not want them ever to be made uncomfortable by hard work, or boredom, or pain of any kind. Every minute in the day they would like to have the children perfectly comfortable and amused."[29] According to Gildersleeve, because this was an impossible task, parents subjected themselves to a tremendous strain that could damage their marriage. In addition, she expressed concern that it was this tendency to strive for comfort that caused couples to have fewer children.

Gildersleeve also remarked on the growing trend in which more women were choosing careers outside the home, a move that clergy warned was causing women to forsake the role of mother altogether. Gildersleeve insisted that this need not be the case:

> I know one prominent and admirable woman who has combined [motherhood and career]. She is a successful industrial engineer and a mother of eleven happy children. She says the secret is to have plenty of children. One child is very difficult; two or three are difficult; but as you get up to six, seven, nine, and ten it becomes simple. The older ones take care of the younger ones, and if you are an efficiency engineer you have

your household organized between them so they do all the
household work.... Mrs. Gilbreth is an extraordinarily healthy,
cheerful, well-balanced unnervous person.[30]

She did admit that other friends had told her that combining careers with
raising young children was much more difficult than Gilbreth had claimed.

Presbyterian pronouncements during this time reflected the common
clerical criticism of the contemporary view of romance, which suggested
that marriage could be one long honeymoon. The ad-interim committee
on divorce reported to the General Assembly of the Presbyterian Church
in 1929 that "this makes pleasure the test of life, rather than duty or
suffering, and when marriage ceases to furnish the expected happiness,
many people feel that they are justified in seeking that happiness elsewhere." In defining what marriage should be, the committee report never
mentioned procreation or children. Instead, it stated that the ideal of marriage had been presented by Christ himself; that ideal was the lifelong
union of one man with one woman. It added: "We hold that marriage is
a holy state, ordained of God, a sacred relationship which is to be held in
honor by all, and we deeply deplore the increasing disregard of the sanctity of the marriage tie."[31]

Though these statements indicate a reverence for tradition in the Presbyterian Church, elsewhere in the report there is evidence of adaptation
to societal changes. Regarding the changing role of women, the committee never mentioned motherhood or children. Instead, it reported that the
family was no longer the basic economic unit, as it had been in the past,
since women had been "put on an equal status with men, and they have
achieved their economic emancipation."[32] There was no criticism of this
development; it was used only as an example of one factor in the rising
divorce rate. In addition, the committee suggested that the assembly consider expanding the possible grounds for divorce to include not only adultery but also cruelty, willful and prolonged desertion, and sex perversion.
There was some opposition to this proposal, but the discussion demonstrated that Presbyterians were answering to demands outside the church
in matters relating to marriage and the family.

The Presbyterian General Assembly's Commission on Marriage,
Divorce and Remarriage subsequently compiled a series of articles on the
subject in a book entitled *Twenty-Four Views of Marriage* "so that the
reader can have the whole problem of human relations presented to him
from the angle not only of the conservative, but also of the liberal, and
even radical."[33] The book included chapters by Bertrand Russell, Walter
Lippmann, sociologist Ernest Groves, and eugenicist Paul Popenoe. One

notable discussion on contraception was presented by George Sherwood Eddy, known for his work with the YMCA and for his recent sex hygiene addresses for young men.

In "The Problems of Marriage" Eddy recommended that before marriage all women "without exception" read Sanger's *Happiness in Marriage*. He wrote: "Had this book alone been read, it would have saved many failures in marriage…. It shows the point at which many women are left unsatisfied in their lives, resulting often in a nervous breakdown, because of the ignorance of both the husband and the wife as to woman's biological part in marriage."[34]

In *Happiness in Marriage* Sanger described birth control as a scientific practice that permitted young husbands and wives to "guide and direct their own destinies and to build up their health, happiness and economic strength." She maintained that one of the most serious consequences of the lack of scientific information was the practice of abstinence, or what she called "keeping away" from the husband. A constant denial of sex because of the overwhelming fear of pregnancy put an unbearable strain on a marriage, according to Sanger:

> The poor distracted, worried and hounded wife dares not permit her husband even the ordinary affectionate expression his heart longs for and which his whole body and soul desires and needs. The wife, harried and panic-stricken, dares not even give him a welcoming smile: she shudders at his touch. She struggles against her deepest impulses, and meets his tender embrace with a frigid resistance. She dreads the homecoming of her husband, for his presence means not peace but eternal conflict in her heart.[35]

Eddy's recommendation may have appeared a bold move, but he still did not condone contraception, at least not its widespread use. He noted later in his discussion that sex as a "single impulse" was unsteady, intermittent, and untrustworthy, and if it was not "completed in comradeship and parenthood it may become selfish and tyrannous."[36] Similarly, even though the Presbyterian Church urged education by making various viewpoints available, it still did not condone contraceptive use. However, the fact that Presbyterians opened the forum for discussion further indicated their willingness to accept changes in society regarding matters of marriage and the family.

Lutherans were less accepting of the changes that were taking place in American society. In its report to the convention of the United Lutheran Church in 1928, the Committee on Moral and Social Welfare stressed the sanctity of marriage in much the same way that the Presbyterians did the following year when it reminded followers that the Church regarded marriage as "a holy estate, ordained of God, and to be held in honor by all" and that it "deeply deplore[d] the increasing disregard of the sanctity of the marriage tie, and solemnly protest[ed] against all teaching and practice which violate this sanctity and are therefore contrary to the revealed will of God."[37] In addition, it criticized the contemporary value placed on individual happiness. However, its willingness to compromise on traditional views of the family was comparatively limited. Regarding the status of the family, the committee agreed that there was a need for more conservative influence to insure the preservation of the family's foundation.[38]

The most apparent difference was demonstrated in the Lutheran committee's critical view of the modern woman:

> There is a growing tendency at the present day to justify the claim of womanhood to the right of supplementing the vocation of motherhood with some other vocation in life. Mothers in increasing numbers are engaging in some remunerative employment or following careers which necessitate their absence from the home for the greater part of the day.... Under any circumstances [this situation] cannot be viewed otherwise than with serious misgivings.... Where the mother's continued absence from the home involves the neglect of children during the most formative period of their lives, no accomplishment in other fields can atone for the harm which is done.[39]

At this point the Church did not raise the issue of contraception, or even criticize women for choosing to have fewer children, or no children at all, in order to maintain a career. It is therefore difficult to determine whether, based on this argument, the Church would change its doctrine regarding contraception. The committee's report on the meaning of marriage illustrated the Church's insistence that the primary purpose of marriage was "for the establishment and maintenance of the family." However, the word choice in that statement was significant. At least in this instance, United Lutherans did not use the term "procreation" as they had in the past.

One Methodist opinion was more explicit regarding the importance of parenthood. In 1927 Pennsylvania minister Spenser B. Meeser described the marriage relationship as an ethical and spiritual union of two people in much the same way that others described the sanctity of marriage. Regarding the changing role of women, Meeser wrote that one serious cause of divorce was the growing opportunity for women in industry and the professions. However, in one of the most liberal remarks by any clergyman of the day he stated that the ability for a woman to earn a living may decrease the number of hasty marriages and save marriage from being a matter of mere economic considerations.[40]

Meeser reinforced the Methodist attitude that the function of procreation lay at the base of the institution of marriage, writing that marriage was "a social compact, concerned with the interests and perpetuation of the race." He added that a good marriage was both a social and divine compact that finds its expression in the child: "The two lives united are further made one in the life of the child. There, in the child, is the attest of nature, society and God to the unity for life of the wedded pair.... In the life of the child is the ethical and metaphysical mystery of the unity of the wedded father and mother."[41]

The following year, Washington, D. C., minister Frank Wilbur Collier elaborated further on Methodist teachings concerning the family.[42] Collier echoed the sentiments of other clergy from various denominations, that couples should not enter marriage seeking only pleasure because there were burdens within marriage that must be endured: "When a young woman gets into an airplane and starts over the ocean she is proclaimed a heroine. But a much more lofty courage is expressed by every mother who brings a child into the world."[43]

More important to the evolution of contraception doctrine was Collier's examination of the purpose of the family. He concluded that the family was based on marriage and that the family existed for the development of the well being of the children. His conclusion was significant because he did not claim that marriage existed in order to create children but to insure the proper raising of children.[44] Here Collier was adopting the view of sociologists that the family was the basic social unit, that its primary function was socialization, and that healthy families were necessary for a healthy society. He was not the only member of the clergy to do this. By the late 1920s it was common for clergy who had condemned the behavioral sciences to continue their condemnation of psychology, but adapt their doctrine, based on sociological teachings.

In addition, Collier noted that there was more to marriage than sexual intercourse. According to Collier, biology and anthropology explained the unconscious purpose of men and women marrying and founding families for the development of offspring. While human offspring could be produced only by sex, he wrote, "Sex is not exhausted in the act of procreation; nor is marriage and the family based directly upon the physiological sex.... [I]t needs no very keen powers of observation to see that history and contemporary life give comparatively few examples among enlightened persons marrying with the main purpose of gratifying sex physiologically. The few who have this purpose have not yet reached the human plane, or they have fallen below it."[45] Collier condemned those who looked to marriage for sexual gratification in a way that was compatible with earlier Methodist commentary that too many Americans were becoming "pleasure-seekers." But he did more than that. By stating that "sex is not exhausted in the act of procreation," he indicated that clerical teaching was opening the door to other possible purposes for sexual intercourse than that of procreation.

The report of the General Conference of the Methodist Episcopal Church held in 1928 reflected further change in Methodist marriage doctrine. First, the Committee on Marriage and Divorce requested that courses be prepared to outline the "practical and spiritual values of marriage" and that such courses be taught in church schools, colleges, and universities. Second, the committee urged young people to seek parental, medical, and pastoral advice "before entering upon a relationship so vital to the maintenance of the home, the State and the Church." Without so stating, this reflected the increasing tendency for clergy to encourage couples to seek the advice of a doctor regarding methods of birth control. The conference's statement on public morals once again condemned materialism and pleaded with Methodists to "live in conformity with the spirit of Christ that by their lives, even in the midst of a wicked environment, they may emphasize decency, sobriety, and self-control." The primary focus of this statement, however, was on the issues of motion pictures, gambling, and alcohol consumption.[46]

Northern Baptists were increasingly open in their discussions of the family and marital relationships during these years. They, too, remarked on the growing number of divorces in 1927 and urged "all pastors and other leaders to employ their best endeavor to assist in stabilizing family life in their communities." They did not limit their efforts to encouraging more restrictive marriage licensing nor to clarifying grounds for divorce. Instead, they allowed their prescription to remain vague, presumably encouraging leaders to do whatever it took to resolve the situation.[47]

The following year, the Social Service Committee elaborated on Northern Baptist concerns regarding family life, noting specific developments in American society that contributed to the breakdown of the family. According to the committee, uniform marriage and divorce laws could help but never solve the problem. Complex social factors affecting the family included an industrial system that took the father from the family, except for brief periods each day; the turning over of childhood training from the family to the public schools, Sunday schools, Boy Scouts, Girl

Scouts, and similar agencies; and the choice for women of careers other than homemaking and teaching.

The committee was not critical of women's new roles, nor did it blame them for the continued decrease in family size. In fact, the committee noted: "They are entering every realm and making good." Instead, the committee considered urbanization the cause of smaller families: "We have moved to the city. About 54 per cent of our population live in cities. This reduces living space but increases living costs, and in many cases limits the family to one child or none."[48] In this report the Northern Baptists became the first Protestant denomination to attribute the decline in family size to the outside force of pressing social factors and not to the evils of individual materialism, hedonistic intentions in marriage, or the dissemination of Sanger propaganda.

The Northern Baptists were committed to bettering society as a whole and enthusiastically supported the Federal Council of the Churches of Christ in America in its effort to address social problems. At the convention in 1929 the Social Service Committee reminded Baptists that principles outlined in the Federal Council's social creed of the churches in 1912 were becoming increasingly important in American society nearly two decades later: "The Kingdom of God, so far as it is related to human life on earth, involves the rule of God in human society; and, in consequence, the constitution of society as a whole on the social principle set forth in the spirit and teaching of Jesus — the principle of good-will. A society so constituted is fundamentally a fraternal, democratic, cooperative commonwealth, having for its essential object the promotion of the highest good of all without exception and without partiality."[49] At this point nearly all conservative and liberal denominations in the United States declared some sort of social action as part of their doctrine and increasingly were including marriage and the family among their concerns.[50]

That same year, the Social Service Committee of the Northern Baptists praised highly the publication of "The Ideals of Love and Marriage," by the Federal Council. The committee noted that the pamphlet was produced after long and extensive study by the Council's Committee on Marriage and the Home, adding that the bibliography included was "probably the finest to be found." Each Northern Baptist pastor was mailed a copy of "The Ideals of Love and Marriage," with additional copies made available from the Social Education Division of the Publication Society.

In 1927 the Federal Council had reported that the recently organized national committee on Marriage and the Home was vigorously studying problems related to marriage in the United States. Committee members, who included Bishop James Cannon, Jr., Dean Howard C. Robbins, Worth

M. Tippy, and Russell J. Clinchy,[51] had been reading extensively; gathering information from denominations throughout the United States, Canada, and Europe; and meeting regularly. Aside from establishing a library of materials, in 1929 the committee published "Ideals of Love and Marriage." The opening paragraph of the thirty-one page booklet brought together many of the contemporary social factors individual clergy or denominations had mentioned throughout the decade:

> Observers of American life cannot fail to be aware of the obsession of the stage and present day literature with sex, the disturbed condition of the home, a disquieting increase in divorce and an apparent growth of laxness in the relation of the sexes. The Great War has unsettled, temporarily at least, an entire range of ideas and customs relating to sex, and the situation has been affected by a widespread and increasing knowledge of contraceptives. ... The motion picture, while possessing very great recreational and educational value, has done great harm by over-stimulating sex emotions. The press, also, notably the tabloid and the emotional press, have played excessively upon the same instinct, especially as regards intimate details of sex intrigues which come into the open in courts or in accounts of tragedies of violence.[52]

The committee recognized that its presentation might be considered conservative,[53] and it was. It reinforced traditional values of Christian monogamous marriage, stating that the "spiritual relationship between the sexes is part of a larger moral order. It is linked with belief in God, with purposefulness in the universe, with sacrifice, with the struggle for human life, with the higher idealism and faith of mankind." It condemned companionate marriage because couples entering into such an agreement were seeking only a pleasurable and often temporary relationship without children, adding that "to those who think first of happiness it should be said that children bring the most exquisite happiness."[54]

Regarding working mothers, the committee recommended that churches increase their focus on the importance of parental obligations. It recognized a trend among the upper classes to have nannies, governesses, and private schools rear their children, and it noted working-class mothers were spending too much time away from their children. In the latter case, however, the report did not blame the mothers but rather the employers for failing to provide adequate wages and flexible schedules that would allow women to be at home when their children were at home. *Ideals of Love and Marriage* did not present anything radically different about Protestant notions regarding the family, nor did it provide any liberal recommendations. However, there were a small number of references to family size that indicate that some religious ideals regarding contraception were changing. First, the committee recommended that industry and society should strive for the institution of a living wage that would make it possible for a working man to maintain a family of five in decency.[55] The ability to choose to have a family of that size is what birth control advocates had been demanding. According to the picture that Sanger and others were painting, only the availability of contraceptive information would allow working-class parents to limit the number of their children to three.

More important, the report suggested that the tendency for some couples to have "too many children" might somehow be remedied. Under the topic "Everyday Needs of a Home," the report concluded that unhappiness in a marriage, sometimes culminating in divorce, was often caused by poverty: "Insufficient income is likely to bring unendurable strain upon husband and wife and upon children also as they grow older. They break under the strain or sink into degradation." It added:

> But fortunately one of the great achievements of modern times is the realization that poverty is remediable. Its roots lie deep in the social order and ramify in all directions — low wages, unemployment, accidents, improvidence, sickness, death, feeblemindedness, vice, lack of training for life and work and overstrain of the family income by too many children. These causes of impoverishment which touch innumerable homes make plain the task with which society is now grappling to abolish poverty and to rescue the home from its devastating effects.[56]

Through its social creed and the endeavors of its various committees, the Federal Council worked on the premise that poverty could be and was being progressively abolished in modern industrial states. In suggesting that one cause of poverty could be found in couples having too many children, this committee implied that some degree of poverty might be alleviated if couples could limit the size of their families.

In addition, *Ideals of Love and Marriage* included an extensive bibliography that suggested readings on the topics of the history of marriage, sex education, economics and the home, and applied eugenics. Still, the committee did not specifically condone the use of contraceptives at this time. Regarding birth control, the committee wrote only that *Ideals of Love and Marriage* was designed to prepare the way for later studies and practical recommendations on such subjects. Even liberal Protestants in the United States were not ready to commit themselves to change on this issue.

Resolutions passed by the Lambeth Conference of Anglican Bishops the following year would make their decision easier.

## Conservative Protestants: Anti–Birth Control, Anti-Catholic

The Southern Baptist Convention raised the subject of divorce at its meeting in 1927, noting that recently published statistics reported that there were 175,499 divorces granted in the United States in 1925 — a gain of 4,497 over those in 1924. They blamed the rise on lax laws, which allowed hasty and unwise marriages. Without referring to the sanctity or the spiritual aspect of marriage, Southern Baptists addressed the importance of stable families in maintaining the social order. "Preserve the Home or Perish" was deemed the battle cry of their efforts to ensure congressional legislation regulating marriage licensing.[57]

Southern Baptists further described what they perceived as their role and their intentions in the political world in 1929. Applauding their success in helping defeat Al Smith in his bid for the presidency, the Commission on Social Service reminded the Convention that it was well within the rights of Baptists to "express the collective judgment of its members concerning matters involving the public morals and the public good ... when they become the antagonists of evil and the protagonists of good, whether in the realm of private morals or public morals."[58] Smith had promised to work to repeal prohibition if elected, a move Southern Baptists regarded as deplorable.

During these years the Southern Baptists said nothing about contraception. This was nothing new, as they had not mentioned it specifically earlier in the decade, mainly because they considered it an unmentionable topic. The fact is even less surprising in light of the anti–Catholic attitude on the part of Southern Baptists. They still stood firmly against birth control, but a public declaration would put them on the side of the Catholic Church. To campaign actively against contraceptives as they had against alcohol — and still against gambling, dancing, motion pictures, and immoral literature — would portray them, along with Catholics, as dictating morals outside their membership.

Sentiments expressed by the Reformed Church in 1929 were nearly identical to those of the Southern Baptists. The Permanent Committee on Public Morals also took credit for helping to defeat Smith and reinforced Christian Reformed principles related to political action. The committee report stated, "We renew our determination to teach with zeal the principles of patriotism, and a loyal obedience to all the laws of the land. We are persuaded that the membership of the Reformed Church in America have [*sic*] ever held to a high level of moral purpose and action, but instruction in righteousness, and temperance, and Sabbath observance must still be given to all." As an example of why such action was necessary, the committee cited recent declarations by John Ryan in the *Commonweal* in which he defended disobedience to the prohibition law in the same way that revolutionaries had rejected British law in 1776.[59]

The reason for the absence of Christian Reformed commentary on the subject of birth control during the latter part of the 1920s was similar to the situation of the Southern Baptists. As conservative Protestants, both denominations still opposed the use of contraceptives, both were involved in social and political action regarding various issues, and both sought to secure public morality. However, public objection to contraceptives would place them in the same court with Catholics.

## Central Conference of American Rabbis Takes Action

Though Sanger exaggerated any Protestant support she had obtained, she appeared to have underemphasized the Jewish support. There developed a significant move toward acceptance of contraception on the Jewish front in 1927 — a move that should have gained more attention than it actually did. In that year Jacob Z. Lauterbach, professor of the Talmud at Hebrew Union College in Cincinnati, presented his "Talmudic-Rabbinic View on Birth Control" to the Central Conference of American Rabbis, as requested. In that report Lauterbach recognized that some rabbis still condemned all forms of birth control, except for abstinence, but called their condemnation "unscientific and not justified in the discussion of such a serious and important question."[60]

Through extensive study and analysis, Lauterbach concluded that:

1. The Talmudic-Rabbinic law does not consider the use of contraceptives as such immoral or against the law. It does not forbid birth control but it forbids birth suppression.
2. The Talmudic-Rabbinic law requires that every Jew have at least two children in fulfillment of the biblical command to propagate the race which is incumbent upon every man.
3. There are, however, conditions under which a man may be exempt from this prime duty: (a) when a man is engaged in religious work like

the study of the Torah, and fears that he may be hindered in his work by taking on the responsibilities of a family; (b) when a man, because of love or other considerations, marries a woman who is incapable of having children, as an old or sterile woman; (c) when a man is married to a woman whose health is in such a condition as to make it dangerous for her to bear children. For consideration for the saving of human life … set aside the obligation to fulfill a religious duty. In this case, then, the woman is allowed to use any contraceptives or even to permanently sterilize herself in order to escape the dangers that would threaten her at childbirth.

4. In case a man has fulfilled the duty of propagation of the race, as when he has already two children, he is no longer obliged to beget children and the law does not forbid him to have intercourse with his wife even in a manner which would not result in conception. In such a case the woman certainly is allowed to use any kind of contraceptive or preventive.[61]

This marked the first detailed doctrinal acceptance of contraception within any denomination, but in the larger birth control debate it got little attention. Instead, Sanger continued to draw attention to letters and public speeches that demonstrated only individual support. Because she worked hard to publicize any religious support she had obtained, it is somewhat puzzling that she did not do so in this case. However, in light of the anti–Semitic atmosphere of the day, it makes sense that she would not wish to bring too much attention to the fact that liberal Jews were now accepting tenets of the birth control activists on an organizational level while Protestants were not.

Even though the decision received little publicity, it is unlikely that she did not know about it. There were enough liberal rabbis who worked closely with her (for example, Goldstein, Mischkind, Weis, and Wise) that word of the Central Conference report would have reached her easily. It is more likely that she resisted drawing attention to the matter. Sanger wanted religious support to help pave the way for public acceptance and eventually for legislation, and because she was appealing to the American mainstream, she would rather have Protestants than Jews behind her.

There is no evidence to indicate that this was a conscious move. It is more likely that this is just one more instance in which Sanger ignored the importance of discussions at the denominational level. Throughout the religious birth control debate, she grasped for individual pronouncements and implied that these people spoke for entire denominations. During 1926 and 1927 the *Review* published only two articles regarding Jews and birth control, and they were both excerpts from the speech given by her long-time supporter, Stephen Wise, at the Sixth Neo-Malthusian and Birth Control Conference in 1925.[62]

## The Decade Comes to a Close

During the late 1920s Sanger put most of her efforts into keeping the light focused on Catholics as the opposition. Increasingly, liberal and mainline Protestants and Jews were examining birth control from a different religious perspective. Still, there was little official denominational support. But regardless of where other denominations stood at this point, Sanger could say that Catholics stood against her.

As Catholic theologians argued their birth control positions as one of natural law concerning all people, they intensified the concerns of a growing number of Americans who feared clerical attempts at legislating morality. The pope had not yet made any official declaration, but Sanger convinced many Americans that he emphatically opposed contraceptives and her efforts to make them legal.

## Notes

1. Edward Alsworth Ross, *Standing Room Only?* (New York: The Century Co., 1927), p. 263.

2. Fuchs, "Election of 1928," pp. 2585–2609. Also see chapter 3, "The Campaign of 1928, a Study in Political Folklore," pp. 25–35, and chapter 4, "The Forgotten Catholic Candidate, Thomas J. Walsh," pp. 38–46, in Paul A. Carter, *Politics, Religion and Rockets: Essays in Twentieth Century American History* (Tucson: University of Arizona Press, 1991); James H. Smylie, "Roman Catholic Church, the State, and Al Smith," *Church History* 29 (1960), p. 321; and Oscar Handlin, *Al Smith and His America* (Boston: Little, Brown, 1958).

3. Rev. John A. McClorey, S.J., *The Republic and the Church: A Series of Lenten Lectures Mainly on Divorce and Birth Control* (St. Louis: B. Herdee, 1927), pp. 9, 97.

4. "School Show Bars Birth Control Body," *New York Times*, April 20, 1928, p. 11.

5. "Mrs. Sanger Calls Catholics Bigots," *New York Times*, April 25, 1928, p. 14.

6. *Ibid.*

7. *Ibid.*

8. The Remer Bill would have made it legal for physicians to provide birth control information to married couples.

9. "The 'Black Plague,'" *The Nation*, March 13, 1929, p. 301.

10. *Ibid.*

11. "The Catholics and Birth Control," *New Republic*, May 29, 1929, p. 35.

12. "Mediaeval Thinking: The Catholic Church and the Modern Mind," *Atlantic Monthly*, January–June, 1928, pp. 664–667.

13. *New Republic*, May 29, 1929, p. 35.

14. "The Reply to Mr. Ward," *New Republic*, May 29, 1929, p. 32.

15. "Correspondence, Catholics and Birth Control," *New Republic*, June 12, 1929, p. 101.

16. E. J. Mahoney, "The 'Perverted Faculty' Argument Against Birth Prevention," *Ecclesiastical Review* 79 (August 1928), p. 133.

17. *Ibid.*, pp. 142–143.

18. *Ibid.*, p. 145.

19. John M. Cooper, "Birth Control and the 'Perverted Faculty' Argument," *Ecclesiastical Review* 79 (November 1928), pp. 527–528.

20. *Ibid.*, pp. 532–533.

21. Joseph V. Nevins, "Education to Catholic Marriage," *Ecclesiastical Review* 9 (September 1928), p. 249.

22. *Ibid.*, pp. 242–243.

23. *Ibid.*, pp. 252–253.

24. Nevins, "Education to Catholic Marriage; Adverse Influences," *Ecclesiastical Review* 79 (December 1928), p. 624.

25. *Ibid.*, p. 630.

26. *Journal of the General Convention of the Protestant Episcopal Church, 1928* (New York: Abbott Press and Mortimer-Walling, 1929), p. 120.

27. *Forthright Opinions Within the Church* (New York: Charles Scribner's Sons, 1928), p. 55.

28. Unmarried herself, Gildersleeve devoted her career to academics and women's issues. She held memberships in the Guggenheim Foundation, the American National Committee on Intellectual Cooperation and the International Federation of University Women, and served as president of the Association to Aid Scientific Research by Women.

29. *Ibid.*, p. 68.

30. *Ibid.*, p. 81.

31. *Minutes Of the Sixty-Ninth General Assembly of the Presbyterian Church in the United States* (Richmond, Va.: Presbyterian Committee of Publication, 1929), pp. 145–147.

32. *Ibid.*

33. Clarence A. Spaulding, *Twenty-Four Views of Marriage* (New York: Macmillan, 1930), x.

34. *Ibid.*, p. 151.

35. Sanger, *Happiness in Marriage* (Garden City, N.Y.: Blue Ribbon Books, 1926), pp. 207–215.

36. Spaulding, *Twenty-Four Views*, p. 155.

37. *Minutes of the Sixth Biennial Convention of the United Lutheran Church in America* (Philadelphia, Penn.: 1928), p. 594.

38. *Ibid.*, p. 583.

39. *Ibid.*, pp. 583–584.

40. Spenser B. Meeser, "Divorce and Remarriage," *Methodist Review*, November 1927, pp. 854–857.

41. *Ibid.*, pp. 868–869.

42. Collier was a professor of social psychology at the University of Maryland until 1924. At the time of this writing he headed the philosophy department at American University.

43. Frank Wilbur Collier, "The Family, Marriage, and Divorce," *Methodist Review*, March 1928, p. 211.

44. *Ibid.*, pp. 211–212.

45. *Ibid.*, p. 212.

46. *Journal of the Thirtieth Delegated General Conferenc of the Methodist Episcopal Church* (New York: Methodist Book Concern, 1928), pp. 623–624, 705–706.

47. *Annual of the Northern Baptist Convention, 1927* (n.p.: American Baptist Publication Society, 1927), p. 148.

48. *Annual of the Northern Baptist Convention, 1928* (n.p.: American Publication Society, 1928), p. 85.

49. *Annual of the Northern Baptist Convention, 1929* (n.p.: American Baptist Publication Society, 1929), p. 120.

50. Only Lutherans were publicly stating that they had no intention of reaching beyond their membership in applying their doctrine to family matters.

51. Others included the Rev. John W. Elliott, Mrs. Jeannette W. Emrich, Mrs. John Ferguson, the Rev. Charles K. Gilbert, the Rev. J. Henry Harms, the Rev. Hubert C. Herring, the Rev. John W. Langdale, Bishop Francis J. McConnell, the Rev. John A. Marquis, Mrs. W. A. Newell, Mrs. I. H. O'Hara, Mrs. John D. Rockefeller, Jr., Mrs. Robert E. Speer, Mrs. Anna Garlin Spencer,

the Rev. Henry W. Sweets, the Rev. Alva W. Taylor, the Rev. Henry St. George Tucker, Mr. George Wickersham, the Rev. B. S. Winchester, and Mrs. W. C. Winsborough.

52. Committee on Marriage and the Home, *Ideals of Love and Marriage* (New York: Commission on the Church and Social Service, Federal Council of the Churches of Christ in America, 1929), p. 5.

53. *Ibid.*, p. 3.

54. *Ibid.*, pp. 9–16.

55. *Ibid.*, p. 19.

56. *Ibid.*, p. 11.

57. *Annual of the Southern Baptist Convention, 1927* (Nashville, Tenn.: Marshall and Bruce, 1927), p. 114.

58. *Annual of the Southern Baptist Convention, 1929* (Nashville, Tenn.: Marshall and Bruce, 1929), pp. 87–89.

59. *Acts and Proceedings of the General Synod of the Reformed Church in America, 1929* (New York: Board of Publication and Bible-School Work, 1929), pp. 209–211.

60. Isaac E. Marcuson, ed., *Central Conference of American Rabbis Yearbook, 1927*, pp. 193, 369.

61. *Ibid.*, pp. 383–384. According to Lauterbach, the emphasis on the husband's role rather than that of the wife was justified because in his command "Be fruitful and multiply," God was speaking to Adam and not to Eve. If anyone was disobeying God's command by using contraception, it would be the husband.

62. Stephen S. Wise, "The Attitude of the Synagogue Towards Birth Control," *Birth Control Review,* May 1926, pp. 158–159; "The Synagogue and Birth Control, " *Birth Control Review,* October 1926, pp. 301–302.

# Chapter Five

# 1930–1931: Lambeth and Its Aftermath

Between the summer of 1930 and the spring of 1931 the public religious debate over birth control reached its high point. Nationwide debates erupted while entire denominations attempted to define their official positions. Ultimately, the power struggles within and among religious organizations led to political battles on the federal level, as Margaret Sanger appealed for Congressional action on the matter.

The Depression brought special attention to the fact that Americans were faced with serious questions about bringing more children into their families. As a result, an increasing number of liberal and mainline clergy pointed to evidence that a large number of couples were already deciding to prevent unwanted pregnancies and that it was proper to recognize that what they were doing was not sinful. Conservative clergy argued that the birth control issue transcended contemporary economic conditions and that modernists were making a serious mistake in adjusting religious doctrine to accommodate the American people's wishes. An editorial in the *Commonweal* described the widespread approval of contraception as the triumph of secularism and the death of the Protestant Reformation.[1]

## Clerical Support on the Rise

By 1930 birth control advocates were increasingly aware that the attitudes of religious America were shifting in their favor. The mavericks who had supported the movement early had not abandoned their positions, and more important, numbers of mainline clergy were voicing their approval. Editors of the *Birth Control Review* devoted their entire May 1930 issue to the topic, entitling the edition "The Churches and Birth Control: A Symposium." As in the past they enlisted the verbal support of individual clergy bold enough to side publicly with the movement. Some of the names were familiar in the Sanger camp; however, the number of supporters was growing dramatically. The *Review* included written commentaries by twenty-one additional Protestant ministers and two Catholics— the Reverend Leo Lehman of the American Catholic Church, which was not affiliated with the Roman Catholic Church, and E. Boyd Barrett, a former Jesuit priest and, at this time, a vehement anti–Catholic writer.

The *Review*'s presentation made the opposition appear weak. The magazine presented only the position of the Catholic John M. Cooper, which was excerpted from his "Birth Control"— a pamphlet that had been issued by the National Catholic Welfare Conference in 1923.[2] Whereas Sanger's strategy during the previous decade had been to portray the Catholic Church's position as a threat to the social fabric of the United States, and one to be feared, she was no longer the driving force behind the *Review*.[3] The new editors were now focusing on the positive support she had gained from other clerics.[4] An editorial opening the *Review*'s "symposium" stated, "We have by no means made a poll of the Churches, but we have found that there are many religious leaders who are pointing the way for their people, and setting the pace for their colleagues."[5]

The *Review* had not altogether abandoned Sanger's criticism of the Catholic Church. The editorial continued:

> No one can deny that the Catholic opposition is the keystone of all the opposition to Birth Control. It permeates into every field. It explains why social workers believe in Birth Control while social agencies do not officially endorse it; why intelligent doctors concede the need for it, both in curative and preventive medicine, while the American Medical Association refuses to declare itself, and contraceptive technique is still not generally taught in medical schools; why politicians and political parties do not take a stand. There are, in each case, Catholic supporters, patients, voters, who must not be antagonized.[6]

However, the *Review*'s anti–Catholicism was not as intense as it had been in previous years. The numerous commentaries by ministers did not focus on the Catholic Church. Instead, they centered their attention on their own "enlightened" positions on birth control, most of which reflected current economic and marital pressures. This was exhibited in excerpts from their comments:

> Reverend John Ray Ewers, D.D., Minster of East End Christian Church, Pittsburgh, Pennsylvania: ...Facing modern economic conditions the average family would be ruined by unlimited

begetting of children. Physicians are able to prescribe methods of control, which permit children to arrive as they are wanted and as they can be financially well taken care of.

Reverend W. Nelson Winter, Pastor of Calvary Evangelical Church, Baltimore, Maryland: ...I am sure that I voice the sentiments of many fellow clergymen when I say that the Church is vitally interested in the question of Birth Control. No longer do we feel that the Great Creator somehow made a terrible mistake when he endowed man with the powerful sexual instinct — we are beginning to see that "what God hath cleansed should not be called common or unclean." We are beginning to realize that sex is the world's greatest dynamic and more closely related to the religious impulse than was formerly realized. How to direct and conserve this potent force is one of the problems of the Church. We feel that voluntary parenthood is decidedly a step in the right direction.

Reverend Paul Jones, Acting Bishop of the Episcopal Diocese of Southern Ohio: ...For the great mass of people our present civilization offers three choices: Marriage and a large family with poverty, undernourishment, demoralization, discord and despair; temporary unions broken by desertion and divorces and the children denied their right to life in a family; or voluntary parenthood where the children are the result of choice determined by the health and strength of the mother and the economic condition of the family. To my mind there is no question but that the last is the only basis for a family life that will give the best results for the parents, the children and society at large.

Reverend Frank S. C. Wicks, Minister of All Souls Unitarian Church, Indianapolis, Indiana: ...Children should be what George Eliot calls the "Symbol of the eternal marriage between love and duty." Love should welcome each child and duty determine when the child shall be born. Let us no longer shift upon God our own ignorance, our own mistakes, but frankly recognize that the responsibility rests upon us.

Reverend Bernard C. Clausen, Minister of the First Baptist Church, Syracuse, New York: ...I believe that our present state of mind on Birth Control represents one of the greatest intellectual accomplishments of modern times. With persistent patience, rare skill, and an avidity for persecution Margaret Sanger and those surrounding her have carried on a magnificent bit of mental strategy, and deserve the laurels usually kept for more gory warriors for the common good.

Reverend E. G. Gallagher, Minister of the First Congregational Church, Waseca, Minnesota: ...There is nothing vulgar about the relationships which bring man and woman together. There is something very noble and sacred in the eyes of God, something too sacred to be peddled by unclean minds. Parents should have a sufficient degree of confidence in their children, to be glad to give the facts leading up to so important a matter as child bearing, or a competent physician should be asked to do this. Add the prerogative, lawfully given to reliable physicians, to instruct married people in the contraceptive methods, and what misery and estrangement would be avoided, what happiness assured to thousands of homes.

Reverend Joseph F. Michael, Pastor of the First Methodist Church, Turkey, Texas: The more I study the Birth Control movement, and see the plight of hundreds of homes into which I go each year, the more I am convinced it is a God-sent movement. At first I was very much opposed, but after several years of observation and prayerful study, it looks decidedly different, and I am completely won over.[7]

The clerical support of the movement that was solicited by the *Review* was varied. However, not all of it ignored the Catholic Church. Woven into the ministers' arguments were charges against the Church. Some of the commentary chastised the Church; some simply mentioned its opposition to birth control. Some spoke of the Church directly; others, such as Dr. Henry Neumann, leader of the Society for Ethical Culture in Brooklyn, merely implied that they were speaking about the Church. According to Neumann, "It is a thousand pities that backward-looking groups are still powerful enough to prevent repealing the laws against spreading the knowledge of Birth Control."[8] Other observations of Catholic doctrine and behavior came from two of Sanger's longtime supporters: Chairman of the Central Conference's Social Service Commission Rabbi Edward L. Israel, and humanist and former Unitarian minister, Charles F. Potter. Israel wrote, "I for one do not condemn [Catholics and Orthodox Jews] for what they believe. My only condemnation is that they refuse to grant others that inalienable right of freedom of belief and conduct in personal life, which does not interfere with another's freedom." Potter wrote, "It is a most significant decade that the Roman Catholic Church now finds itself on the defensive in the matter of Birth Control. A new generation has risen within the church who demand a reason for the vigorous opposition to Birth Control which so frequently characterizes Catholic leaders."[9]

Two new clerical supporters addressed Catholic behavior. The Reverend Bradford Young, who was assistant minister of the Church of the Holy Trinity in Brooklyn, stated, "Even active Roman Catholics, to my knowledge, use and approve contraceptives. Certainly the time has come when the hypocrisy and the injustice of denying the poor and uneducated what is freely enjoyed by the rich and well-tutored shall be abolished."

The Reverend Ernest Caldecott, minister of All Souls Church in Schenectady, New York, wrote, "My experience takes me into the homes of those who have more children than they can care for, mostly Catholics. ... He who advocates sexual intercourse only for purposes of propagation may be sincere, but he is certainly not sensible."[10] Regardless of what degree of criticism the ministers expressed, all of them tended to separate the religious birth control debate into two camps—the "enlightened" and the "backward."

## Denominational Support

Clerical support for Sanger's work had grown significantly. Not only had the numbers increased, but the dimensions of her backing had widened. No longer were a few radical clergymen the only ones speaking out; now she could depend on mainline Protestants. More important, three religious organizations had granted their approval during recent denominational conferences.[11] They included the Universalist General Convention, the New York East Conference of the Methodist Episcopal Church, and the Central Conference of American Rabbis.[12]

In October of 1929 the Universalist General Convention adopted the report of its Committee on Birth Control at its annual meeting. That committee concluded that misconceptions regarding contraceptive use — confusing it with abortion and obscenity — had initiated passage of the Comstock Law in 1873 and had inhibited proper understanding of the subject. In its report the Committee on Birth Control concluded that voluntary parenthood was "one of the most practicable means of race betterment" and recommended:

1. That this Convention urge the immediate repeal of such federal and state laws as interfere with the prescription of contraception by physicians; and
2. That where legal barriers do not exist, socially minded persons be urged to establish in every center of population clinics where those needing it may receive contraceptive advice under medical supervision.[13]

In May of 1930 the equally liberal American Unitarian Association granted its approval. After considerable study of marriage by the Department of Social Relations, the Unitarians recognized, "It is becoming increasingly clear that, in the interest of social betterment, racial progress and a more wholesome family life, parenthood should be undertaken with due regard for the mother's health and the children's welfare, both physical and moral," and voted to recommend "to its constituent churches and members an earnest consideration of the fundamental social, economic and eugenic importance of birth control to the end that they may support all reasonable efforts in their communities for the promotion of the birth control movement."[14]

The first official religious sanction came from the New York East Conference of the Methodist Episcopal Church, which adopted the report of its Social Service Committee at its meeting in April of 1930. It is apparent from the committee report that Methodists had drawn the same conclusion that Reform Jews and Universalists had thus far: that the religious community should recognize responsible contraceptive use as acceptable. In addition, clergy could cooperate with the medical community in ensuring that couples made educated and morally responsible decisions when choosing to prevent pregnancy. The Methodists' report read: "It is the clear duty of the churches to offer to their young people an opportunity to consult some qualified adviser — the minister, perhaps, or a physician, the director of religious education, or other specialist — who, besides having a clear grasp of the fundamental principles of sex morality, would have also an appreciation of modern tendencies and would be in a position to offer rational advice."

It recommended: "In the interest of morality and sound scientific knowledge we favor such changes of the law in the States of New York and Connecticut as will remove the existing restrictions upon the communication by physicians to their patients of important medical information on Birth Control."[15]

The Central Conference of American Rabbis reinforced its position condoning contraceptives two months before Lambeth. In June of 1930 the rabbis voted to include the following in their program:

> We recognize the need of exercising great caution in dealing with the delicate problem of birth regulation in view of the widespread disregard of the old sanctions affecting the institution of marriage and of the family. We earnestly desire to guard against playing into the hands of those who would undermine the sanctity of these time-honored institutions through reckless notions and practices. We are especially mindful of the noble tradition obtaining among the Jewish people with respect to the holiness of domestic relations.

But, the rabbis added: "At the same time, we are keenly aware of the many serious evils caused by a lack of birth regulation among those who by reason of lack of health or of a reasonable measure of economic resources or of intelligence or all of these, are prevented from giving to their children that worthy heritage to which all children are entitled. We, therefore, urge the recognition of the importance of intelligent birth regulation as one of the methods of coping with social problems."[16]

The issue of economics to which the rabbis referred proved important in various denominational debates over contraception. The Great Depression was affecting the way social observers and policy makers were discussing all aspects of society, including issues of the family and the topic of birth control. The Central Conference had condoned contraceptive use before the effects of the Depression had set in, but in the rabbis' discussion in 1930 the economic question was raised. By including the phrase "a reasonable measure of economic resources," they added to the growing amount of religious literature that recognized that average families were finding it increasingly difficult to bring additional children into the world.

If one sees the religious shift as a sudden sweeping one that begins in August of 1930 and follows through into the spring of 1931 with numerous Protestant and Jewish groups jumping on the bandwagon, then it appears that the Depression must have contributed tremendously to that shift. But as seen in previous chapters religious arguments were already opening to changes in doctrine that focused primarily on the purpose of marriage in response to the "decline of the American family"—a development that intensified during the 1920s.

The actual effects of the Depression appear even less significant after looking more closely at various facets of the Lambeth decision and the Central Conference decision. The encyclical letter on marriage and sex presented at Lambeth indicated the bishops were concerned about the effects of the Depression on the family but implied that any decisions made regarding the family should transcend the current economic situation. More specifically, according to the encyclical, personal economic difficulties should not weigh in a couple's decision whether or not to have a child:

> When healthy parents refuse for selfish reasons to have children in homes where there is, or by self-denial may be, provision for them, they deny to both Church and nation lives, which, with a Christian training, might be of priceless value to the community. We are familiar with the difficulties. We deeply sympathize with those who have burdens which are hard to bear. But we appeal to the whole community of the Church to remember that in home life, as in personal life, we are called to take up the cross, to endure hardness, and to count upon the enabling power of the Spirit of God. And indeed when the

sacrifice is made for the sake of the family, that cross becomes a crown.[17]

The opening sentence of this statement is strikingly reminiscent of even the most conservative criticism in years past of parents who chose to have fewer children. The widespread effects of the Depression were forcing churches to restructure their condemnation of materialism, but the essence of that condemnation was still there.[18]

In 1930 the Central Conference of American Rabbis did not specifically address the issue of personal economic hardship brought on by the Depression or the impact of such on a couple's decision to have a baby. The rabbis had already formulated their position on birth control going into the 1930 meeting, and that position was based solely on an analysis of Talmudic teaching that transcended contemporary trends. Discussion of the topic during the mid–1920s concluded only that the responsibility for making such a decision was better left to couples and their physicians. Therefore, the onset of the Depression did not weigh in the decision to allow the use of artificial means of contraception. However, in 1930 the subject was addressed with the global economic crisis in mind.

This time the discussion centered primarily on the desire to include the subject of birth control in the social justice program. However, the subject was discussed along with the larger issue of economics in a way that brought Malthusian principles to light for the first time in ten years. Rabbi James G. Heller maintained that any position on birth control should be considered part of the social justice program: "The question of birth control is not only one of the most pressing social problems, but it has many repercussions in the field of international war and peace, the pressure of population on food supply, the morals of our homes, the prevalence of poverty, real and relative, the distribution of wealth in general, etc., etc. Personally I feel that a rational policy of birth control has much to do with promoting what we are accustomed to speak of as the sanctity of the home."[19]

The onset of the Depression was largely responsible for the rebirth of Malthusian discourse. The essence of Malthusianism that centered on numbers and resources had fit well into the global conditions present before, during, and immediately after World War I. During the economic boom of the 1920s such principles no longer seemed to apply — at least in the United States — and birth control advocates generally refrained from using Malthusian arguments. However, conditions during the 1930s provided proof for many that population control was in order.

It is also important to note that just as some of the birth control arguments used during this time were not new to the debate, neither were some of the players. This was true in the case of the Central Conference of American Rabbis. Serving on the Commission on Social Justice at the time the rabbis defined their position on birth control were three of Sanger's earliest religious supporters: Sidney E. Goldstein, Stephen S. Wise, and Edward L. Israel. The action taken by the Central Conference was important, but by no means did it represent the attitudes of all American Jews. Conservative and Orthodox Jews had yet to voice their opinions.

## *Lambeth Decision*

Two months after the pronouncement by the Central Conference, the bishops at the historic Lambeth conference announced their stand. Lambeth conferences had been called approximately every ten years by the Archbishop of Canterbury, some attracting more attention than others. The conference of 1930 attracted a tremendous amount of attention, as its birth control resolution spurred a worldwide debate calling into question the powers of the bishops at Lambeth. At the same time, it drew worldwide attention to the issue of contraception.

During that conference the bishops reversed their position of 1920, which had specifically condemned the distribution and use of artificial contraceptives. In August of 1930 the bishops voted 193 to 67, with 46 abstaining, to pass the following resolution:

> Where there is a clearly felt moral obligation to limit or avoid parenthood, the method must be decided on Christian principles. The primary and obvious method is complete abstinence from intercourse (as far as may be necessary) in a life of discipline and self control lived in the power of the Holy Spirit. Nevertheless, in those cases where there is such a clearly-felt moral obligation to limit or avoid parenthood, and where there is a morally sound reason for avoiding complete abstinence, the Conference agrees that the other methods may be used, provided that this is done in the light of the same Christian principles.[20]

After examining how vague many of the clerical positions had been in the years leading up to Lambeth, it is easy to see why the attention of birth control historians has been drawn to this decision. Although the Lambeth decision was not an especially controversial one, the comparatively direct statement reflected a definite shift in doctrine.

The resolution did grant approval of contraceptive use aside from abstinence, but the approval was clearly limited. First, the bishops' decision was far from unanimous. Historians often describe the vote as "3 to 1," failing to mention the 46 abstentions. In addition, various passages within the resolution reminded followers that the primary purpose of marriage was procreation, that the duty of parenthood was "the glory of married life," and that the benefit of a family was "a joy in itself." There was no sweeping change in the way Anglican bishops viewed marriage; nothing they stated represented anything radical. Still, the bishops helped demonstrate the way the religious world was expanding its definition of the purpose of marriage. This was especially evident in their additional recognition that "intercourse between husband and wife as the consummation of marriage [had] a value of its own within that sacrament."[21] Though other clerics had hinted at such a consideration in years past, now a denomination's official stand recognized a value of sexual intercourse as an end in itself, which could strengthen the bond between husband and wife.

There were numerous factors in the secular and religious worlds that contributed to the changing clerical stance on birth control — factors that were present for at least a decade. In the eyes of some contemporaries, however, the reasons for change appeared to be much more simple. For instance, the editors of *Outlook and Independent* immediately provided a brief and unnoticed, yet insightful, commentary on one reason behind the Lambeth decision. They noted: "There is reason to believe that the conference reversed itself over its decision of ten years ago because the majority of the delegates this year are married, whereas in 1920 the bachelors preponderated over the married episcopate."[22] Undoubtedly, birth control historians would deny that what they have considered a landmark decision could have been made on such a simple basis. Still, the argument that the Catholic Church has never approved of contraception because Catholic clergy remain unmarried has been raised at least since Sanger brought this view to light. A more important factor in the Lambeth decision was the presence of Dean William Inge — eugenicist, Malthusian, and longtime Sanger supporter. By 1930 it appeared that he was finally able to convince a majority of his colleagues that individual and social need weighed heavily in the birth control question.[23]

## Modernist Commentary

Protestant publications, which had remained strikingly silent on the subject during the 1920s, published numerous articles addressing contraception after Lambeth. Two editorials appeared in the preceding year. The first was written by the outspoken liberal Presbyterian minister Harry Emerson Fosdick. Fosdick's modernist stance on other issues had already made him a lightning rod for the wrath of fundamentalists during the decade, so his liberal position on birth control came as no surprise. But even he recognized that there were few bold enough to condone contraception, stating that "all but a few religious leaders are antagonistic, apathetic, or timorous about the matter." Still, his support of the movement appeared far from radical to secular America by this time. Fosdick wrote, "To have as many children as can be well brought up, to space them with due regard to the mother's health, to have them come when they are wanted and because they are wanted — to encourage, in a word, a sane, scientific control over this most important part of human life — is the ideal."[24]

The *Outlook and Independent* subsequently published an editorial by Yale sociology professor A. G. Keller. His argument raised questions regarding birth control that had never before been raised and addressed them in a manner that would have shocked more conservative Protestants. But *Outlook and Independent* editors introduced the editorial simply as one in which Keller found "little to worry about in birth-control," mentioning that Keller was the "distinguished co-author of 'The Science of Society'" and had been "a regular and popular contributor to this weekly editorial page."

At the time of publication on April 16, 1930 — four months before the Lambeth decision — the effects of economic distress were already evident, and Keller introduced relevant Malthusian principles in his argument. But he went further. Claiming that it was impossible to prevent dissemination of information, Keller maintained it would be more beneficial to concentrate efforts on anticipating the effects legalizing contraception would have on relations both inside and outside of marriage. Without an agenda prescribed by Malthusians, eugenicists, Sanger followers, conservative clerics, or liberal clerics, Keller wrote matter-of-factly:

> It is feared that the removal of the threat of pregnancy will lead to laxness in extra-marital relations. It may; but, if that is so, there will at least be fewer illegitimate children, which is something. There is a lot of chatter nowadays about repressions, inhibitions, (apparently always disastrous), fancy sublimations. perils of *dementia precox*, and so on; but, as suggested in a previous editorial, this is not so cosmic or durable a phase as some excitable or notoriety-seeking folk would have us believe. There are other deterring considerations against looseness aside from fear of the scarlet letter. No one can prove that there is not an

orgy of universal debauchery in the offing; but some of us cannot see the signs of it.

He added:

> As for the matrimonial relation, there need be no concern over the introduction of the "companionate marriage," for it is here already; and the sensible view seems to be prevailing that it is nobody's business if married people do not want children for a while, or ever. Doubtless knowledge of contraception tends to lessen the birthrate, but that is not bad in itself. If such knowledge becomes widely disseminated — not confined, like decent liquor, to the well-to do — its service in making out of the hit-or-miss family a better planned enterprise may be incalculably beneficial.[25]

Just before the Lambeth decision, the editors of *Outlook and Independent* were finally willing to give attention to birth control.

Following Lambeth, the editors no longer hid behind outside editorial writers but addressed the topic themselves. An article of September 26, 1930, essentially summarized the archbishop of Canterbury's interpretation of Lambeth, which concluded that there existed circumstances in which there was "a moral obligation to control the number of children, as when birth would involve great danger to health, when it is financially impossible to provide for another child, or when additional children may render a prematurely exhausted mother incapable of doing her duty to the existing family," and that the use of artificial contraception was permissible in those exceptional cases. But following this summary was a brief commentary indicating that editors had considered it unnecessary to comment until this time.

According to the article, despite what religious leaders were saying or doing about contraceptives, Americans in general were using them. The article stated:

> The fact is that artificial birth control among the married is now generally sanctioned by intelligent public opinion for ordinary as well as extraordinary cases. The fact is, again, that modern men and women demand, and cannot be prevented from exercising, complete freedom to limit their families according to convenience — "mere convenience," if you will. The fact is, finally, that they regard birth control by complete abstinence as an impracticable and doubtful ideal.

The article concluded that listing these facts suggested that the churches still had "far to go before they assume[d] the attitude toward birth control already taken for granted among most intelligent women."[26]

The *Christian Century* also commented on the Lambeth decision, declaring that moral leaders had been slow to address the matter of birth control, which deserved to be "faced with a degree of frankness and intelligence." The modernist position of this publication manifested itself in its description of contraception as a modern issue:

> The limitation of offspring naturally could not be practiced in a pre-scientific age when neither the reasons for nor the methods of control had received any serious consideration. There was no economic motive for it in the pioneer period when children were an asset rather than a liability; when any child ten years of age was worth his keep for the chores he could do around the house and barn, and a boy of fifteen was as good as an extra "hand" on the farm. Large families could not fail to meet with general approval when population was so sparse and the call of the frontier for occupants so urgent that multiplication seemed a social duty, or when the need of soldiers for the king's wars made it seem a patriotic duty.

The article continued:

> The church, as usual, provided a religious sanction for a procedure which had been found to have a social value through a long period, and sanctified it as an "ideal." To have a large family was to be blessed of the Lord; not to have one was to be unfortunate and to be under suspicion of his disfavor; deliberately to avoid having one was sin. It is greatly to the credit of religion that it so habitually gives its sanction to practices which have proved themselves to be socially valuable; but it acts slowly in raising a useful custom to the rank of a divinely ordained duty, and still more slowly in reversing its decision when the custom in question loses its utility under changed conditions or even becomes detrimental to the general welfare.[27]

The article presented both sides of the religious birth control debate, noting that those who favored it were "interested primarily in the welfare of concrete individuals in specific situations"—a position that "risks becoming an individualistic opportunism which may not, in the long run, serve the interests of the largest number of individuals." This hardly appears to be a sanction of contraceptive use. However, the article concluded that "the Christian conscience, sensitive alike to inherited values and to considerations of human welfare under present conditions, must learn at least to deal honestly with it in the privacy of its own thought."[28]

Providing additional evidence that the position of this publication was considerably liberal was a brief mention of one aspect of the birth control debate. In a few sentences the *Christian Century* took a far more liberal stand than any denomination had taken up to this point. The passage referred to the opposition's claim that available birth control information could easily fall into the hands of unmarried couples. Most denominational discussions had centered on the concerns of married couples—contraceptive use by those unmarried was not even a consideration. The *Christian Century*, however, maintained that it was obvious that "sinners, both actual and potential," already knew about it. What should have been of greater concern, stated the article, was that by attempting to deny those people contraceptive information, the opposition was using pregnancy — and ultimately a child — as a threat or punishment for the "sin," which was "a degrading use of childhood."[29]

The attention received by the Lambeth Conference helped pave the way for denominations that were leaning toward acceptance but were hesitant to take the more controversial stand. As determined already, there were openings in various denominational arguments that allowed for the prevention of pregnancy in some cases, even if they did not officially condone the use of artificial contraceptives. Liberal Protestant denominations followed the lead of the Lambeth bishops and adopted doctrine similar to that of the Anglicans. Some conservatives who remained opposed to contraceptive use quietly protested the Lambeth decision, while others were more vocal in their opposition. But whatever positions denominations had taken in the past, most reacted by attempting to clarify or modify their stands within the year. To determine more precisely who was sanctioning contraceptive use and when, it is important to look at denominational pronouncements made immediately before, during, and after the Lambeth decision.

## *Federal Council Stirs Debate*

A more liberal position on various issues was heard from the Federal Council of the Churches of Christ in America, which considered itself the voice of Protestant America. However, a definite stand on birth control did not come easily. Interchurch cooperation lay at the foundation of the Federal Council, and officials were well aware of the controversy surrounding the topic. Hesitating to take a stand, the council continued its study.

The Committee on Marriage and the Home, which published *Ideals of Love and Marriage* in 1929, gained official representation from the Presbyterian General Assembly's Committee on Marriage, Divorce, and Re-Marriage, and the Protestant Episcopal Commission on Divorce. In 1930 the committee developed a course for young adults entitled "Preparation for Marriage" and began working on a statement regarding the "Moral Aspects of Birth Control." Though there was no formal indication at this time how liberal the position on contraceptive use would be, the committee was working closely with the American Social Hygiene Association, a longtime proponent of birth control.[30]

Pronouncements made by Presbyterians and Episcopalians at this time did not condone the widespread use of contraceptives. In his report to the Presbyterian General Assembly in 1930 Ralph Marshall Davis, chairman of the Commission on Marriage, Divorce, and Re-Marriage condemned modern attitudes promoting unrestricted use of preventives, pointing to contemporary philosophy: "If you can't be good, be hygienic." In his detailed statement he especially criticized extreme limitation of family size:

> The widespread use of contraceptives for the total prevention, rather than for the reduction of the number of children, certainly produces distinct losses of personality. Granting physical and mental competency, to frustrate the coming of children to the Christian home is to frustrate a certain normal development that the Christian monogamic marriage assumes. ... Easy divorce proceedings and easy means of preventing conception have an intimate connection that will never be given the public. There may be a place for the contraceptive under medical advice, but it still remains that a baby in the home now and then is a splendid escape for those suffering from an uneventful married life.[31]

The position of Episcopalians in 1930 was less clear. The Commission on Divorce conducted an extensive study, surveying eight hundred Episcopalian, Presbyterian, Baptist, Methodist, and Congregational ministers in an effort to understand the causes of divorce. The commission report introduced the importance of the study by raising rhetorical questions such as, "What should be the attitude of husband and wife toward child bearing?" and "What should be the attitude on birth control?" but the questionnaire did not address these.[32]

Even though the Anglican Communion, of which Episcopalians were members, voted for approval at Lambeth, American Episcopalians remained divided. For example, Bishop Ernest M. Stires of the Protestant

Episcopal Diocese of Long Island, an American delegate to the Lambeth Conference, voted in favor of the resolution, saying, "In this matter, the church has acted with vision, understanding and great courage and it will be discovered that it has strengthened its real foundation with a spirit of reverence that has never been surpassed. It has measured up to the light and needs of the twentieth century." The Right Reverend Paul Matthews, Episcopal Bishop of New Jersey, voted against the measure. He later commented, "I think the statement was somewhat too broad. In England this question is much to the fore, and it is discussed with considerable frankness. That is not so of America. We are often accused of being Puritanical and prudish, but I think, in matters of this kind, it is an advantage to be prudish.... Too many bars have been let down abroad already. I think they are behaving loosely over there. Loosely is the word."[33] Evidence that some Episcopalian bishops remained critical of contraception in 1931, after various denominations had approved of its use, is found in their report on the "Solemnization of Holy Matrimony." Under new canonical law ministers were required to have couples sign the following before conducting a marriage ceremony:

> We A. B. and C. D., desiring to receive the blessing of the Church upon our marriage, do solemnly declare that we hold Christian marriage to be a lifelong physical and spiritual union of husband and wife, for the purpose of mutual fellowship, encouragement and understanding, for the procreation (if it may be) of children and their physical and spiritual nurture, and for the safeguarding and benefit of society. And we engage ourselves, the Lord being our helper, to make every effort to realize the Christian ideal, and to avail ourselves of means of grace thereto as taught and provided by the Christian Church.[34]

To Episcopalians procreation was still a primary purpose of marriage.

In part, the Federal Council's Committee on Marriage and the Home had a difficult time developing a comprehensive report on contraception because of the varying attitudes among committee members. In addition, committee members did not want to offend conservatives among the larger organization's members. The latter is evident in the form taken in the final draft of "Moral Aspects of Birth Control," which committee chairman Dr. Howard C. Robbins presented to the Federal Council in February of 1931. First, the report reinforced general religious teachings that were common among conservatives: "In conception we are in the presence of the wonder and mystery of the beginnings of human life. In this mystery the two mates, knowingly or unknowingly, are acting creatively with God. When so understood, the circumstances and incidents of conception, growth and finally of birth are astonishing manifestations of divine power, and inexpressibly beautiful." Quoting from the Bible, the report attempted to assure conservative Protestants that this was not a broadly liberal statement:

> In the sex relations between husband and wife we are also in the presence of another mystery. "From the beginning of the creation God made them male and female," said our Lord. "For this cause," He continued, "shall a man leave his father and mother and shall cleave to his wife: and they twain shall be one flesh." We have here the passing of shame and the realization of the meaning of sex in the divine economy, which make the union of the two mates a supreme expression of their affection and comradeship.[35]

Though this statement did not appear to offend tradition, it demonstrated a growing emphasis on sex as integral to the marital relationship, rather than as an act meant only for procreation. The report stated in more specific terms: "There is general agreement ... that sex union between husbands and wives as an expression of mutual affection, without relation to procreation, is right. This is recognized by the Scriptures, by all branches of the Christian Church, by social and medical science, and by the good sense and idealism of mankind."[36] Committee members did not agree on method. The majority, with a vote of 21 to 3,[37] agreed that the "careful and restrained use of contraceptives by married people is valid and moral." The minority contended that abstinence was preferred.[38]

Recognizing that no consensus existed among clergy — that Catholics opposed it and that Anglican bishops dissented at Lambeth — the committee maintained that further study was needed: "Guidance should be sought from the Holy Spirit, the Lord and Giver of Life. It should be expected that guidance will find expression through the researches and experience of physicians and men of science as well as through the corporate conscience of the Church." The only declarations the committee made as a whole were that Protestants should not (1) attempt to impose their positions on the rest of society through legislation or (2) attempt to prohibit physicians from dispensing information.[39]

On March 20, when the committee's report was made public, Sanger was quoted as responding: "Today is the most significant one in the history of the birth control movement."[40] Sanger understood the importance of gaining Federal Council approval and had worked diligently through executive secretary Worth M. Tippy. She provided anonymous monetary donations and secretly scheduled expert speakers to argue her case.[41] The editors of the *Outlook and Independent* considered the Federal Council pronouncement equally important, immediately praising the position: "What that document does is to bring the attitude of America's Protestant churches, so far as it can be expressed by the Federal Council, into line with the opinions and practices of their most intelligent members, into line with the best liberal and scientific thought of the day. This is an immense and exhilarating advance.... Since the mountain of secular opinion will not come toward Mahomet, the church, Mahomet is going toward the mountain."[42] Because the Federal Council represented some twenty-two million American Protestants, the decision was important. However, Protestants were far from united on this issue.

The *Federal Council Bulletin*, in its determination to promote a peaceful relationship among denominations, reprinted "Moral Aspects of Birth Control," introducing it as a statement of "guarded approval." The *Bulletin* did recognize the decision was not unanimous regarding method but emphasized that it was unanimous in "calling attention to the necessity for 'some form of effective control of the size of the family and spacing of children.'"[43] The following month the *Bulletin* acknowledged that the report had "evoked wide public interest." But it criticized only the Catholic response, giving the impression that this was the only protest. A quote from *The Baptist* defended "Moral Aspects of Birth Control":

> It is the judgment of a company of men and women, conscientious and competent, who for many months have made an intelligent study of a confessedly difficult subject of wide social and economic significance and of important moral implications, and who have given the product of their study in a disinterested manner to the public. As such, it should be gratefully received. More than that is impossible and more than that they would not desire. The nature of the subjects involved is such that it is peculiarly true of them that every individual must ultimately face and settle them for himself. Let all the light that may be shed upon them from every angle be welcomed.[44]

In addition, the *Bulletin* quoted from other Protestant publications in its defense as commending it as representing "a frank and courageous facing up to one of the most pressing of present-day problems" ([New York] *Christian Advocate*), as expressing "the noblest kind of Christian spirit" (*Christian Leader*) and as being "a sensible and Christian statement" (Southern Methodist *Christian Advocate*).[45]

The *Literary Digest* quoted from some of the same publications, painting a picture where Protestant waters were not quite that calm. According to the *Digest*, the New York *Christian Advocate*, a Methodist publication, reminded observers that the Methodist General Conference had not yet agreed on a birth control position. When the General Conference did address the issue, the *Christian Advocate* predicted, "Opinion will be divided, not so much as to the basic morality of birth control, as to the dangers flowing from the general dissemination of information regarding the use of contraceptives. It will not be possible to sweep away the fear that such knowledge, however desirable and proper under certain circumstances, is also liable to perverse use to immoral ends."[46]

*The Churchman*, an Episcopalian journal, also recognized this fear that liberal religious leaders were "hoping to save the race by the promiscuous advocacy of sexual gratification without the burden of children." However, *The Churchman* continued, "Nothing could be less fair to the guarded declarations of Lambeth and the Federal Council, which uphold the Christian ideal of self-control, but cautiously agree that there are exceptional conditions—human nature what it is—when human health and happiness seem to demand that the Church should lift its age-long ban, and permit, even indorse, what once seemed to be a sin, and what, in many cases, is still a sin."[47]

The most liberal responses were heard from Unitarians and Universalists. The Unitarian *Christian Register* asked, "What has birth control to do with religion?" maintaining "it is fundamentally a hygienic and economic matter, as well as a matter of personal choice." The Universalist *Christian Leader* recognized that "doctors, ministers, editors, teachers, moralists—always are divided," continuing: "What we assert is that whatever harm there may lie in publishing information, or alleged information, infinitely greater harm results from suppressing it. There is no human right to the status of ignorance. If we moralists can not induce people to use knowledge wisely, considerately, unselfishly, so much the worse for us, but the way of knowledge must not be blocked."[48]

It was not until September of that year that the *Federal Council Bulletin* reported the actual action taken on the part of denominational assemblies in response to "Moral Aspects of Birth Control." However, the publication blamed "divergent views" among Protestants on misleading interpretations of the report in the daily press, "which treated it as if it had claimed to be an official utterance for the Protestant denominations.... The fact was often overlooked that the report was not a pronouncement at all, but rather a detailed study setting forth with equal care the point of view both of those who favored birth control and those who did not."[49] The *Bulletin* admitted that denominations took a variety of action. In a joint meeting the National Council of the Congregational Churches and the General Convention of the Christian Church adopted a resolution "giving enthusiastic approval" to the study and commending the general program of the council. The General Synod of the Reformed Church in America remained in the council "by an almost unanimous vote." The Executive Committee of the Northern Baptist Convention stated its conviction that "some symbol of the essential unity of Protestantism" is necessary and that "in this juncture the Federal Council is most suitable as such a symbol." However, the Convention maintained that the statement on birth control was not to be understood as speaking for the Baptist denomination and adopted a resolution designed to set up safeguards in the issuing of future statements.[50] The General Assembly of the United Presbyterian Church continued its membership in the council, as did the General Assembly of the Presbyterian Church in the U.S.A. However, the latter voted that it "disapprove[d] of ecclesiastical pronouncements on birth control." The General Assembly of the Presbyterian Church in the U.S. (Southern) withdrew from the council.[51]

## Denominations Forced to Face the Issue

Publication of "The Moral Aspects of Birth Control" forced a number of denominations to face the topic of birth control head-on. One was the Northern Baptist Convention. In 1930 the Social Service Committee reported on the status of the family, reiterating earlier findings:

> The family is the basic unit of society and, if it crumbles, there is no foundation left. It is, therefore, alarming to some to note that the rate of marriages decreased with regularity from 1923 to 1928, and if this rate is maintained for the next fifty years, the institution of marriage will have practically passed from American life. The other item in the picture is the increase in the divorce rate, which in 1887 was .47 of a divorce in each one thousand population. By 1925 this had increased to 1.52 a thousand, and three years later the rate was 1.62. What will it be in 1950? Should we be interested?[52]

Nearly a year before the Federal Council's statement, this conference demonstrated little concern among Northern Baptists regarding birth control. A better picture of the Baptist position is found in *The Art of Living Together*, written by A. W. Beaven, pastor of the Lake Avenue Baptist Church in Rochester, New York. Within his address of the larger topic of marriage, Beaven criticized couples who chose to remain childless:

> We are living at a time when the absence of parenthood by married couples is one of the serious problems that we face. We

would refer ... to actual avoidance of parenthood that grows out of selfishness or exists because of the desire for freedom on the part of the wife. It should be said frankly that married life undertaken with a definite intention of the avoidance of parenthood, because of the selfish or pleasure-loving desires of the two is a gigantic sin against the laws of nature, against the future of the race, and against the ideals of the Christian home.

His criticism of one-child families was nearly as severe:

The limitation of the family to one should be carefully weighed by the people who today feel that one child is enough. Certain things ought to be considered. Not only is it in question because the family of one fails to do the home's share toward propagation of the race, but because of the child itself. A child raised as the only one in a family is placed under a very serious handicap. One of the great functions of a home is to socialize the child....Through [a baby's] contacts with its fellows it develops the social instincts and these contacts create the necessity of limiting its rights in view of the rights of others.

However, even though Beaven maintained "a larger number of children make possible a family life that is richer through the lifetime of that entire generation," he added that quality in parenting was more important than quantity. He wrote, "It is not simply more parenthood but better parenthood we need."[53]

In 1931 the Northern Baptist Convention finally addressed birth control directly, at least as a response to the Federal Council's publication. Though the general convention reminded Baptists and others that the council's position did not necessarily reflect their own, council delegates praised the Committee on Marriage and the Home "whether it voices the sentiments of either a minority or a majority, has at least brought forth the earnest thoughts of a few able and devout souls."[54]

By 1931 Northern Baptists made a notable effort to study family issues by creating its own Committee on the American Home. The intention was "to outline the general principles for a study of the home; to define its purpose and those characteristics which would best fit it for that purpose; to suggest steps in a progressive adaptation to constantly changing conditions and demands; to urge pastors and Christian teachers to provide instruction, encouragement and inspiration for the founding of happy Christian homes; to assist young people in making a serious study of home life before establishing homes of their own."[55] A singular phrase contained in that statement of purpose — "to suggest steps in a progressive adaptation to constantly changing conditions and demands"—indicated that Northern Baptists might be more inclined to approve of contraceptive use than they had previously implied. The committee's advice to ministers suggested that they might support young couples' choices in matters of birth control by providing information. Though the term "contraceptives" is missing from the directive, the message was clear:

> He has an opportunity to meet wisely the questions which his young people have wanted to have answered, but have not dared ask; he can inform himself by much careful reading and study; he can invite their confidence at a time when their need of guidance is great; and when the wedding is over, he will find it possible to continue as friend and adviser, by correspondence and by personal visits. Perhaps his own counsel can be reinforced or extended through the use of some book or pamphlet listed herewith, and which he may present or recommend.[56]

The committee suggested a number of pamphlets, noting that the American Social Hygiene Association would be of help. That agency had been a longtime proponent of legalizing the distribution of accurate contraceptive information.[57]

In addition, the Judson Press published *The Home Beautiful*, a manual to educate Baptists in matters of marriage and the family. Author Mary M. Chalmers provided a biblical interpretation of marriage and noted the joys of bringing children into the world. However, she also recognized the benefits of limiting family size: "There are certain facts observable in our civilization of today. The birth-rate tends to decrease as the standard of living rises. In an industrial civilization, the parent cannot adequately care for so large a family as he can in an agricultural country. Infant mortality is not nearly so high as it was when very large families were the rule. The tendency of today is for the child to remain a dependent in the home for longer and yet longer periods." Chalmers urged parents and the church to provide information to young adults, emphasizing self-control and the "inspiration of high ideals."[58] She, too, provided an extensive list of suggested readings.

The Presbyterian reaction to "Moral Aspects of Birth Control" was more negative. During the General Assembly of the Presbyterian Church in the U.S.A. (Northern) held the previous year, the Commission on Marriage, Divorce, and Remarriage presented its position, which linked "easy divorce proceedings" with "easy means of preventing conception." It further noted that the institution of marriage "finds its primary justification in the establishment and maintenance of the Christian home in which children shall be born and nurtured in the Christian faith."[59]

In 1931 committee chairman Ralph Marshall Davis repeated much of the same statement to the General Assembly. The definition of marriage had not changed, and it appeared that contraceptive doctrine had not changed. However, there was no peaceful agreement among the presbyteries. Instead of simply reiterating the previous year's stand, the Committee on Marriage, Divorce, and Remarriage announced that it intended to present a report similar to the Federal Council's "Moral Aspects of Birth Control," a move that created a fury lasting four days. Responding to protests, the committee omitted references to contraception in its report.[60]

Still, the committee emphasized the need for education and informed ministers of the publication of its *Twenty-Four Views of Marriage*, which included excerpts from already published books and articles "so that the reader can have the whole problem of human relations presented to him from the angle not only of the conservative, but also of the liberal, and even the radical."[61] In addition, the committee included a bibliography of several works by various clergy, sociologists, and physicians.

The dispute did not end there. Based on their opposition to any liberalization or moderation of the traditional view of birth control, several ministers demanded withdrawal from the Federal Council and nearly achieved it. With a majority voting to remain, the General Assembly agreed that the Council should "be instructed hereafter to hold its peace on questions of delicacy and morality, until the General Assembly has had an opportunity of expressing its opinion upon them," adding, "Any other course than continued cooperation with the Federal Council would in our judgment be inconsistent with the great traditions, the principles and the spirit of our Church and would deprive us of the privilege and of our share in the duty of the Evangelical Churches in our country to go forward with the great tasks which confront us in these new days."[62]

The General Assembly of the Presbyterian Church in the United States (South) did not remain in the Federal Council. Voting 175 to 79, the assembly voted to withdraw in protest over the birth control measure.[63] Conservatives pointed to the decision as proof that striving for a consensus within the "Protestant Church" on moral, economic, and political questions was futile.[64]

Methodists were similarly divided on the issue. Though the New York East Conference had condoned contraceptive use, most Methodists still objected to it.[65] Attempts to develop a single position on which Methodists could agree manifested themselves in a report presented at the Sixth Ecumenical Methodist Conference in Atlanta in October of 1931. At that conference Methodist Protestant minister J. C. Broomfield reported on the subject, "Marriage, Home, and Family." Broomfield reminded colleagues that "the business of Methodism is not to accommodate itself to the changing environment and standards of earth, but to get back to the Book, and to proclaim the 'Thus saith the Lord' on this all-important question."[66] Broomfield's address did not limit itself to traditional Methodist teachings, but he did take a conservative stand on birth control.

Broomfield condemned modern American society for promoting obscenity and new freedom for women. With regard to contraception, he directly linked the dissemination of information to a changing attitude toward marriage:

> We have access to literature that leads all the way from sex-brute lust up to romantic love as the basis of marriage, home and family. Confining ourselves to the days in which we are living, the first thing confronting us is *the new abandon* with which we write and talk on subjects cognate to the theme we are discussing, such as the science of eugenics, the education of youth in matters of sex, birth control, the use of contraceptives, companionate marriage, etc. Some one has said, "This is a sex-obsessed age, stimulated by such agencies as the movies, and encouraged by the use of contraceptives."

Citing recent statistics, Broomfield pointed to changing expectations of women and the devaluation of children: More divorces were being sought by women than by men; 4.5 percent of divorces are sought in the first year of married life, 6.6 percent in the second year, and 40 percent between the third and seventh year — indicating that the "coming of children ha[d] made marriage irksome."[67]

Within Broomfield's suggestions for remedy, a notable shift in attitude emerged. Straying from his position that Methodist doctrine should not adapt itself to contemporary developments, he recognized that American cities were becoming increasingly congested. In addition, modern government had taken over many responsibilities of the urban family, causing some to refer to the home as merely a "boarding-house and breeding place." According to Broomfield, the decay of American society was responsible for the decay of the family: "The immigrant family settles in the United States as a social unit; but, where there are children in the family, this unity gradually is broken up through the Americanization process of the public schools, and the new social surroundings."[68] Remarkably, the position of mainline Protestants had shifted to such an extent during the previous decade, that they were looking to immigrants as an exemplary group attempting to maintain strong family tradition.

Still, Broomfield's position on birth control remained conservative.

He praised the *Ladies' Home Journal* for abandoning its practice of publishing "sex-knowledge." "In the course of time ... this influential publication virtually confessed it had made a mistake, and that after all old-fashioned modesty had proven itself a better safeguard of morals than the sex-knowledge it had been advocating." With regard to marriage his remarks were equally conservative and similar to what Catholics were saying. Broomfield stated, "It is not enough to teach the ideals that have arisen out of the experiences of the race. There are divine and eternal principles that must be upheld."[69]

He quoted the Presbyterian definition of marriage, outlined at conferences of the General Assembly in 1930 and 1931, as one of the best:

> Marriage is an institution ordained of God for the honor and happiness of mankind, in which one man and one woman enter into a bodily and spiritual union, pledging each to the other mutual love, honor, fidelity, forbearance, and comradeship, such as should assure an unbroken continuance of their wedlock as long as both shall live. This institution finds its justification in the establishment and maintenance of the Christian home in which children shall be born, and nurtured in the Christian faith.[70]

Broomfield's concluding statement appeared similarly conservative: "With marriage recognized as a divine institution, with God honored in the home in family worship, with children given their God-ordained place in marriage, and with sex-relations kept as a mutual expression of comradeship and affection, then marriage will remain the happiest and noblest, and most enduring of human relationships."[71] As conservative as his report was, by considering marital sex "a mutual expression of comradeship and affection," Broomfield acknowledged that it could exist as something more than an act of procreation.

Lutherans protested the Federal Council's pronouncement even more vehemently. The United Lutheran Church had maintained a consultative relationship with the council but, as with other Lutherans, never participated as members. Publication of "Moral Aspects of Birth Control" nearly resulted in the breaking of all ties. The United Lutheran Synod of New York argued that the report "expressed views distinctly opposed to the moral and spiritual teachings of the Lutheran Church" and considered severing its relationship with the Federal Council. The concern "was not merely a matter of birth control, although it was birth control that crystallized the issue."[72] In observing that the Council's declaration had "thrown the religious world into a ferment," the *Literary Digest* quoted

Frederick H. Knubel, president of the United Lutheran Church in America, who contended that it was significant that the agitation for birth control occurred at a time "notorious for looseness in sexual morality" and that "the fact creates suspicion as to the motives for the agitation."[73]

Lutherans, too, continued their study of the American family, demonstrating their concern for the divorce rate. In doing so United Lutherans called for stricter divorce laws and once again defined what they considered the meaning and purpose of marriage. In that definition the emphasis on children was clear: "In the first place, [marriage] is the divinely appointed way for the establishment and maintenance of the family.... In the second place, marriage is intended by God to assist the individual to realize the highest ends of being, not only from the temporal, but also from the spiritual point of view."[74]

## Conservative Protestants' Protest Intensifies

The Missouri Synod Lutherans' position remained even more conservative. They had never held membership in the Federal Council, in part because of the Synod's resistance to social action, in part because of its comparatively conservative ideology. They made no concessions on birth control. One editor referred to the Federal Council statement as "a lapse into paganism," and following a Congressional hearing, J. Frederic Wenchel described Sanger's "camp followers" as unmarried and largely Jewish.[75]

The General Synod of the Reformed Church voted to continue its membership in the Council; however, it gave several reasons for considering severing ties: "The prominence of certain non-evangelical leaders in the work and activities of the Council," the "Modernistic tendencies revealed in both the preaching of its official spokesman[76] as also in its official publications," and "its unnecessary pronouncement of 'Birth Control' and 'Usurpation of Authority' as revealed in the 'deliverance' upon a moral question such as Birth Control."[77]

Synod representatives voted to remain in the Federal Council only after reinforcing its stand — and one taken by the Council — that the birth control report simply reflected results of a study and did not represent the view of all its members: "Such reports are not to be construed as declarations of the policy or attitude of the Council or of its Administrative Committee, or of the denominations but rather as means of information for helping church members to arrive at their own conclusions."[78]

One group that neither clarified nor modified its stand was the Southern Baptist Convention. At the height of publicity surrounding religion and birth control, during their annual conference in 1931, Southern Baptists still did not mention the topic. Their only discussion of marriage surrounded a condemnation of the growing "divorce evil," which they blamed on lax divorce laws, especially in the state of Nevada.[79] In 1932 Southern Baptists continued to criticize the widespread availability of divorce, adding that a general lack of uniformity in both marriage and divorce laws contributed to the nation's high divorce rate. Though they again failed to mention birth control, their report on marriage indicated a concern for eugenics, noting that strict marriage regulation would control the propagation of unfit children. In the same statement they made clear that they stood far apart from the Catholic Church on matters of marriage and the family:

> The Roman Catholic Church holds that marriage is one of the "sacraments of the church" and that the church has exclusive authority and control over it, being free even to declare void a marriage duly and only celebrated by authority of the state. Baptists, along with all other non–Catholic Christians and citizens, freely recognize the authority of the state.... Marriage is a civil matter. The state has power and authority to say what classes of persons shall marry and what shall not. This applies to race, age, physical or mental health and all matters affecting the peace and happiness of those who enter the marriage relation, their probable offspring and the public. To ... question the right of the state in this matter would be to take the position of the Vatican, or to favor "common law" marriage.[80]

One of the more direct statements made by conservative Protestants on the subject of contraception was presented in the *Moody Bible Institute Monthly*. Only briefly noting the topic within the larger context of the family, fundamentalist minister Richard W. Lewis of Fresno, California, appeared less concerned with initiating legislation or formulating public policy than with reinforcing biblical teaching. Recognizing that contemporary trends were forcing religious leaders to address the American family, Lewis wrote:

> In all human history never has the family been so prominently before the public as now. Fifty years ago nearly everybody seemed to take the home as a matter of course. It was looked upon as a sacred institution.... In former days no one appeared to find fault with the Bible idea that marriage is of divine origin, and the bonds thereof too sacred for human hands to break asunder with levity. In those days every husband was considered the head of his house, the priest of his home. With such views there was stability about the home not found in our day.

His solution: "We shall need to seek a remedy for the serious homesickness in our wonderful country, and that remedy can be found in only one book — the Bible."[81]

Lewis proposed a nationwide program of lectures to address various topics regarding the family, including the roles of husband and wife, disciplining children, and religious education. His list of proposed lectures suggested there was no room for modern interpretation on any topic, including contraception. That one was to be titled: "Is There Justification for Birth Control? 'Be Fruitful and Multiply.'"[82]

## Catholic Reaction

Catholic opponents to birth control responded with full force to the Protestant developments,[83] beginning with the Lambeth resolution, and the response was international in scope. Belgian Jesuit theologian, Arthur Vermeersch and Cardinal Francis Bourne, archbishop of Westminster, challenged it, Bourne declaring that, by their decision, the Anglican bishops had forfeited any claim to be "authorized organs of Christian morality."[84] However, much of the reaction was uniquely American. Fulton J. Sheen of the Catholic University responded to the Federal Council decision by declaring that the advocates of birth control should no longer call themselves Christian: "The same group of persons who are continually urging law enforcement have made bootleggers of the citizens and are now trying to make bootleggers of the storks."[85]

An editorial published in *America* in August of 1930 reaffirmed the Catholic stance against the "grave evil of contraception." It added that in the Anglicans' argument that the method of contraception should be decided "on Christian principles," they might just as easily have said that the practice of theft, murder, or lying also should be based "on Christian principles." The editorial went on to say that the argument struck against the very heart of Christianity: "It shows that the Bishops and the Anglican Church do not know what Christianity is. It disqualifies them from any pretense to spiritual leadership, and from every claim as teachers of Christianity. In the Name of Our Lord Jesus Christ they have dared approve a vile practice which degrades womanhood, promotes promiscuous licentiousness, destroys the family, undermines the State, and makes all Hell rejoice."[86]

Once the dust had settled, officials of the Catholic Church found it necessary to make an official statement expressing its unchanging stand on the issue. *Acta Apostolicae Sedis* 22: 560 stated:

> The Catholic Church, to whom God himself has committed the integrity and decency of morals, now standing in this ruin of morals, raises her voice aloud through our mouth, in sign of her divine mission in order to keep the chastity of the nuptial bond free from this foul slip, and again declares: any use whatever of marriage, in the exercise of which the act by human effort is deprived of its natural power of procreating life, violates the law of God and nature, and those who do such a thing are stained by a grave and mortal flaw.[87]

*Acta Apostolicae Sedis* 22: 559 stated, "Since therefore the conjugal act is destined primarily by nature for the begetting of children, those who in exercising it deliberately frustrate its natural effect and purpose, sin against nature and commit a deed which is shameful and intrinsically vicious."[88]

A more detailed expression of the Church's stand came in the form of *Casti Connubii: On Christian Marriage*, the encyclical of Pope Pius XI on Christian marriage, which was issued December 31, 1930. The encyclical repeated identically some passages of *Acta Apostolicae Sedis* and further explained the gravity of committing this "sin against God," both on the part of the couple and on the part of priests who acknowledge the use of contraception:

> We admonish ... priests who hear confessions and others who have the care of souls, in virtue of Our supreme authority and in Our solicitude for the salvation of souls, not to allow the faithful entrusted to them to err regarding this most grave law of God; much more, that they keep themselves immune from such false opinions, in no way conniving in them. If any confessor or pastor of souls, which may God forbid, lead the faithful entrusted to him into these errors or should at least confirm them by approval or by guilty silence, let him be mindful of the fact that he must render a strict account to God, the Supreme Judge, for the betrayal of his sacred trust, and let him take to himself the words of Christ: "They are blind and leaders of the blind; and if the blind lead the blind, both fall into the pit."[89]

The pope added that concern that the mother's life might be in danger if faced with pregnancy or childbirth was no excuse for using contraceptives:

> As regards the evil use of matrimony, to pass over the arguments which are shameful, not infrequently others that are false and exaggerated are put forward. Holy Mother Church very well understands and clearly appreciates all that is said regarding the health of the mother and the danger to her life. And

who would not grieve to think of these things? Who is not filled with the greatest admiration when he sees a mother risking her life with heroic fortitude, that she may preserve the life of the offspring which she has conceived? God alone, all bountiful and all merciful as He is, can reward her for the fulfillment of the office allotted to her by nature, and will assuredly repay her in a measure full to overflowing.[90]

Quoting the Book of Genesis and the writings of St. Augustine, the pope gave no indication that the church would bend to contemporary circumstances.[91]

John Ryan concluded in his analysis of *Casti Connubii* in the *Ecclesiastical Review*,

"In other words, no consideration of consequences nor of changed circumstances can make this sort of act morally lawful. It is wrong in itself, always and everywhere." As to the pope's comments to the priests, Ryan admitted to knowing of priests who had absolved penitents who confessed to "addiction to birth control practices." Ryan wrote, "It is difficult to understand how any priest could follow this course in the face of the explicit instruction of the Congregation of the Penitentiaria, 10 March, 1886, to the effect that confessors are obliged not only to refuse absolution to penitents who refuse to avoid this sin for the future, but also to interrogate penitents whom they have reason to suspect as guilty." He added that the clarity of the encyclical should prevent priests from pleading ignorance any longer.[92]

The majority of Catholic theological debate following the encyclical did not center so much on the general use of contraception as on the method used. *Acta Apostolicae Sedis* and *Casti Connubii* seemed to leave the door open to abstinence when they condemned the experiencing of the conjugal act, which "by human effort is deprived of its natural power of procreating life." This opened up the debate on "rhythm," or periodic abstinence during times when the woman was believed to be fertile. The question of abstaining during fertile days of the menstrual cycle had been debated since St. Augustine had condemned it. During the 1930s, however, new ideas surrounding the use of the rhythm method were taking shape. Research in 1930 by Dr. Ogino of Japan and Dr. Knaus of Austria had provided new information leading to what were considered more accurate calculations of female fertility.[93] The publicity surrounding that research accompanied by the serious economic effects of the depression might well have spurred Catholic approval of periodic abstinence.[94]

Official approval was not granted, but consent was given by enough high-ranking authorities for Catholics to consider the method approved.

Ryan presented the most convincing evidence when he interpreted the encyclical as permitting the use of the rhythm method by "any married person with a serious reason for avoiding offspring."[95] Ryan and other Catholics applied periodic abstinence to what they considered a papal directive based on laws of nature that considered intercourse a natural process. The use of rhythm became widespread among Catholics, who claimed that neither participant had done anything themselves to interfere with the natural process.[96]

Catholic debate also addressed other methods of birth control. Ryan condemned the use of sterilization, adding that recent scientific evidence had proven that the procedure did not prevent "feeblemindedness" as had been claimed by those prescribing it in order to prevent pregnancy.[97] In his "Canonical Notes on the Encyclical Letter on Christian Marriage" Valentine Schaaf claimed that the time had come for the pope to clarify the Church's opposition to abortion, since the scientific community had made intricate advances in methods of abortion not yet specifically addressed by the Church.[98]

In addition, specific questions arose surrounding the use of *coitus interruptus*, or the method of withdrawal. Ryan was unclear whether the encyclical had specified that a woman had sinned if she had intercourse with a man during which the man practiced withdrawal. Earlier teaching had declared the woman a sinner, even if she had consented to it during duress. In his interpretation James H. Kearney said he understood the reason for confusion and concluded that there were times when the situation was grave enough for a woman to tolerate the act of withdrawal of her husband. Yet, he said, there was still no excuse for a woman to tolerate the use of a condom by her husband, nor was there an excuse for a man to tolerate the use of a diaphragm by his wife.[99] Although no other denomination engaged in such detailed discussion regarding method, as with other denominations, the debate appeared to stop when it came to the use of mechanical devices or chemicals.

## *The Politics of Resistance*

The *Ecclesiastical Review* was written essentially for clergy, and its primary writers, such as Ryan, interpreted the theological intricacies of Catholic doctrine for priests and bishops. The *Commonweal*, on the other hand, was read widely by Catholic laypersons, and focused on the more emotional American public debate following the Federal Council's publication of "The Moral Aspects of Birth Control." A *Commonweal* editorial published on April 1, 1931, agreed with the *New York Herald Tribune*'s assessment of the pronouncement as "almost revolutionary" but noted that the revolutionary significance reached beyond the birth control debate:

> It may come to be recognized as the liquidation of historic Protestantism by its own trustees; the voluntary bankruptcy of the Reformation. If the theses nailed by Luther to the church door at Wittenberg three centuries ago marked the birth of the Reformation, the theses of the Federal Council, when considered in connection with the similar approvals of contraception by the Anglican bishops at Lambeth, and by the Methodist Episcopal Church and the Unitarians in this country, may mark the death of the Reformation.

The cause of death for the Reformation, according to the *Commonweal* was an unconditional surrender to secularism: "[Protestantism] came into organized existence as a revolt against the doctrine of authority in religion. It dissolves into secularism in the same fashion. Private judgement in religion thus completes its fatal cycle."[100]

In subsequent weeks Edward Robert Moore, director of the Division of Social Action of the Archdiocese of New York, wrote several articles for the *Commonweal*, expressing various reasons for opposing contraception, and eventually a book entitled, *The Case Against Birth Control*, with an introduction by Patrick Cardinal Hayes. Less provocative than the original *Commonweal* article, Moore's arguments disputed various claims made by birth control advocates. He noted that even the Federal Council admitted that opinion in the medical profession was divided on the safety of contraception. Furthermore, wrote Moore, the Federal Council recognized that there was an "element of uncertainty" with regard to effectiveness. Clearly in response to the suggestion that intelligent, reasoning, and enlightened Americans condoned birth control, Moore concluded, "Contraception is a medical technique that is condemned by many distinguished members of the medical profession. Thinking people will not overlook this fact when they have occasion to evaluate propaganda in its favor emanating from lay groups."[101]

## Battle in Congress

Moore specifically opposed the Gillett Bill, which was introduced in Congress in February of 1931. Sanger had armed herself for a legislative battle in Washington by establishing the National Committee for Federal

Legislation for Birth Control. Between 1931 and 1934 there were five congressional hearings on various forms of birth control legislation, and at many points during the hearings, the testimony reflected an ongoing battle between Sanger and Ryan. Sanger was effective in her lobby as congressmen were deluged with letters of support. Ryan's support was equally as strong, however, as he was able to match Sanger witness for witness throughout the hearings.[102] During her testimony Sanger depended heavily on arguments of providing medical service, protecting the health of women and lowering infant mortality. Ryan used arguments such as the effect of the declining birthrate on the building trades and real estate business, but he concentrated primarily on issues of national morality.

The Gillett Bill challenged the Tariff Act of 1922 and would have legalized the importation and dissemination of contraceptives. In his argument, published in the *Commonweal*, Edward Moore quoted Dr. W. C. Woodward, director of the Bureau of Legal Medicine of the American Medical Association, who maintained birth control advocates were misleading the public by referring to the Gillett Bill as the "Doctors' Bill" because it was viewed as specifically protecting physicians. According to Woodward, "to prevent any misunderstanding, you are informed that the American Medical Association has taken no part in the preparation of this bill or in procuring its introduction. The association has expressed no opinion with respect to the principles and purposes of the bill."[103]

An earlier editorial in the *Commonweal* had reminded readers that although the National Catholic Welfare Conference had appeared as the strongest opposition to the Gillett Bill, it was not the only organization that opposed the measure. Dr. Howard Kelly, Johns Hopkins University professor emeritus of gynecology, and Dr. Henry Catell, editor of *International Clinics*, led the medical opposition at Senate hearings. In addition, the Southern Baptist Convention, the Religious Liberty Association, the Lord's Day Alliance, and the Methodist Board of Public Morals testified against the bill.[104] Though few conservative Protestant groups wanted to publicize the fact that they were on the same side as the Catholic Church on the matter of birth control, Catholic officials continued, as they had since 1921, to publicize any stand by Protestants that was similar to their own. However, such sympathetic groups were becoming increasingly rare.

Lobbyists for birth control were able to present larger numbers of religious supporters to Congress during the Gillett Bill hearings. Humanist Charles Potter testified that several religious organizations—from the liberal Unitarians and Universalists to those he considered to be the conservative Anglican bishops at Lambeth—approved of contraceptive use because they recognized the morality of birth control. Potter contended that a growing number of clerics understood that birth control was better for the child, the parents, and the community. It tended to prevent war and abortions, and it substituted "the higher morality of intelligent responsibility for the lower morality induced by fear of consequences.[105]

Addressing any opposition that might exist among the entire Judeo-Christian population in the United States, Rabbi Sidney Goldstein argued that birth control was not contrary to the laws of God. He admitted that it did contradict the command "increase and multiply," but he added: "I call your attention to the fact that the first time this creed occurs is in the first chapter of the book of Genesis, when there were two people in the Garden of Paradise; and the second [and only other] time it occurs is just after the flood when, according to the census taker, there were only eight people on the face of the earth."[106]

In other testimony the debate was divided along Catholic/non–Catholic lines by Sanger. A statement issued by the National Catholic Welfare Conference had argued that the proposed law would supersede state law, making it impossible for individual states to legislate according to their own wishes. Furthermore, according to the NCWC, because no state legislature had repealed or weakened existing state legislation, "it seems that there is no real popular demand for this proposed legislation."[107] The Bureau of Jewish Social Research condemned the Catholic statement — via a letter presented to the Senate Judiciary Committee by Sanger — for attempting to speak for the morality of the population outside the Church. The Bureau letter added: "In his recent encyclical the Pope endorses the so-called "natural" methods of birth control sanctioned by the Catholic Church. Senate bill 4582 will permit other discoveries which science has determined as hygienically valid. We hope that the Congress of the United States will recognize the legitimate needs of the majority of its citizens."[108]

Sanger had a difficult time finding a sponsor for the bill, and the hearings demonstrated the reluctance among congressmen to speak publicly on the subject of birth control. Heywood Broun, columnist for the *New York Herald Tribune*, commented, "Birth control is in the eyes of politicians political dynamite. If they support it they may lose some votes. If they oppose it, they may lose some votes. There is nothing a politician hates more than losing votes. He would much rather the subject never came up."[109] On March 4, 1931, the Gillett Bill died in committee.

Even though their early attempts in Congress had failed, by 1931 birth control advocates were benefiting from denominational support for their cause. They continued to employ their strategy of presenting the Catholic Church as the enemy, which aided in drawing more liberal and mainstream Protestant and Jewish clerics into their camp. In addition, as more religious figures condoned birth control, Sanger and her supporters found it easier to define the Catholic Church as the outsider. As the decade progressed, the Church found fewer denominations on their side who remained as clearly opposed to artificial contraception.

# Notes

1. "The Birth Control Revolution," *Commonweal*, April 1, 1931, pp. 589–593.

2. John M. Cooper, "Catholic Principles and Teaching on Birth Control," *Birth Control Review*, May 1930, pp. 146–147.

3. She had lost control of the *Review* and of the American Birth Control League in 1929. See Gordon, p. 271.

4. Other birth control advocates continued to single out Catholics. See Caroline Hadley Robinson, *Seventy Birth Control Clinics: A Survey and Analysis Including the General Effects of Control on Size and Quality of Population* (Baltimore: Williams and Wilkins, 1930).

5. *Ibid.*, p. 131.

6. *Ibid.*

7. "The Roll-Call: Twenty Opinions," *Birth Control Review*, May 1930, pp. 132–140.

8. *Ibid.*, p. 133.

9. *Ibid.*, pp. 136, 143.

10. *Ibid.*, pp. 134–135.

11. Though, in my opinion, official denominational approval was more important than acceptance by individual clergy, it does not appear to have been so important to Sanger. Excerpts from convention reports were buried in the *Review*. It is possible that editors of the *Review* did not think the "legalese" of the reports was as convincing as the eloquent writings of the ministers.

12. The *Review* did not mention the Unitarian resolution because it was passed three weeks after this publication.

13. *Birth Control Review*, May 1930, p. 150.

14. *Annual Report of the American Unitarian Association for the Fiscal Year May 1, 1929–April 30, 1930* (Boston: American Unitarian Association, 1930), pp. 41, 67–68.

15. *Ibid.*, p. 149, *New York Times*, April 8, 1930.

16. Isaac E. Marcuson, ed., *Report of the Central Conference of American Rabbis, 1930*, pp. 78–79. Even though little recognition was granted to the rabbis' decision, they understood they were the first to officially accept contraceptive use. In 1930 the report of the Commission on Social Justice stated, "Since the Central Conference of American Rabbis took the leadership in expressing an attitude on this important subject, three other large religious groups have already followed our lead with similar and even more emphatic declarations." They did not name the three religious groups. See p. 78.

17. *The Lambeth Conferences*, p. 151. This commentary reflected similar Roman Catholic sentiment expressed during the Depression that attempted to provide spiritual guidance to couples suffering financial hardships who might be tempted to use artificial means of birth control.

18. For a study of birthrates during the 1930s, see Samuel A. Stouffer and Paul T. Lazarsfeld, *Research Memorandum on the Family in the Depression* (New York: Arno Press, 1972), pp. 121–123. Stouffer and Lazarsfeld conclude that the Depression had little effect on the general birthrate because it had been declining at a more rapid pace during the previous decade. Susan Ware, in *Holding Their Own: American Women in the 1930s* (Boston: Twayne, 1982) and other women's historians in subsequent works have concluded that a more significant factor in the low birthrate was the postponement of marriage during the Depression.

19. *Central Conference of American Rabbis, 1930*, p. 83.

20. *The Lambeth Conferences (1867–1930)*, p. 166. See also St. John-Stevas, *The Agonising Choice*, p. 74.

21. *Ibid.*, pp. 165–166.

22. "Birth Control and the Church," *Outlook and Independent*, August 27, 1930, p. 661.

23. Chesler, p. 548. For an overview of varying opinions on the Lambeth decision from representatives of the Anglican Communion, see Paul Matthews, "Lambeth and Birth Control," *American Church Monthly*, October 1930, pp. 253–257; Francis J. Hall, "Is the Use of Contraceptives Ever Right?" *American Church Monthly*, January 1931, pp. 63–72; Wilhelmine P. Willson, "An Analysis of Marriage and Sex Philosophy," *American Church Monthly*, November 1931, pp. 380–385.

24. Harry Emerson Fosdick, "Religion and Birth Control," *Outlook and Independent*, June 19, 1929, p. 301. See also "Twenty Opinions," p. 132.

25. A. G. Keller, "Birth-Control," *Outlook and Independent*, April 16, 1930, p. 619.

26. "On Birth Control," *Outlook and Independent*, September 26, 1930, pp. 485–486.

27. "Voluntary Parenthood," *Christian Century*, September 3, 1930, pp. 1053–1054.

28. *Ibid.*, p. 1054.

29. *Ibid.*

30. *Federal Council of the Churches of Christ in America, Annual Report, 1930* (New York: n.p., 1930), pp. 35–36.

31. Ralph Marshall Davis, "Romance and Religion: Report of the Presbyterian Commission to the General Assembly," in Spaulding, pp. 122–127.

32. *Report to the General Convention of the Protestant Episcopal Church of the Joint Commission to Study the Whole Problem of Divorce — Its Conditions and Causes*, in Spaulding, p. 429.

33. *Birth Control Review*, October 1930, pp. 276–277.

34. *Journal of the General Convention of the Protestant Episcopal Church in the United States of America, 1931*, p. 73.

35. *Federal Council of the Churches of Christ in America, Annual Report, 1931*, p. 81. Also in "Birth Control: Protestant View," *Current History*, April 1931, pp. 97–100.

36. *Ibid.*, p. 82.

37. For voting record see report.

38. *Ibid.*, pp. 82–84.

39. *Ibid.*

40. "Federal Council on Birth Control," *Outlook and Independent*, April 1, 1931, p. 458.

41. Chesler, p. 319; Kennedy, p. 155.

42. "Federal Council on Birth Control," *Outlook and Independent*, April 1, 1931, p. 458.

43. "The Churches and Birth Control," *Federal Council Bulletin*, April 1931, p. 19.

44. "Concerning the Report on Birth Control," *Federal Council Bulletin*, May 1931, p. 2.

45. *Ibid.*

46. "Dangers of Birth Control," *Literary Digest*, May 16, 1931, p. 24.

47. *Ibid.*

48. *Ibid.*

49. "The Council and Denominational Assemblies," *Federal Council Bulletin*, September 1931, p. 19.

50. *Ibid.* See also *New York Times*, June 6, 1931, p. 13; *Annual of the Northern Baptist Convention, 1933*, p. 115, in Kennedy, p. 155.

51. *Bulletin*, September 1931, p. 19.

52. *Annual of the Northern Baptist Convention, 1930*, pp. 147–148.

53. A. W. Beaven, *The Fine Art of Living Together* (New York: Richard R. Smith, 1930), pp. 131–134.

54. *Annual of the Northern Baptist Convention, 1931*, p. 141.

55. *Annual of the Northern Baptist Convention, 1932*, p. 135.

56. *Ibid.*, p. 138.

57. *Ibid.*, p. 141. See also Graham and Katharine Baldwin, "Youth and the World Today: Sex and Christian Living," *The Baptist*, March 28, 1931, p. 402. For one of the most liberal and approving responses to "Moral Aspects of Birth Control," see Russel J. Clinchy, "Birth Control — An Exposition of the Federal Council Report," *Congregationalist*, May 28, 1931, p. 714.

58. Mary M. Chalmers and Owen C. Brown, eds., *The Home Beautiful: An Elective Course for Parent Groups* (Philadelphia: Judson Press, 1931), pp. 42–43.

59. *Minutes of the General Assembly of the Presbyterian Church in the U.S.A., 1930* (Philadelphia: Office of the General Assembly, 1930), pp. 80, 86.

60. *General Assembly of the Presbyterian Church in the U.S.A., 1931, Part I, Journal and Statistics* (Philadelphia: Office of the General Assembly, 1931), p. 345; *New York Times*, April 27, 1931, p. 1; May 5, 1931, p. 16; May 20, 1931, p. 21; May 28, 1931, p. 29; May 29, 1931, p. 2; May 31, 1931, p. 1; June 2, 1931, p. 21; iKennedy, pp. 156–157.

61. Spaulding, *Twenty-Four Views of Marriage*, x.

62. *Minutes of the General Assembly of the Presbyterian Church in the U.S.A., 1931*, pp. 104–105.

63. *Minutes of the Seventy-First General Assembly of the Presbyterian Church in the United States, 1931* (Richmond, Va.: Presbyterian Committee of Publication, 1931), p. 28.

64. "Presbyterians Withdraw from Federal Council of Churches," *Christian Fundamentalist*, July 1931, pp. 20–21.

65. *New York Times*, April 8, 1930, p. 30; April 12, 1931, p. 1.; *Christian Advocate*, April 2, 1931, p. 421; November 19, 1931, p. 1422. See Kennedy, p. 157.

66. *Proceedings of the Sixth Ecumenical Methodist Conference, 1931*, p. 203.

67. *Ibid.*, p. 204.

68. *Ibid.*, p. 205.

69. *Ibid.*, p. 206.

70. *Ibid.*, p. 207; See also *Minutes of the General Assembly of the Presbyterian Church in the U.S.A., 1930*, p. 86; *Minutes, 1931*, p. 72.

71. *Proceedings of the Sixth Ecumenical Methodist Conference, 1931*, p. 208.

72. *Lutheran*, April 2, 1931, p. 15; *New York Times*, June 4, 1931, p. 2. See Kenney, pp. 158–159.

73. "More Shooting at the Stork," *Literary Digest*, April 11, 1931, p. 18.

74. *Minutes of the Seventh Biennial Convention of the United Lutheran Church in America, 1930*, p. 104.

75. Graebner, "Birth Control and the Lutherans," p. 315; Walter A. Maier, *Walther League Messenger*, 39 (1931), p. 552; *Lutheran Witness*, 50 (1931), p. 174.

76. The synod was most likely referring to Reinhold Niebuhr, chairman of the Committee on Social Service.

77. *The Acts and Proceedings of the General Synod of the Reformed Church in America, 1931*, p. 946.

78. *Ibid.*, p. 947.

79. *Annual of the Southern Baptist Convention, 1931* (n.p.: n.p., 1931), pp. 123–124.

80. *Annual of the Southern Baptist Convention, 1932* (n.p.: n.p., 1932), p. 92.

81. Richard W. Lewis, "A Family Forum," *Moody Bible Institute Monthly*, May 1931, p. 447.

82. *Ibid.*

83. Tentler, p. 4.

84. St. John-Stevas, p. 74.

85. "More Shooting at the Stork," p. 18.

86. "Anglicans Approve Contraception; Editorial," *America*, August 30, 1930, p. 488.

87. St. John-Stevas, pp. 83–84.

88. *Ibid.*

89. Encyclical, *Casti Connubii*, December 31, 1930, 2: 57.

90. *Ibid.*, 2: 58.

91. *Ibid.*, 1: 11; 2: 55.

92. John A. Ryan, "The Moral Teaching of the Encyclical," *Ecclesiastical Review*, March 1931, pp. 265–266.

93. Elizabeth B. Connell, "Contraception by Periodic Abstinence or Lactational Anovulation," in Stephen L. Corson, Richard J. Derman, and Louise B. Tyrer, eds., *Fertility Control*, (Boston: Little, Brown, 1985), p. 328.

94. Samuel A. Stouffer and Paul F. Lazarsfeld, *Research Memorandum on the Family in the Depression* (New York: Arno Press, 1972), p. 137.

95. Ryan, "The Moral Aspects of Periodical Continence," *Ecclesiastical Review*, 1933, p. 29; Noonan, p. 443; Chesler, p. 321.

96. This interpretation was applied to oral contraceptives shortly after their introduction in the United States, nearly leading to Catholic approval of "the pill" because it did not interfere with the natural process of sexual intercourse.

97. Ryan, "The Moral Teaching of the Encyclical," p. 268.

98. Valentine Schaaf, "Canonical Notes on the Encyclical Letter on Christian Marriage," *Ecclesiastical Review*, March 1931, pp. 272–273.

99. James H. Kearney, "Sinned Against Rather Than Sinning," *Ecclesiastical Review*, March 1931, pp. 503–508. For additional Catholic opinion on the contraceptive question, see Reginald Ginns, "Financial Control and Birth Control," *Catholic World*, August 1930, pp. 605–608; Ginns, *Catholic World*, pp. 349–351; Vincent Joseph Flynn, "Sangre Azul," *Catholic World*, February 1931, pp. 547–550; "Proposals Regarding Birth Control," *Catholic World*, March 1931, p. 749; *Commonweal*, March 4, 1931, p. 479; "The Birth Control Revolution," *Commonweal*, April 1, 1931, pp. 589–593; Edward Roberts Moore, "Futures in Food," *Commonweal*, April 22, 1931, pp. 679–682; Moore, "Doctors Differ on Birth Control," *Commonweal*, April 29, 1931, pp. 713–716; "Birth Control Publicity," *Commonweal*, May 6, 1931, pp. 2–3; Moore, "The Malice of Contraception," *Commonweal*, May 20, 1931, pp. 68–71.

100. "The Birth Control Revolution," *Commonweal*, April 1, 1931, pp. 589–593.

101. Edward Robert Moore, "Doctors Differ on Birth Control," *Commonweal*, April 29, 1931, pp. 713–716.

102. Kennedy, p. 233. Also see *Hearings Before a Subcommittee of the Committee on the Judiciary, United States Senate, on S. 4582, February 13 and 14, 1931* (Washington, D.C.: Government Printing Office, 1931); *Hearings Before a Subcommittee of the Committee on the Judiciary, United States Senate, on S. 4436, May 12, 19, and 20, 1932* (Washington, D.C.: Government Printing Office, 1932); *Hearings Before the Committee on Ways and Means, House of Representatives, on H. R. 11082, May 19 and 20, 1932* (Washington, D.C.: Government Printing Office, 1932); *Hearings Before a Subcommittee of the Committee on the Judiciary, United States Senate, on S. 1842, March 1, 20, and 27, 1934* (Washington, D.C.: Government Printing Office, 1934).

103. Moore, pp. 713–714.

104. *Commonweal*, March 4, 1931, p. 479.

105. *Hearings on S. 4582, February, 1931*, pp. 11–13.

106. *Ibid.*, p. 19.

107. *Ibid.*, pp. 77–80.

108. *Ibid.*, p. 80.

109. *New York Herald Tribune*, October 15, 1930; cited in Chesler, p. 329.

# Chapter Six

# 1932–1937: Conservatives Hold Strong, Catholics Hold Stronger

From 1932 to 1937 birth control advocates continued to lobby Congress through Sanger's National Committee for Federal Legislation for Birth Control. Legislators responded by introducing various bills in the House and Senate that attempted to amend tariff and postal laws to allow for easier access to contraceptives and contraceptive information. None of the legislation was passed, but the hearings gained national attention, giving both sides the opportunity to state their cases to the American public.

In these years Americans also watched the economic picture worsen. Financial hardship on the American family during the Great Depression brought further attention to the issue of birth control. Facing unemployment and the threat of not being able to feed or clothe existing members of the family, millions of married couples in the United States faced the serious question of whether to risk bringing a new life into an already desperate situation. For the first time in U.S. history the birthrate fell below the replacement level, dropping from 21.3 live births per 1,000 population in 1930 to 18.4 by 1933.[1]

Both of these developments—congressional debates and the Depression—further divided the religious forces on the issue of birth control. Though some denominations aside from the Catholic Church continued to voice their opposition to artificial contraceptive use and lobbied against legalizing contraception, they did not make themselves as visible as Catholic spokespersons did. Consequently, birth control advocates pointed to the intensified lobbying efforts on the part of Catholics as a growing threat to the personal and political freedoms of Americans.

## Mainline Protestant Declarations

As the focus of the public debate centered on the Catholic opposition, Protestant pronouncements became rare. However, this did not mean that all Protestant debates had ended in a consensus support of birth control. Quite the opposite was true. The move toward widespread approval in 1930 and 1931 generated a growing number of attacks on contraceptive use, from both conservative and mainline Protestants.

At its conference in 1934 the Federal Council once more attempted to project an image of harmony among Protestant churches, reporting that denominations were cooperating on issues such as race and labor and, of course, family welfare. Recognizing that "'Moral Aspects of Birth Control' has helped to shed light on a most difficult problem on which there is no unanimity of judgment," the Federal Council noted, "Twenty-five years ago there was no concerted program for strengthening Christian family life. Today the Federal Council provides a united educational leadership in this field.... The publications, 'Ideals of Love and Marriage,' 'Mixed Marriages,' and 'Safeguarding Marriage,' have had a wide use."[2] December of 1933 had marked the twenty-fifth anniversary of the Federal Council, and it reported growing harmony: "The old era of divisive, unrelated, competitive denominations is definitely passing. The new day of cooperation, of fellowship, of a practical working unity had dawned."[3]

*Safeguarding Marriage* was the most recent educational endeavor of the Committee on Marriage and the Home. The pamphlet was published in 1935 and reflected the council's intention to pacify those it had alienated with its report on birth control. It focused on preventing hasty and careless marriages, discussing "the sex question" with restraint. The report suggested that marital intercourse as an expression of love need not contradict biblical teachings: "A sensible and realistic view is that sex will be highly important to [people entering marriage] and that it is possible for them to achieve an increasingly successful adjustment by developing a mature artistry of love-making which uses biological differences as means of mutual joy-giving so that the expression of Scripture is fulfilled that in marriage "the two shall become one flesh." Regarding the spacing of children, *Safeguarding Marriage* suggested ministers might consider teaching couples to make parenthood voluntary rather than accidental but also teach them to "avoid unsatisfactory and dangerous methods of birth control."[4]

Still, a number of writings held more critical views of contraception. One important work was written in 1935 by the evangelical J. A. Huffman, dean of Taylor University's School of Religion. *Building the Home Christian* was primarily a Northern Baptist guide preparing young adults for marriage. In what was, by far, one of the most frank Protestant discussions of the social well being of the home, Huffman explained the fundamental importance of understanding the "race debt":

> That two persons should be united in marriage, to enjoy the most intimate social relations, carries with it a definite debt to the race of which they are a part. Unless men and women are willing to acknowledge and pay that debt, they have blundered in signing the contract to pay, by entering into the social pact of marriage. ... No dictatorial attitude is meant in taking this position relative to the marriage relationship. Neither is the role of a condemning judge assumed. But the debt to the race assumed in a marriage can be easily seen. The rearing of two children by husband and wife simply balances the account. It is only beyond two children that any race contribution has been made whatsoever.[5]

However, his prescription was not limitless. Calling unwanted pregnancy the "social accident" and a crime against childhood, Huffman declared that every child had a right to be well born. The solution was planning:

> Perhaps it would be easier to practice a false modesty here; to pass the subject entirely by, and leave the whole matter, as is usually done, to chance. But is this the best, the truly Christian, way? The race debt, and a race contribution, has been recognized and insisted upon. Beyond that, the number of children which shall be reared in any home is a private matter, resting with God and the parents. But for the sake of the children yet unborn, and in defense of their social rights, let it now be determined, once and for all, that every child shall be wanted and cherished. This is the truly Christian way in relation to the social rights of the child.[6]

The discussion among United Lutherans demonstrated their hesitance to endorse birth control. For example, in 1932 the United Lutherans' Committee on Moral and Social Welfare included "sex-laxity" among the numerous social ills that needed attention:

> Nothing in the moral experience of man is more difficult than the maintenance of that purity and sanctity against the urges of the strong animal passions, inseparable from sex consciousness. When the animal, sex passions are allied with other evil motives, like the money-motive, the worldly social-ambition motive, etc., it is no wonder that they manifest their corrupting

> power in obscenity, gross sex immorality, easy divorce and the
> practical repudiation of marriage as a sacred institution. Let it
> be noted that in the New Testament lists of social evils, sex-
> immorality is always put in the first place.

From this passage, one might conclude that the committee was speaking only of the most sinful acts of prostitution and adultery. However, Lutherans were speaking also of "lustful" intercourse within a marriage, noting that it was in the "purity of sex-feeling" and the "sanctity of sex-function" that the character of the family was determined.[7]

## *Missouri Synod:* For Better, Not for Worse

Members of the Missouri Synod reinforced conservative Lutheran ideals regarding parenthood throughout the Depression, one member noting that "more babies would solve a lot of our economic problems."[8] But by 1935 they were willing to address the topic of contraception directly. Walter A. Maier of the Concordia Seminary in St. Louis published *For Better, Not for Worse*, the first full-length Missouri Synod marriage manual. In his chapter "The Blight of Birth Control" Maier responded to contemporary declarations concerning overpopulation, child development, eugenics, and maternal health, rejecting claims by others that birth control was a moral necessity.[9]

By the third printing of *For Better, Not for Worse* Maier had attacked Sanger's claim that the absence of birth control was partly responsible for the Depression. He noted that a committee report of the American Medical Association convention in 1936 admitted that it found "no evidence available to justify the broad claim that dissemination of contraceptive information will improve the economic status of the lower-income groups."[10] Maier called birth control "an outrage against nature," stating, "The love of children is a basic gift of nature, and for Christians this gift is sanctified by the high and holy regard which their faith places upon childhood. Interference with these natural fundamentals must provoke a cataclysm of tremendous proportion."[11]

Regarding the effects of contraceptive use on a marriage, Maier wrote, "Birth control must be condemned because, immoral, it promotes immorality. In emphasizing the way of escape from the consequences of marriage, it has of course thrown open the door to licentiousness by reducing the unwelcome consequences of promiscuous relations before and after marriage." To prove his point, he cited statistics that he said demonstrated that birth control was a stimulus for divorce. According to Dr. Alfred

Cahan's *A Statistical Analysis of American Divorce*, Maier wrote, 63 percent of all divorces in 1930 and 1931 were issued in childless marriages, 20 percent in marriages with one child, 9 percent in marriages with two children, 3 percent in marriages with three children, and 1 percent in marriages with more than three children.[12]

Maier demonstrated one of the most conservative attitudes of the 1930s when he reminded couples that procreation was the primary purpose of marriage: "The Church must maintain its emphatic avowal of Christian marriage as God's institution for the propagation of the human race. It must insist that, whenever the divine command 'Be Fruitful and multiply' is evaded for selfish purposes and through the employment of methods suggested by birth control, divine displeasure is invoked." However, his use of the phrase "for selfish purposes" indicated his pronouncement was conditional. He did agree that in the "infrequent and exceptional" conflicts between childbirth and maternal health, couples could seek the advice of the clergy and a Christian physician and even consider artificial methods. Still, periodic abstinence was preferable. With the "spiritual forces of Christianity" and the "power of effective prayer," restraint was possible.[13] By the 1940s, Synod theologian Alfred Rehwinkel was examining the position of humanity as subject to nature but maintaining the ability to modify and limit nature. He argued that the biblical quotation "Be fruitful and multiply" was not a command, but a blessing.[14]

## *Fundamentalists: Look to Scripture*

Fundamentalist Protestants wavered little, if any, in their birth control teaching. In *What God Hath Joined Together* minister William Cooke Boone expressed one Southern Baptist opinion. In his chapter entitled "God's Gift, the Baby" Boone substantiated his position with biblical quotations such as "Lo, children are an heritage of the Lord. ... As arrows in the hand of a mighty man, so are the children of youth. Happy is the man that hath his quiver full of them: they shall not be ashamed, but shall speak with their enemies in the gate."[15] He declared, "No home is complete without a baby. No married couple can enter into the true glory of love, except as that love is blended and centered in a little child. It is God's plan that marriage should be completed and sanctified in the high privilege of parenthood. The baby is God's gift that enriches and deepens the love of a man and woman for each other as nothing else can. This is the high and holy, the divine purpose of the institution of marriage." Boone also made it clear that one child was not enough: "It is far better for the family to divide what they have among several children than to spend it all on one, no matter how little it is. It is far better for father and mother to look after several, and not a great deal more trouble, than to give their time and attention to one. There is great danger that our small families with one or two children, will not have the training in those great principles of unselfishness, service, and love that the large families of our grandparents had."[16] In pointing out that the birth rate of "American native stock" was decreasing rapidly, threatening "our American heritage of high standards and ideals," Boone embraced Protestant anti–birth control principles of the previous two decades. This was common among fundamentalist Protestants during the 1930s. A noted eugenicist made note of this sentiment in his appeal to Dr. Arthur J. Barton, chairman of the Southern Baptist Convention, when calling for support of the birth control movement. Guy Irving Burch informed Barton that he now supported the legalization of contraceptives but had formerly worked to prevent the American people from "being replaced by alien or Negro stock, whether it be by immigration or by overly high birth rates among others in this country."[17]

The common criticism of materialism continued among conservative Protestants. One example is evident in the writing of Chicago fundamentalist Harold L. Lundquist. In 1937 Lundquist placed much of the blame for what he perceived as the declining status of the American family on working women and on materialism, or "more love for luxuries than children." In addition, he criticized the "flippant" attitude that deemed the home unnecessary "since we are born in a hospital, reared in a boarding school, courted in an automobile, married in a church, spend our days in an office or on the golf course, attend some place of amusement at night, die in a hospital and are buried from a funeral home."[18]

## *Argument Among Jews*

The deepening Depression and the continued public debate on contraception also caused Conservative and Orthodox Jews to examine their birth control teaching. Though Orthodox Jews generally maintained their stand, Conservatives responded to the "present conditions." Instead of continuing to oppose contraceptive use in spite of the economic situation, as conservative Protestants and Catholics had, Conservative Jews reconsidered their teaching. In 1932 the Conservatives' Rabbinical Assembly of the Jewish Theological Seminary of America created its Committee on Social Justice, which included family relations among the issues it addressed.[19] In 1935 the assembly published a comprehensive statement on contraception, granting approval of its use. The statement was presented as follows:

> As rabbis, we are deeply concerned with the preservation and extension of the human values inherent in the institution of the monogamous family. Careful study and observation have convinced us that birth control is a valuable method for overcoming some of the obstacles that prevent the proper functioning of the family under present conditions. ... Hence we urge the passage of the legislation by the Congress of the United States and the State Legislatures to permit the dissemination of contraceptive information by responsible medical agencies. We maintain that proper education in contraception and birth control will not destroy, but rather enhance, the spiritual values inherent in the family and will make for the advancement of human happiness and welfare.[20]

The committee concluded that Jewish law could be interpreted "as not opposing the use of contraceptives, whenever the question of health was involved."[21] Although the Conservatives' decision came several years after that of the Central Conference, their statement reflected the conclusions drawn by more liberal denominations, especially those by liberal Protestants. The Rabbinical Assembly adapted doctrine — just as some Protestants had — to society's "present conditions," demonstrating concern for the contemporary state of the family.

Orthodox Jews remained steadfast in their opposition to birth control but allowed the practice of abstinence when pregnancy posed a threat to a woman's health or to the health of an infant she was already breast-feeding. Orthodox Rabbi David Miller presented one of the few descriptions of Orthodox opinion during these years in his *The Secret of the Jew: His Life — His Family*, which was published in 1930. Even his description was brief, noting that for observant Orthodox Jews birth control was generally unnecessary. According to the rules of *Nidah-Tvilah*, a woman was to experience seven "clean" days following her "menstrual malady" before having sexual intercourse with her husband. The purpose of this was to insure that the womb was sanitary before conception took place. Miller wrote: "She is then in her prime and full blossom. Her mate by that time has regained his vitality, and his sexual interest has been renewed." He added, "When fertilization takes place under *such favorable conditions*, it naturally results in the most select seeds and products. Children who have a good healthy start in life while young, can better cope with and overcome the obstacles and enemies to health which inevitably confront them in their natural life." Miller contended that because the number of days a woman could engage in intercourse was limited, there was less of a chance she could become pregnant.[22] He wrote, "The Jewish religion, as a rule, does not approve of direct birth control. Nevertheless, the observant Jewish woman thus enjoys, to a certain extent, the control of and the protection from surplus births, and the giving of birth is less likely to be in vain."[23]

In 1940 Sanger supporter Sidney Goldstein answered critics of birth control in his *Meaning of Marriage and Foundations of the Family, a Jewish Interpretation*. Goldstein could no longer simply single out the Catholic Church as the opposition without recognizing that Orthodox Jews held similar beliefs. To the Orthodox argument that birth control would lead to race suicide, Goldstein responded: "It is true that since the adoption of the birth control program the birth rate in every civilized country has dropped rapidly; but so has the death rate. The population is not composed of those who are born but of those who survive; and there is still a margin between births and deaths that should remove all fear of race suicide." To the position that birth control was a desecration of marriage, he answered: "There is no evidence whatever to show that the standards of life in families in which birth control is an acknowledged procedure are lower than in families with an unchecked birth rate. The sanctity of marriage does not depend upon conception or contraception but upon the spirit of consecration with which men and women enter the marriage bond." He contended that those who maintained birth control violated God's law were basing their argument on "the command quoted from the myths in the earlier chapters of the Bible." "Science teaches us, however, that the lower down we go in the scale of evolution the less restriction there is upon the reproductive process; and the higher we rise the more restraint appears from stage to stage. In other words, through birth control or contraception we are given sight and intelligence to what in nature is a blind and groping instinct."[24]

## Catholic Doctrine and the Depression

The nature of Catholic teaching changed during the 1930s. The Church never abandoned its condemnation of artificial contraceptives, but comparatively few Catholic pronouncements published between 1932 and 1936 dealt with theological debate. Immediately following the Lambeth decision and the Federal Council's publication of the "Moral Aspects of Birth Control," Catholic debate had centered on moral and religious discussions of natural law. In subsequent years, however, they focused on the

Church's response to the Depression, a response that essentially condemned materialism and, at times, the American social and economic structures.

To Catholic theologians economic necessity was no excuse for the use of artificial contraception. For instance, P. J. Ward suggested that contemporary emphasis on materialism had caused couples to lose sight of God's purpose in the blessing of offspring when they claimed that "no child has a right to be born unless there is the means of providing it with a measure of worldly goods and opportunities."[25] The eleventh annual convention of the National Council of Catholic Women held in 1931 reinforced its stand against birth control, repudiating the "new form of propaganda for this evil under the guise of economic necessity in the present condition of unemployment and distress" and renewing its "unqualified condemnation of this vicious un-Christian social evil."[26]

In March of 1931 R. E. Howard, who referred to himself as the only Catholic member on the board of directors of his local welfare association, claimed he was eager to take positive action in supplying relief to the indigent but objected to one caseworker's stance on birth control. The caseworker reasoned that the people who appeared to be in constant need were the "alcoholic, the mentally deficient and the criminally inclined" and that these were people who many times bore unwanted children. She saw it as imperative that the welfare association provide such parents with contraceptives; thus, "only can we at the same time decrease the number of unfit and of undesirables in the community, and make our own work more fruitful and permanent in results," though she added that she certainly would not use this approach with Catholic clients. Howard responded, "This is not exactly a matter that concerns Catholics. Scientific birth control is not wrong because it is forbidden by the Catholic Church. It is forbidden by the Catholic Church because it contravenes the law of nature and of God."[27]

The Church's answer to the difficult question of bringing new life into the desperate world of the Depression remained simple. The phrase "God does not command the impossible" was applied to both of the Catholic alternatives—abstinence or additional children. According to Ryan, "Those who accept either alternative will be stronger in character, better citizens and vastly more in accord with the purposes of God, than parents who resort to birth-control practices."[28] Pope Pius XI recognized the seriousness of the situation facing parents in *Nova Impendet*, his encyclical on the economic crisis issued October 2, 1931: "More vehement still becomes our commiseration as we gaze at the multitude of little children who 'ask for bread when there is no one to break it for them' (Jer. Thren. iv, 4). These little ones, in their innocence, are bearing the worst of the burden. Squalid and wretched, they are condemned to watch the vanishing of the joys proper to their age, and to have their rightful laughter hushed upon their young lips as they gaze with bewilderment around them."[29] The pope's prescription for this crisis was charity and prayer.

American Catholics saw the answer to such desperation in reform of the present social condition. They did not believe it was necessary to work in the interests of the individual but in the interests of society. By 1931 the National Council of Catholic Women had voted that members of the Church should cooperate with government to combat unemployment and extend relief to the needy. The council saw major changes as necessary because the economic condition hampered virtuous living, bred discontent, and threatened the stability of government.[30]

The call for social reform during the Depression did not contradict earlier teachings of the Church. Forty years earlier Pope Leo XIII helped plant seeds for later minimum wage legislation in his labor encyclical *Rerum Novarum*. *Casti Connubii* reinforced the same obligation to provide a decent wage for workers, suggesting that failure to do so "is at the root of much of the modern desecration of Christian marriage." In his interpretation of the economic factors presented in *Casti Connubii*, Paul Blakely wrote that a wage that provided even the minimum in food, clothing, and shelter was not enough. In addition to its failure to provide any savings to insure against future sickness or unemployment, it made marriage and children impossible.[31] Cardinal Hayes saw solutions in reordering the nation's economy and social structure to make it possible to have children and to rear them in keeping with their needs. Hayes blamed the poor distribution of wealth and demanded "less capitalistic control" of the labor market, higher wages, and better housing to relieve the burdens of large families among the poor.[32] This kind of rhetoric was common among Catholic social activists and further alienated the Church from mainstream Protestants who had warned Americans that Catholics were incapable of staying out of governmental affairs.

The fundamentals of Catholic contraceptive doctrine did not differ much from the teachings of moderate and conservative Protestants and Jews. No denomination recommended incessant childbearing, especially in a condition of poverty. Rather, the conflict primarily centered around the method of preventing pregnancy. With the permission of various bishops in the early 1930s, American Catholics were practicing periodic abstinence, and the "rhythm" method provided the answer for Catholics in the aftermath of the birth control debate.[33] The first serious Catholic examinations of the rhythm method began in the Midwest, in particular with

Dr. Leo Latz, a physician and faculty member of Loyola of Chicago's medical school.

Dr. Latz was reportedly asked by a Jesuit priest, a fellow Loyola faculty member,[34] to investigate recent research by Ogino and Knaus into women's fertility cycles,[35] in order to develop a practical method of periodic abstinence. Subsequently, Catholic couples embraced Latz's 1932 book, *The Rhythm*, and it sold sixty thousand copies in the first two years of publication.[36] However, the book was still highly controversial, as there was no official Catholic sanction of the rhythm method. Though Latz gained the approval of Chicago's Cardinal George Mundelein, and donated all proceeds to the Church, the controversy led to his dismissal from his teaching position at Loyola.[37]

The method was again described in the widely read 1934 booklet entitled *Legitimate Birth Control: According to Nature's Law, in Harmony with Catholic Morality*, by The Rev. John A. O'Brien, Chaplain of Catholic Students at the University of Illinois. Huntington, Indiana's, Our Sunday Visitor Press published *Legitimate Birth Control* for Catholic parishioners, dedicating it to "Mothers, the Unsung Heroes of Our Race, Who Go Down Into the Valley of the Shadow of Death, and Out of Their Travail and Sacrifice Give Life to the World." O'Brien wrote the book in response to "thousands of letters" asking for "further explanation" following his November 1933 article entitled "The Church and Birth Control," which appeared in the weekly *Our Sunday Visitor*. O'Brien criticized the Church's enemies who he said portrayed the Church as "obscurantist," arguing that the Church in fact "welcomes every new truth," in this case, the "additional law of nature"—rhythm.[38]

In the extensive "Church and Birth Control" article O'Brien maintained that the practical significance in recent findings was that "Almighty God, the author of the laws of nature, has provided natural means for the regulation of the number of offspring.... They show that ample time, indeed more than half of the monthly period, is available for the exclusive attainment of the secondary ends of marriage, mentioned by the Hold Father, as 'mutual assistance, and the fostering of mutual love.'" O'Brien also quoted Loyola professor Rev. Joseph Reiner, S.J., who claimed that "Divine Providence has come to the assistance of mankind at critical periods by unfolding nature's secrets. It seems to be doing that in the present crisis by enabling scientists to discover the rhythm of sterility and fertility." And according to Dr. Latz, they could expect "the married lives of many couples will be vastly enriched with the values, physical, psychic, and moral, of married life, as it was intended by the creator." In addition, Latz saw the accepted use of rhythm as a means to curb the rate of abortion, which was estimated in the United States at seven hundred thousand per year by Dr. Hugo Ehrenfert, chairman of a White House committee formed to study "Abortion in Relation to Fetal and Maternal Welfare."[39]

Following O'Brien's *Legitimate Birth Control*, Indiana's Bishop John Francis Noll published *Catechism on Birth Control*, in which he decried Protestants who shifted toward approval of artificial contraceptives. Referring to birth control as "mutual masturbation," Bishop Noll cited numerous biblical passages — all of which referred in one way or another to succumbing to passions of the flesh — which he claimed prohibited it on grounds that it violated natural law.[40] He went on to condemn the Federal Council of Churches and individual moderate and liberal Protestant denominations for their acceptance of Birth Control. He had already chastised them in a pamphlet entitled *The Catholic Church vs. the Federal Council of Churches of Christ in America* immediately following the Council's shift on contraception.[41]

By the mid–1930s, the dividing line in Catholic minds was drawn between "artificial methods" and "rhythm," and the religious debate over birth control in general was drawn between Catholics and non–Catholics. But there still remained strong common threads that were being ignored among all denominations. Even the most liberal religious teaching regarded abstinence as the preferred method. Above all, they agreed, no one should intentionally prevent conception for trivial or selfish reasons. And regarding the purpose of marriage, most Protestants, Jews, and Catholics were limiting their emphasis on procreation while maintaining their insistence that marriage was a spiritual union and a lifelong commitment to be entered into seriously. Little attention was given to these similarities during the vicious debates before Congress.

## *More Public Attacks*

Outside the Congressional hearings, anti–Catholicism had been demonstrated in other writings, which some claimed had been part of an effort to aid lobbyists in this new congressional battle.[42] For instance, in 1932 the National Committee on Maternal Health, a longtime proponent of birth control, published *Medical Aspects of Human Fertility*. The committee presented the booklet as a well-researched survey of opinion obtained primarily from the scientific community. Included among its reports, the organization noted numerous instances of Protestant and Jewish support. However, for an outline of Catholic opinion, the author suggested only John F. Moore's *Will America Become Catholic?*[43]

It is difficult to understand why the author would have chosen this work above all others as the one in which "the Roman Catholic position is set forth in some detail."[44] It is possible that he or she confused it with Edward Moore's *The Case Against Birth Control*. Also published in 1931 this was a work produced by a Catholic theologian that did outline the Catholic position. More likely, members of the Committee on Maternal Health wanted to strengthen its case for legalizing contraceptives. John Moore was not Catholic and until the publication of this popular book was a relatively unknown writer and editor of the *Railroad Association Magazine*. In *Will America Become Catholic?* he did discuss the Church's position on birth control but did it with the intention of instilling greater fear in the American public.

Moore claimed that this work was "not propaganda but an inquiry into the actual situation." But he concluded that through immigration, evangelism, and now propagation American Catholics might finally achieve the dream of the outspoken Archbishop John Ireland of St. Paul, Minnesota, who proclaimed in 1889: "Our work is to make America Catholic! If we love America, if we love the Church, to mention the work suffices. Our cry shall be, 'God wills it!' and our hearts shall leap with Crusader enthusiasm."[45]

Birth control advocates certainly had *The Nation* on their side. In 1932 *The Nation* devoted nearly an entire issue to the birth control debate, publishing a series of articles supporting the legalization of contraception. The authors of the articles describing the opposition to legalization maintained that opposition was directed by the Catholic Church. Sanger accused the Pope of separating himself from the real world by looking down from his "watch-tower." "In that remote tower he sits comfortably, takes counsel from a pile of old books and from bachelor advisers, and then writes scolding sermons about the marriage problems of intelligent people. I wish he could come down into real life for a few weeks, walk the earth and mingle with the poor."[46] Journalist Robert S. Allen called the Catholic opposition, which "Mrs. Sanger and her associates continually encounter," "without a doubt the greatest single obstacle to be overcome."[47] Charlotte Perkins Gilman added:

> Every religion believes itself to be the Truth, and warmly desires to increase its membership, not intelligence and ability being requisite, but numbers. On no account does it wish to check the increase of constituents, and low mentality among converts offers no obstacle.... Thus we find individual fundamentalists strongly opposed to any prudential checks to the increase of population, and in particular the immense authority of the hier-

archy of the Roman Catholic church forbidding as a sin the use of contraceptives. Members of this faith not only are forbidden to practice birth control themselves, or even to study the facts and figures as to its social necessity, but they are urged to prevent other people from studying the question.[48]

## *Congressional Battles Continue*

The debates in Congress over legalizing the importation and distribution of contraceptives further divided the religious debate into a Catholic and non–Catholic one. The Gillett Bill had been defeated, but the American Birth Control League and the Voluntary Parenthood League did not give up, as they found alternative approaches to Congress. The Tariff Act of 1930 had strengthened, at the federal level, provisions against the importation of foreign-made products, including contraceptives. Also known as the Hawley-Smoot Tariff Act, the measure was a prescription intended to cure economic ills in the United States.

With the passage of Hawley-Smoot, birth control advocates saw another chance to publicly challenge birth control restriction at the federal level. By 1932 they had also seen a growing support for their movement from various Protestant and Jewish denominations. In 1932, when Senator Henry D. Hatfield of West Virginia introduced legislation similar to the Gillett Bill, birth control advocates attempted to separate the opposing forces into the "enlightened" side and the "Catholic" side.

There were similarities in some of the actual testimony before the Senate. On Sanger's behalf Rabbi Edward Israel entered lists of religious supporters as evidence during hearings before the Senate Judiciary Committee. In addition to various state groups and individual churches, Israel's list included the following larger organizations: Central Conference of American Rabbis; General Council of the Congregational and Christian Churches; Middle Atlantic Conference of Congregational and Christian Churches; Universalist General Convention; Woman's Auxiliary of Episcopal Triennial Convention, Denver, Colorado; Federal Council of the Churches of Christ in America; Lambeth Conference of Anglican Bishops; American Unitarian Association; Laymen's League of Unitarian Church; and "Methodist Episcopal leaders at convention in Delaware, Ohio."[49]

In addition to publicizing religious support, Israel insisted on lambasting religious opposition. In a prepared statement Israel criticized dogmatic religion for its opposition to birth control. Though he did not name the Catholic Church, his implication was clearly understood: "I speak of no one religion. Dogmatic religion has opposed all marks of progress of the mind of man, such as embodies birth control in its intelligent aspects to-day [*sic*], when they do not agree with it. It fought at one time against the teaching of the idea that the world moved around the sun. It burned men at the stake for daring to teach that idea. It has fought against the teaching of the theory of evolutionary development of physical life."[50] New York University professor and noted eugenicist Henry Pratt Fairchild did not raise the topic of religion but focused on demographic issues illustrative of anti–Catholicism in previous decades. Fairchild maintained that the United States' economic troubles were caused by overpopulation, much of which was now a result of reproduction. According to Fairchild, "We have restricted, and I believe very wisely, the flow of immigration from foreign countries into this Nation of ours.... Also there is the question of quality in immigration. We have handled that by our selective restrictions for immigration." He added, "Now we have got to face the situation from our internal aspect. We have got to regulate the increase of our own population within our own borders, and we have to be careful that such increase as does take place comes from the better elements of society."[51]

During hearings on the same legislation before the House Ways and Means Committee, religion played a more significant role with religious leaders using secular arguments and laypersons raising the issue of religion. The opposition found an ally in Congressman John W. McCormack of Massachusetts, who refuted many of the arguments presented by birth control lobbyists. McCormack weakened Malthusian arguments by getting Rabbi Sidney Goldstein to admit that Thomas Malthus did not advocate contraception. Furthermore, humanist Charles Potter yielded to McCormack's contention that his references to Japanese aggression — which Potter blamed on overpopulation — did not apply in the United States.[52]

When Charlotte Perkins Gilman attempted to employ the common practice of singling out the Catholic Church as the opposition, the following interaction ensued:

> MRS. GILMAN [speaking].... The religious objection is really the biggest one and the only one that makes any organized fight. It is held by many pious persons that the use of contraceptives is wrong. The Catholic Church, in particular, considers it a sin. They have a right to believe it is a sin. They forbid it to all their communicants as a sin. They have a right to forbid it to their communicants. They have no right to forbid it to people who are not their communicants and who do not believe it to be a sin. To interfere with the legislation of the country in the interests of a particular church is not fair.

MR. MCCORMACK. Mr. Chairman, is this an attack on the
Catholic Church? I would like to know.

THE ACTING CHAIRMAN [Charles R. Crisp, Georgia]. Do
not let us get into this sort of issue, Mrs. Gilman.

MRS. GILMAN. It is no attack. It is a statement of fact.[53]

Though Catholics continued their struggle to remind Americans
through their testimony that they were not alone in their opposition to
birth control, as the hearings went on it became increasingly evident that
they made up the vast majority of the opposing force. Some of the strongest
testimony supporting the stand of Catholics came from the Reverend
William Sheafe Chase, who represented himself as the Superintendent of
the International Reform Federation. However, in a subsequent hearing,
Clarence True Wilson, who acted as vice president of the International
Reform Association and executive secretary of the Methodist Board of
Temperance, supported birth control advocates and noted that Chase had
spoken only for himself and not for his organization.[54]

In addition to the testimony by Goldstein and Potter, Sanger also had
clerics and religious laypersons who were newcomers to her camp make
presentations of support for the Hatfield Bill. They included Mrs. Alexander Wolff, who spoke for the National Council of Jewish Women, and the
Reverend Russell J. Clinchy, who represented the Department of Social
Relations of the National Council of Congregational Churches. L. Foster
Wood, professor of ethics at the Colgate-Rochester Divinity School, presented statements of support from the Federal Council, the New York East
Conference of the Methodist Episcopal Church, the Universalist General
Convention, and American Unitarian Association, and the Special Commission on Marriage, Divorce, and Remarriage to the General Assembly
of the Presbyterian Church in the U.S.A. When the Hatfield Bill failed to
pass, the National Committee for Federal Legislation for Birth Control had
the bill reintroduced by Senator Daniel Hastings. Many of the same arguments that had been used by both sides in the past were used again. However, the growing severity of the Depression significantly influenced much
of the debate.

Claiming that birth control could help relieve the Depression, Sanger
argued, "Population is pressing upon the relief agencies, upon the dole,
upon the other fellow's job. ... What is to become of the children? Of the
millions whose parents are today unemployed?" She also supplied figures
showing that families with no employed workers had birthrates 48 percent higher than did families with one or more employed workers; therefore, unwanted children were becoming an increasing burden on the
taxpayer.[55] But, responded Ryan, a declining birthrate would be the death

of our society rather than the solution to the problems of the Depression.[56]

In general, Catholics had embraced the New Deal, and by the time of the Hastings Bill hearings they were gaining political strength in Franklin Roosevelt's administration. Roosevelt had recognized political potential in appealing to the Catholic electorate, and New Deal policies in his first term in office represented what Catholic social activists had been preaching for decades. Cardinal Hayes praised Roosevelt's reform policies, noting their similarities to Catholic teachings. Among his various appointments of prestigious Catholics to government posts, Roosevelt appointed Ryan to the Industrial Appeals Board of the National Recovery Administration and to the President's Committee on Farm Tenancy, and he was consulted in the writing of the Social Security Act.[57]

This new close relationship between Catholics and the federal government provided additional ammunition for the birth control lobbyists' battle. To many Americans this relationship validated their fears about Catholic church-state philosophy. Having already failed before Congress, lobbyists sharpened their attacks on the Church as the enemy. Most of their testimony during hearings of the Hastings Bill in the Senate, and the similar Pierce Bill in the House, addressed the medical, social, and economic benefits of birth control. But within their statements many of them singled out the Church's own lobbying efforts as what had held up passage of any legislation.

During the Pierce Bill hearings, the *New York Times* described the opposition as "almost solidly Catholic," to which the self-proclaimed leader of the opposition replied with a letter to the editor. H. Ralph Burton claimed it was he, a non–Catholic attorney from Washington, who led the opposing forces. He reminded readers that representative United Lutherans, Evangelical Lutherans [Augustana Synod], Southern Baptists, Episcopalians, and Methodists provided statements against the legislation along with Catholics. However, when the Pierce Bill died in the House Judiciary Committee, Sanger blamed the Catholic Church, in particular, Father Charles Coughlin. Coughlin used the medium of radio as his pulpit and had gained a wide, loyal audience of Catholics and non–Catholics through his Detroit-based program. The solutions he proposed for economic ills and the attacks he made on various aspects of American society were based more on emotion than on reason, and by the late 1930s, many had written him off as a lunatic. At this point his appeal was viewed as a threat by those who feared Catholic political power, and he had joined in the birth control debate. Sanger accused Coughlin of using his radio influence to have his listeners deluge senators with letters opposing the recently proposed

World Court, contributing to its failure. She claimed he did the same to defeat the Pierce Bill in the House of Representatives.[58]

Senate testimony on the Hastings Bill reflected birth control lobbyists' continuing focus on the Catholic Church. Sanger was successful in introducing a number of supporters who held her view of the Church's tactics. According to Ira S. Wile, a New York pediatrician and frequent lecturer, "If there is any form of action more likely to increase a belief that Catholicism has the power to control political opinions and to limit freedom of speech, then [sic] the efforts of the Catholic church to hamper legislation demanded by the great majority of the people of this commonwealth, I cannot imagine what it is." Wile continued: "That any minority group of our population should be able to bring about a situation stultifying to intelligent citizens is a sad commentary upon our boasted democracy, our intellectual honesty, and our pretensions to foster the 'new deal.'" Blanche H. deKoning, executive secretary of the Grand Rapids, Michigan, Anti-Tuberculosis Society, added, "My work throws me constantly in contact with people of all classes and religions and I am amazed to find out how much of the general run of Catholics have changed their minds about this matter in the last few years. They have refused to be dictated to by their priests and the Pope, none of whom have ever known the problem of economic pressure, of feeding hungry mouths, of clothing and educating little children, or of giving a square deal to motherhood."[59]

Sanger herself had demonstrated restraint during previous congressional hearings when it came to her comments on the Catholic Church. But testimony presented during the hearings on the Hastings Bill demonstrated that she had not yielded in her position. While it is true that the vast majority of her statements had nothing to do with the Catholic Church, Sanger also subtly chastised Church authorities when describing various methods of contraception: "No one objects to continence. We have no objection whatsoever to certain religious orders claiming that is the only method the church can sanction. There is nothing in the law against it. They may practice it and we say that is their own affair. Their own individual right."[60] In making these statements, she was simply articulating what she had claimed all along — that the Church was infringing on the individual rights of non–Catholics.

Behind the scenes Sanger's comments were much less reserved. This was made evident when Thomas E. Boorde, pastor of Temple Baptist Church in Washington, D. C., and representative of the Home Mission Board of the Southern Baptist Convention, entered into testimony a copy of a letter written by Sanger. Boorde criticized birth control lobbyists for making the debate appear to the American public as a question of

"Protestantism against Catholicism," using the letter as evidence of Sanger's strategy of antagonism. The letter called for support from every "Friend, Coworker, and Endorser," and outlined the status of the Congressional hearings. "Each and everyone [sic] of our speakers presented the case with logic, reason, and courtesy, bringing forth the facts of science from various angles. There was no doubt that the common sense and justice and humanity of the question was on our side," wrote Sanger. She continued:

> The opposition, on the other hand, started off their bombast by an insulting tirade by Father Coughlin, the radio "passion flower" priest from Detroit. Coughlin's aggressive disregard and disrespect for any government outside of Vatican City was obviously demonstrated in his behavior in sitting before the Judiciary Committee. Of course, one of the Congressmen, quick to recognize the arrogance of Coughlin's behavior requested permission from the chairman after, but not until, the priest had been seated.
>
> Then began the fireworks of this celibate priest, insulting American womanhood, intimating that those who had small families through birth control were "fornicators" and prostitutes of the marriage bed. These and other abusive remarks were followed by an array of Catholic opponents including another priest and three House Representatives. Needless to say the object of this spectacle was not to present facts to the committee but to intimidate them by showing a Catholic block of voters who (though in the minority in the United States) want to dictate to the majority of non–Catholics as directed from the Vatican in social and moral legislation.
>
> American men and women, are we going to allow this insulting arrogance to bluff the American people? Or, are we going to assert our conviction now by demanding of our Representatives that they take action in refusing to be intimidated and bring this bill before Congress. [sic][61]

While it was not true that the Catholic Church represented the only religious force working against Sanger, it was clear the Church had increasingly fewer allies by the mid–1930s. No other religious denomination — however conservative — had been nearly as outspoken in its position nor as organized in its legislative battles. Furthermore, as time went on, larger numbers of liberal and mainline denominations and other religious groups publicly supported the ideals of the birth control advocates. By 1934 Mrs. Thomas Hepburn, the legislative chairperson for the National Committee on Federal Legislation for Birth Control,[62] could submit an impressive list of clerical supporters to the Senate Judiciary Committee. What she referred to as a partial list of official religious endorsements included "ten national organizations, 13 state Unitarian organizations, 7 Methodist, 7 Presbyterian, 218 Congregationalist, 1 Baptist, 36 Liberal, 1 United Church, 1 Universalist, 2 All Souls, 2 Jewish, 2 Humanist, 1 Episcopalian, 10 miscellaneous," and "310 organizations representing many thousands of individuals." She did acknowledge that in addition to Roman Catholics, Orthodox Jews and "certain divisions of Lutherans and Baptists" remained opposed.[63] As extensive as the religious support — as well as other support — was, it did not convince Congress to act. By 1935 Congress had refused to deal with the birth control issue any longer, at least in part because contemporary law was not hampering such practice. It was understood that doctors were regularly breaking the law with impunity.[64]

Some considered John Ryan, the National Catholic Welfare Conference, and other Catholic organizations and individuals the victors in the congressional debate because no substantial legislation regarding birth control reform was passed into law. In reality, however, there was evidence that Ryan privately supported a "doctor's bill" because it would have provided strict medical control of contraceptives. He was quoted as saying, "Of course you understand that the Catholic Church can take no conciliatory attitude publicly or officially towards birth control. It would be misunderstood. The press would play havoc with the situation."[65] By this time the momentum in the religious division of the debate was so strong that even Ryan recognized there was no room for reconsideration of the Church's position. The anti–Catholicism of the birth control movement had been so successful in portraying the Church as the enemy because of its political action that Catholics ultimately entrenched themselves in defense of their right to be politically active. Similarly, birth control activists had used the public arena so successfully to condemn the Church's adherence to traditional teaching that Catholics found themselves refusing to waver on their position in that same arena.

## Victory in the Courts

While birth control advocates had focused their efforts on legislative action, victory came unexpectedly in the courts. In the 1930 case before New York's U.S. Circuit Court of *Youngs Rubber Corporation v. C. I. Lee and Co., Inc.,* Judge Thomas Swan felt pressure to express his views regarding the legality of the interstate transportation of contraceptives, though the case initially concerned little more than settling a trademark dispute.

Judge Swan recognized that neither federal law nor any state laws prohibited the sale or manufacture of contraceptives. He added that even in the case of transport, it was impossible to know whether their ultimate use would be illegal or not, since it was legal for a doctor to dispense condoms for the prevention of disease. In three cases between 1931 and 1934 Judge John M. Woolsey of the Federal District Court for the Southern District of New York granted permission for the distribution of two books on contraception written by Marie Stopes and of *Ulysses* by James Joyce, which contained explicit passages describing the use of contraceptives.[66] Sanger took advantage of victories to force liberalization of the laws even further.

She was able to do this in 1936 with the case of *United States v. One Package of Japanese Pessaries*. In 1932 a Japanese physician, whom Sanger had met at a birth control conference, mailed her a package of pessaries. After customs confiscated the package, Sanger's attorney Morris Ernst suggested she have the physician mail it again, this time to physician Hannah Stone. He correctly predicted that a court battle would ensue, and they could fight it based on medical exemption. The court ruled in Stone's favor, with Judge Augustus Hand announcing that the right of authority for dispensing contraceptives lay with the medical community. Hand wrote, "[The law's] design, in our opinion, was not to prevent the importation, sale, or carriage by mail of things which might intelligently be employed by conscientious and competent physicians for the purpose of saving life or promoting the well-being of their patients."[67] Ernst said in commenting on the case, "Nowhere in its opinion did the court specifically state under what circumstances a doctor was to be free to prescribe a contraceptive. The inference was clear that the medical profession was to be the sole judge of the propriety of the prescription in a given case, and that as long as a physician exercised his discretion in good faith the legality of his action was not to be questioned."[68] The American Medical Association voted in 1937 to recognize contraception as "proper medical practice," and though Sanger had not begun the struggle with the help of the AMA, nor to benefit the AMA, it was clear that she had won her battle. The court's decision was representative of the growing sentiment among many religious denominations that the matter of contraceptive choice was best left to the expertise of physicians.

## Notes

1. Susan Ware, *Holding Their Own: American Women in the 1930's* (Boston: Twayne, 1982), p. 7.

2. *Federal Council of the Churches of Christ in America, Annual Report, 1934*, pp. 5–11.

3. *Ibid.*, p. 5.

4. Committee on Marriage and the Home, "Safeguarding Marriages" (New York: Department of the Church and Social Service, Federal Council of the Churches of Christ in America, 1935), pp. 27–29.

5. J. A. Huffman, *Building the Home Christian* (Marion, Ind.: Standard Press, 1935), p. 35.

6. *Ibid.*, pp. 37–38.

7. *Minutes of the Eighth Biennial Convention of the United Lutheran Church in America, 1932*, p. 411. It was not until 1956 that United Lutherans specifically permitted "conception control." See *Minutes of the Twentieth Biennial Convention of the United Lutheran Church in America*, 1956, p. 1138; Kennedy, p. 159.

8. R. P. Young, *Lutheran Witness*, 1939, p. 306; Graebner, p. 315. See also Martin Sommer, *Lutheran Witness*, 1936, p. 52; Theodore Graebner, *Lutheran Witness*, 1931, pp. 119–120; Maier, *Walther League Messenger*, 1938, p. 603.

9. Maier, *For Better, Not for Worse: A Manual of Christian Matrimony* (St. Louis, Mo.: Concordia Publishing House, 1939 [1935]), pp. 377–394.

10. *Ibid.*, p. 395.

11. *Ibid.*, p. 397.

12. *Ibid.*, pp. 399–400.

13. *Ibid.*, pp. 410–412. For supporting Missouri Synod opinion see John H. C. Fritz, *Pastoral Theology* (n.p., 1945); Louis Nuechterlein, "Series on the Christian Marriage Relation," *Concordia Pulpit for 1940* (St. Louis: Concordia Publishing House, 1939).

14. In 1959 Rehwinkel's position permitting the use of contraceptives was published. See Graebner, pp. 320–322.

15. Psalms 127:3; William Cooke Boone, *What God Hath Joined Together: Sermons on Courtship, Marriage, and the Home* (Nashville, Tenn.: Broadman Press, 1935), p. 79. For an identical reference by the Missouri Synod Lutherans, see Graebner, p. 311.

16. Boone, pp. 79–82.

17. Cited in Chesler, p. 343.

18. Harold L. Lundquist, "The Decline of the American Home," *Moody Bible Institute Monthly*, November 1937, pp. 115, 123. Conservative Protestants accepted the use of artificial birth control by the late 1960s. See Walter O. Spitzer and Carlyle L. Saylor, eds., *Birth Control and the Christian: A Protestant Symposium on the Control of Human Reproduction* (Wheaton, Ill.: Tyndale, 1969).

19. *Proceedings of the Rabbinical Assembly of the Jewish Theological Seminary of America, Thirty-second Annual Convention*, vol. 4 (New Rochelle, N.Y.: Press of the Little Print, 1933), pp. 358–363.

20. Isaac Landman, ed., *The Universal Jewish Encyclopedia*, vol. 2 (New York: KTAV Publishing House, 1969), p. 381. See also *Proceedings of the Rabbinical Assembly of America, Thirty-fifth Annual Convention*, vol. 5, p. 168.

21. *Proceedings ... Thirty-Fifth Annual Convention*, p. 168.

22. Recent medical observations regarding the "fertile period" weakened his argument, since the eighth day virtually marks the beginning of ovulation.

23. David Miller, *The Secret of the Jew: His Life — His Family* (Oakland, Calif.: by author, 1930), pp. 186–193. For the most comprehensive Jewish work on contraception, see David M. Feldman, *Birth Control in Jewish Law: Marital Relations, Contraception, and Abortion as Set Forth in the Classic Texts of Jewish Law* (New York: New York University Press, 1968). Also see Louis M. Epstein, *Sex Laws and Customs in Judaism* (New York: KTAV Publishing House, 1967 [1948]).

24. Sidney E. Goldstein, *Meaning of Marriage and Foundations of the Family, a Jewish Interpretation* (New York: Bloch Publishing, 1940), pp. 52–57.

25. P. J. Ward, "Analysis of the Encyclical of Pope Pius XI on Christian Marriage; with Study Outline," *N.C.W.C. Review*, February 1931, pp. 4–5.

26. "Unemployment and Relief; Resolution Adopted by National Council of Catholic Women," *N.C.W.C. Review*, November 1931, p. 16.

27. R. E. Howard, "Welfare Work and Birth Control," *America*, March 15, 1931, p. 553.

28. Ryan, "Moral Teaching of the Encyclical," p. 267.

29. Encyclical, *Nova Impendet*, October 2, 1931, p. 2.

30. "Unemployment and Relief," *N.C.W.C. Review*, November 1931, p. 16.

31. Paul L. Blakely, "Marriage Encyclical and Wages," *America*, January 24, 1931, pp. 384–385.

32. Kennedy, p. 147. For additional rhetoric regarding the Depression, see Lawrence B. de Saulniers, *The Response in American Catholic Periodicals to the Crises of the Great Depression, 1930–1935* (New York: University Press of America, 1984).

33. In 1951, Pope Pius XII officially declared that the rhythm method was permissible, provided there was serious reason for it. The serious reason, however, might be medical, eugenic, economic, or social. See St. John-Stevas, p. 89.

34. Though unnamed in Latz's obituary, the priest was probably Joseph Reiner, S.J., who wrote the introduction to Latz's book.

35. *Chicago Sun Times*, May 4, 1994, p. 79. In Leo Latz biographical file, Loyola University of Chicago Archives.

36. *Ibid.*; Ellen Skerrett, "Tales Recall Pain, Piety of Post-War Marriages," *The New World*, September 17, 1993, review of Alice Halpin Collins, *The Rhythm Girls*, privately printed.

37. *Chicago Sun Times*, May 4, 1994, p. 79; Leo J. Latz, M.D., "The Latz Foundation — Its Aims and Achievements," *Lincare Quarterly*, December 1934, pp. 8–15, a clipping in the Office of the President, Samuel Knox Wilson, 20–24, Loyola University of Chicago Archives.

38. The Rev. John A. O'Brien, *Legitimate Birth Control: According to Nature's Law, in Harmony with Catholic Morality* (Huntington, Ind.: Our Sunday Visitor Press, 1934), p. 15.

39. John A. O'Brien, "The Church and Birth Control," *Our Sunday Visitor* (Fort Wayne, Indiana, edition), November 26, 1933, pp. 3–5.

40. Romans 8:12–13; Galatians, 5:24; 1 Peter 4:2; 1 Thessalonians 4:4–5; and Romans 1:24–27.

41. John Francis Noll, *Catechism on Birth Control* (Huntington, Ind.: Our Sunday Visitor Press, 1938), pp. 6, 10–36; Noll, *The Catholic Church v. the Federal Council of Churches of Christ in America* (Huntington, Ind.: Our Sunday Visitor Press, 1931).

42. Wilfrid Parsons, S. J., "The Great Birth-Control Plot," *America*, February 6, 1932, pp. 427–429.

43. *Medical Aspects of Human Fertility, a Survey and Report of the National Committee on Maternal Health, Inc.* (New York: National Committee on Maternal Health, 1932), pp. 10–11.

44. *Ibid.*, p. 11.

45. John F. Moore, *Will America Become Catholic?* (New York: Harper and Brothers, 1931), vii, 1, 237–242.

46. Sanger, "The Pope's Position on Birth Control," *Nation*, January 27, 1994, p. 104.

47. Robert S. Allen, "Congress and Birth Control," *Nation*, January 27, 1932, p. 105.

48. Charlotte Perkins Gilman, "Birth Control, Religion, and the Unfit," *Nation*, January 27, 1932, pp. 108–109. For other arguments see Henry Pratt Fairchild, "Birth Control and Social Engineering," pp. 105–107; C. V. Drysdale, "Asiatic Conflict and Overpopulation," pp. 107–108; Adolphus Knopf, M.D., "Birth Control in Disease," pp. 109–110; George B. Lake, M.D., "The Spiritual Aspect of Birth Control," pp. 110–111; William Allen Pusey, M.D., "Birth Control and Sex Morality," pp. 111–112; John Dewey, "Education and Birth Control," pp. 112–113; Morris L. Ernst, "How We Nullify," pp. 113–114.

49. *Hearings on S. 4436, May, 1932*, p. 20.

50. *Ibid.*, pp. 20–21.

51. *Ibid.*, p. 60.

52. *Ibid.*, pp. 27–31, 50–52.

53. *Ibid.*, p. 56.

54. *Ibid.*, pp. 88–97; and *Hearings on S. 1842, 1934*, pp. 69–70.

55. The findings of Stouffer and Lazarsfeld, cited in chapter six, dispute this.

56. Kennedy, pp. 235–237; *Hearings on S. 1842, 1934*, pp. 14–32, 103–111.

57. David J. O'Brien, *American Catholics and Social Reform: The New Deal Years* (New York: Oxford University Press, 1968), pp. 47–55. Also see Patrick Cardinal Hayes, "The Principles of the Common Good," *Catholic Mind*, July 22, 1933, p. 261.

58. *New York Times*, January 20, 1934, p. 17, col. 1; January 29, 1934, p. 14, col. 7; February 6, 1935, p. 15, col. 3.

59. *Hearings on S. 1842, 1934*, pp. 60–61.

60. *Ibid.*, p. 17.

61. *Ibid.*, pp. 136–138.
62. And mother of Katharine Hepburn.
63. *Hearings on S. 1842, March 1, 20, and 27, 1934*, pp. 8–14.
64. Kennedy, p. 241.
65. *Ibid.*, pp. 236–237.
66. *Ibid.*, p. 250; Chesler, *Woman of Valor*, p. 331.
67. *U.S. v. One Package*, 86 F. 2d 737 (1936), pp. 5–6; Chesler, pp. 372–373.
68. Kennedy, p. 250.

# Chapter Seven

# Conclusion

By the late 1930s the struggle for federally legalized dissemination of contraceptives had come to an end. The majority of the nation's clergy reconsidered their positions that procreation was the primary purpose of marriage and that legalizing contraceptives would only further the moral decay of American society. Denominations recognized that there was substantial moral ground for legalization. By the 1930s they expressed moral obligation to allow couples to limit the numbers of their children. The topic of Sanger's speech that she was prohibited from giving on November 13, 1921, "Birth Control, Is It Moral?," had accurately predicted where the religious debate would ultimately arrive.

But the shift did not lie primarily in attitudes of individual morality. Rather, in this new age, notions of what was best for society is what was at stake. Early-twentieth-century faith among modernists that social progress was in their hands played a key role in the religious debate over birth control. The notion prevailed that population could be properly managed if the task was undertaken rationally and with scientific and medical expertise. The inferior stock could be prevented from weakening the American population if their numbers were restricted. Poverty could be alleviated by insuring that the poor did not worsen their situation by having more children. Marriages could survive if couples entered into marriage after a waiting period and with clerical counseling, a marriage manual, and a discussion with the family physician. Clerical leaders eventually concluded that conception was potentially under human control and did not necessarily have to be left strictly in the hands of God.

Not all denominations arrived at the same conclusion. As illustrated, some actively resisted this trend toward modernism. Various groups of conservative Protestants and Jews, as well as Catholics, maintained that having sexual intercourse while purposely attempting to prevent conception was sinful. They ignored psychologists' warnings that abstinence might have a detrimental effect on the individual and on the marriage relationship. Representing much of the lower classes, they decried materialism rather than suggest the use of artificial contraceptives to improve one's economic status. They preached that the pressures of marriage could be dealt with through prayer. Their insistence on maintaining traditional contraceptive teaching stemmed from a general resistance to adapt doctrine to social changes, which lay in direct opposition to modernism. There was little that could persuade conservative Protestant, Jewish, and Catholic clerics to acknowledge conception as anything but a gift from God.

But Catholics stood apart from the others in the eyes of the nation. The fact that Orthodox Jews and fundamentalist Protestants would not change their basic teachings did not matter to Americans as much as the fact that Catholics would not change theirs. Catholic positions on birth control were viewed as something with which to contend. The reasons for this were clearly rooted in the religious-political challenges that were driven by anti–Catholicism. At the same time, Catholics did exert their influence in the battle over legalization, as they, too, viewed it as a social question that they had a democratic right to address politically.

Birth control activists, led by Margaret Sanger, quite successfully portrayed the Catholic Church as something to fear in the contraceptive debate. This was possible because of the anti–Catholicism that was already present in the United States. It was also possible because Catholic authorities made statements and took action early in the movement that birth control activists could point to as evidence that they were the enemy. Sanger ignored critics who said she would achieve success more quickly if she stopped antagonizing Catholics, and in doing so she accelerated much of the non–Catholic support of her movement. Mainline and more liberal Protestants and Jews preferred being viewed as progressive, modern thinkers, who were concerned about society's well-being, rather than old-fashioned and authoritative, as Catholics were considered.

But while a degree of liberalism allowed them to change their positions on contraception, their ultimate goal was one of social control. America's clergy did not accept the use of contraceptives by unmarried couples or suggest that women should be granted unlimited reproductive rights. They essentially wanted to insure results such as declines in divorce rates, in juvenile delinquency, and in dollars spent on relief programs. More important, their intentions were rooted in racial improvement or at least the prevention of race degeneracy. In these respects it was conservatism that aided in clerical support of birth control legislation.

Furthermore, it was the conservatism of the 1920s that helped create a religious birth control debate in which Catholics became the outsiders. Social conservatives wanted to prevent a growing Catholic population from changing the social fabric of the United States. Economic conservatives sought to solve the problem of poverty by restricting the numbers of poor. Catholic social activists suggested various methods of redistributing the nation's wealth, further upsetting conservatives. Political conservatives wanted to keep newcomers from actively participating in the political system and were suspicious of Catholics who held such ambitions.

By 1931 economic conditions justified the legalization in many American minds, but politicians feared losing Catholic votes if they supported it. This gave birth control activists additional proof that Catholics had bred so extensively, that they may have become an invincible voting block. Success in the courts in 1936 took the pressure off the politically timid who could not take a public stand. It also took the pressure off the timid among American clergy who could not wholeheartedly condone contraceptive use. Leaders of the birth control movement had hoped for support from all clerics to ease passage of legislation, but court decisions in favor of birth control made that support unnecessary.

In the following decades birth control activists continued to fight the Catholic Church, and the Church continued to fight back. Any tendency by Church authorities to bend on their contraceptive teaching was overshadowed by official statements that contended the Church was not changing its position. Furthermore, as the movement increasingly became an international one, activists pointed to the pope as blocking their efforts to alleviate overpopulation in Catholic Third World countries.

The religious debate over birth control certainly became a different kind of debate. But again, it has been a debate that is understood as one with Catholics on one side and non–Catholics on the other. Still, other forces have continued to play roles in recent decades (for example, ideas of social control, eugenics, and racism), and there is plenty of room for further research in order to understand the complex nature of the religious debate over birth control since the "Sanger years."

# Bibliography

## Periodicals

America, 1915–1932.
American Church Monthly, 1930–1931.
[American] Ecclesiastical Review, 1910–1933.
American Journal of Sociology, 1907–1911.
American Mercury, 1924.
Annals of the American Academy of Political and Social Science, 1907.
Atlantic Monthly, 1908–1928.
The Baptist, 1920–1931.
Biblical World, 1913.
Birth Control Review, 1921–1930.
Catholic Charities Review, 1912–1920.
Catholic Mind, 1934.
The Catholic World, 1912–1931.
Christian Advocate, 1931.
Christian Century, 1917–1930.
Christian Fundamentalist, 1931.
Christian Workers Magazine, 1917.
Commonweal, 1931.
Congregationalist, 1931.
Congressional Globe, 1873.
Current History, 1931.
Current Literature, 1910–1920.
Current Opinion, 1915–1922.
The Dial, 1913.
Dublin Review, 1911.
Eugenics Review, 1920.
Federal Council Bulletin, 1931.
Fortnightly Review, 1910–1920.
Harper's Weekly, 1915–1924.
Hibbert Journal, 1914.
Independent, 1909–1926.

Journal of Heredity, 1915.
Journal of Hygiene, 1929–1930.
Journal of Political Economy, 1911.
Journal of Social History, 1969.
Ladies' Home Journal, 1910–1923.
The Lincare Quarterly, 1934.
Literary Digest, 1912–1931.
London Times, 1906.
Lutheran Church Review, 1920.
Lutheran Quarterly, 1914–1923.
Lutheran Witness, 1917–1939.
Methodist Review, 1927–1928.
Moody Bible Institute Monthly, 1931–1937.
The Nation, 1921–1934.
N.C.W.C. [National Catholic Welfare Conference] Review, 1931.
Nature, 1911.
New Republic, 1915–1929.
New York Times, 1921–1935
The Nineteenth Century, 1905–1913.
North American Review, 1894.
Our Sunday Visitor, 1933.
The Outlook, 1910–1931.
Popular Science Monthly, 1910–1920.
Reformed Church Review, 1915–1926.
Review and Expositor, 1920.
The Standard, 1916.
The Survey, 1910–1930.
U.S. Catholic Historian, 1997.
Walther League Messenger, 1931–1938.
Westminster Review, 1910–1930.
Woman Rebel, 1914.

## Reports, Documents, Proceedings

Acts and Proceedings of the General Synod of the Reformed Church in America, Embracing the Sessions of June 1920, 1921, 1922. New York: The Board of Publication and Bible School Work.

213

*Acts and Proceedings of the General Synod of the Reformed Church in America, 1923–1925, 1926–1928, 1929, 1931.*

American Social Hygiene Association, *First Annual Report, 1913–1914.* New York: American Federation for Sex Hygiene, 1914.

*Annual of the Northern Baptist Convention, 1916, 1927–1933.*

*Annual of the Southern Baptist Convention, 1911, 1912, 1918, 1920, 1923–1927, 1929, 1931–1932.*

*Annual Report of the American Unitarian Association, For the Fiscal Year May 1, 1929–April 30, 1930.* Boston: American Unitarian Association, 1930.

*Central Conference of American Rabbis, Thirty-Seventh Annual Convention, 1926.*

*Central Conference of American Rabbis Yearbook, 1927.*

*The Child in the City: A Series of Papers Presented at the Conferences Held During the Chicago Welfare Exhibit, May 11–25.* Chicago: Department of Social Investigation, Chicago School of Civics and Philanthropy, 1912.

*Cummins-Vaile Bill, Congress of the United States, Joint Subcommittee of the Judiciary Committees, of the Senate and House of Representatives, April 8, 1924.*

*A Digest of the Acts and Proceedings of the General Assembly of the Presbyterian Church in the United States, 1861–1944.*

Encyclical, *Casti Connubii,* December 31, 1930.

Encyclical, *Nova Impendet,* October 2, 1931.

Eugenics Record Office, *Bulletin No. 8, Some Problems in the Study of Heredity in Mental Diseases.* Cold Spring Harbor, N.Y.: 1912.

Eugenics Record Office, *Bulletin No. 10A, Report of the Committee to Study and to Report on the Best Practical Means of Cutting Off the Defective Germ-Plasm in the American Population — The Scope of the Committee's Work.* Cold Spring Harbor, N.Y.: 1914.

*Federal Council Bulletin,* April 1931, May 1932, September 1931.

*Federal Council of the Churches of Christ in America, Annual Report, 1930, 1931, 1934.*

*First Annual Report of the New York Society for the Suppression of Vice, Feb. 11, 1875 Report of the Sex Education Sessions of the Fourth International Congress on School Hygiene and of the Annual Meeting of the American Federation for Sex Hygiene, Buffalo, New York, August 1913.*

*Hearings Before a Subcommittee of the Committee on the Judiciary, United States Senate, on S. 4582, February 13 and 14, 1931.* Washington, D.C.: U.S. Government Printing Office, 1931.

*Hearings Before a Subcommittee of the Committee on the Judiciary, United States Senate, on S. 4436, May 12, 19, and 20, 1932.* Washington, D.C.: U.S. Government Printing Office, 1932.

*Hearings Before the Committee on Ways and Means, House of Representatives, On H. R. 11082, May 19 and 20, 1932.* Washington, D.C.: U.S. Government Printing Office, 1932.

*Hearings Before the Committee on the Judiciary, United States Senate on S. 1842, March 1, 20, and 29, 1934.* Washington, D.C.: U.S. Government Printing Office, 1934.

*Journal of the General Convention of the Protestant Episcopal Church in the United States of America, October 11–27, 1916; October 7–24, 1925; 1931.*

*Journal of the General Convention of the Protestant Episcopal Church, 1928.* New York: Abbott Press and Mortimer-Walling, 1929.

*Journal of the Thirtieth Delegated General Conference of the Methodist Episcopal Church.* New York: Methodist Book Concern, 1928.

*Journal of the Twenty-Ninth Delegated General Conference of the Methodist Episcopal Church.* New York: Methodist Book Concern, 1918.

*Journal of the Twenty-Seventh Delegated General Conference of the Methodist Episcopal Church Held in Saratoga Springs, New York, May 1–29, 1916.* New York: Methodist Book Concern, 1916.

*The Lambeth Conference, 1908, 1920.*

*Minutes of the Eighth Biennial Convention of the United Lutheran Church in America, 1932.*

*Minutes of the Fifth Biennial Convention of the United Lutheran Church in America, October 19–27, 1926.* Philadelphia: United Lutheran Publication House, 1926.

*Minutes of the General Assembly of the Presbyterian Church in the U.S.A., 1925, 1930, 1931.* Philadelphia: Office of the General Assembly, 1925, 1930.

*Minutes of the Seventh Biennial Convention of the United Lutheran Church in America, 1930.*

*Minutes of the Sixth Biennial Convention of the United Lutheran Church in America.* Philadelphia, 1928.

*Minutes of the Sixth Ecumenical Methodist Conference, 1931.*
*Minutes of the Sixty-Ninth General Assembly of the Presbyterian Church in the United States.* Richmond, Va.: Presbyterian Committee of Publication, 1929.
*Minutes of the Twentieth Biennial Convention of the United Lutheran Church in America, 1956.*
*Proceedings of the First Conference of Catholic Charities.* Washington, D.C.: Catholic University of America, 1910.
*Proceedings of the Rabbinical Assembly of the Jewish Theological Seminary of America, Thirty-Second Annual Convention.* New Rochelle, N.Y.: Press of the Little Print, 1933.
*Proceedings of the Rabbinical Assembly of America, Thirty-Fifth Annual Convention, 1936.*
*Report of the Central Conference of American Rabbis, 1930.*
*Report of the Fifth International Neo-Malthusian and Birth Control Conference.* London: William Heinemann, 1922.
*Report of the Sex Education Sessions of the Fourth International Congress on School Hygiene and of the Annual Meeting of the American Federation for Sex Hygiene, Buffalo, New York, August, 1913.* New York: American Federation for Sex Hygiene, 1913.
*Report to the General Convention of the Protestant Episcopal Church of the Joint Commission to Study the Whole Problem of Divorce — Its Conditions and Causes.* S.I.: Commission?, 1928.
*Sixth International Neo-Malthusian and Birth Control Conference, Vol. IV, Religious and Ethical Aspects of Birth Control.* New York: American Birth Control League, 1926.
*U.S. v. One Package*, 86 F. 2d 737 (1936).

# Books and Articles

Appleby, R. Scott. *"Church and Age Unite!": The Modernist Impulse in American Catholicism.* Notre Dame, Ind.: University of Notre Dame Press, 1992.
Athengoras, *Embassy for the Christians*, in *Patrologiae Cursus Completus ... Series Graeca.* Paris: J. P. Migne, 1857–1899.
Baker, John R. "The Spermicidal Powers of Chemical Contraceptives I; Introduction, and Experiments on Guinea-Pig Sperms, *Journal of Hygiene* 29(1929–1930): 323–329.
Barker-Benfield, G. J. *The Horrors of the Half-Known Life: Male Attitudes Toward Women and Sexuality in Nineteenth Century America.* New York: Harper and Row, 1976.
Batten, Samuel Zane. "The Redemption of the Unfit." *American Journal of Sociology*, September 1908.
_____. *The Social Task of Christianity: A Summons to the New Crusade.* New York: Fleming H. Revell, 1911.
Batzill, Hartmann, ed., *Decisiones Sánctae Sedis deusuet abusu matrimonii.* Torino: Marietti, 1944.
Beals, Carleton. *Brass-Knuckles Crusade: The Great Know-Nothing Conspiracy, 1820–1860.* New York: Hastings House, 1960.
Beaven, A. W. *The Fine Art of Living Together.* New York: Richard R. Smith, 1930.
Beckley, Harlan. *Passion for Justice: Retrieving the Legacies of Walter Rauschenbusch, John A. Ryan, and Reinhold Niebuhr.* Lousiville, Ky.: Westminster/John Knox Press, 1992.
Bierstedt, Robert. *American Sociological Theory: A Critical History.* New York: Academic Press, 1981.
Billington, Ray Allen. *The Origins of Nativism in the United States, 1800–1844.* New York: Ayer, 1974.
Blacker, C. *Birth Control and the State.* New York: E. P. Dutton, 1926.
Bontemps, Arna, and Jack Conroy. *Anyplace But Here.* New York: Hill and Wang, 1966.
Boone, William Cooke. *What God Hath Joined Together: Sermons on Courtship, Marriage, and the Home.* Nashville, Tenn.: Broadman Press, 1935.
Bristow, Edward. *Purity Movements in Britain Since 1700.* London: Gillard MacMillan, 1977.
Broderick, Francis J. *Right Reverend New Dealer, John A. Ryan.* New York: Macmillan, 1963.
Brodie, Janet Farrell. *Contraception and Abortion in Nineteenth Century America.* Ithaca, N.Y.: Cornell University Press, 1994.
Bromley, Dorothy Dunbar. *Catholics and Birth Control: Contemporary Views on Doctrine.* New York: Devin-Adair, 1965.

Buhle, Mari Jo. *Women and American Socialism, 1870–1920.* Urbana: University of Illinois Press, 1981.

Carter, Paul A. *Politics, Religion and Rockets: Essays in Twentieth Century American History.* Tucson: University of Arizona Press, 1991.

Cashman, Sean Dennis. *America in the Gilded Age: From the Death of Lincoln to the Rise of Theodore Roosevelt.* New York: New York University Press, 1988.

Chalmers, Mary M., and Owen C. Brown, eds. *The Home Beautiful: An Elective Course for Parent Groups.* Philadelphia: Judson Press, 1931.

Chandrasekhar, S. *"A Dirty, Filthy Book": The Writings of Charles Knowlton and Annie Besant on Reproductive Physiology and Birth Control and an Account of the Bradlaugh-Besant Trial.* Berkeley: University of California Press, 1981.

Chase, Allan. *The Legacy of Malthus: The Social Costs of the New Scientific Racism.* Chicago: University of Illinois Press, 1980.

Chen, Constance M. *"The Sex Side of Life": Mary Ware Dennett's Pioneering Battle for Birth Control and Sex Education.* New York: New Press, 1996.

Chesler, Ellen. *Woman of Valor: Margaret Sanger and the Birth Control Movement in America.* New York: Simon and Schuster, 1992.

Commander, Lydia Kingsmill. *The American Idea.* New York: Arno Press, 1972.

Committee on Marriage and the Home. *Ideals of Love and Marriage.* New York: Commission on the Church and Social Service, Federal Council of the Churches of Christ in America, 1929.

_____. *Safeguarding Marriages.* New York: Department of the Church and Social Service, Federal Council of the Churches of Christ in America, 1935.

Cooper, John M. *Birth Control.* Washington, D.C.: National Catholic Welfare Council, 1923.

Corson, Stephen L., Richard J. Derman, and Louise B. Tyrer, eds. *Fertility Control.* Boston: Little, Brown, 1985.

Crackanthorpe, Montague. *Population and Progress.* London: Chapman and Hall, 1907.

_____. "The Friends and Foes of Eugenics." *Fortnightly Review,* October 1912, pp. 740–748.

Cross, Robert D. *The Emergence of Liberal Catholicism in America.* Cambridge, Mass.: Harvard University Press, 1958.

Curry, William Lee. "Comstockery: A Study in the Rise and Decline of Watchdog Censorship," Ph.D. dissertation, Columbia University, 1957.

Davidson, Randall T., comp. *The Five Lambeth Conferences.* New York: Macmillan, 1920.

Davis, Henry, S. J. *Eugenics and Its Methods.* New York: Benziger Brothers, 1930.

Dennett, Mary Ware. *Birth Control Laws: Shall We Keep Them, Change Them, or Abolish Them?* New York: Grafton, 1926.

de Saulniers, Lawrence B. *The Response in American Catholic Periodicals to the Crises of the Great Depression, 1930–1935.* New York: University Press of America, 1984.

DeVilbiss, Lydia Allen. *Birth Control, What Is It?* Small, Maynard, Publishers, 1923.

Dimont, Max I. *The Jews in America: The Roots, History, and Destiny of American Jews.* New York: Simon and Schuster, 1978.

Divine, Robert A. *American Immigration Policy, 1924–1952.* New Haven, Conn.: Yale University Press, 1952.

Drysdale, C.V. *The Small Family System: Is It Injurious or Immoral?* New York: B. W. Huebsch, 1917.

Earp, Edwin L. *The Social Engineer.* New York: Eaton and Mains, 1911.

Eighmy, John Lee. *Churches in Cultural Conflict: A History of the Social Attitudes of Southern Baptists.* Knoxville: University of Tennessee Press, 1972.

Epstein, Louis M. *Sex Laws and Customs in Judaism.* New York: KTAV Publishing House, 1967 [1948].

Erie, Steven P. *Rainbow's End: Irish-Americans and the Dilemma of Urban Machine Politics, 1840–1985.* Berkeley: University of California Press, 1988.

Evans, Sara M. *Born for Liberty: A History of Women in America.* New York: Free Press, 1989.

Feldman, David M. *Birth Control in Jewish Law: Marital Relations, Contraception, and Abortion as Set Forth in the Classic Texts of Jewish Law.* New York: New York University Press, 1968.

Feldman, Egal. *Dual Destinies: The Jewish Encounter with Protestant America.* Urbana: University of Illinois Press, 1990.

Fosdick, Harry Emerson. *Adventurous Religion and Other Essays.* New York: Harper and Brothers, 1926.

Foster, William Trufant, ed. *The Social Emergency: Studies in Sex Hygiene and Morals.* Boston: Houghton Mifflin, 1914.

Fritz, John H. C. *Pastoral Theology.* St. Louis, Mo.: Concordia Publishing House, 1945.

Gage, Matilda Joslyn. *Woman, Church & State: The Original Expose of Male Collaboration Against the Female Sex.* Watertown, Mass.: Persephone Press, 1980 [1893].

Gerber, David A., ed. *Anti-Semitism in American History.* Urbana: University of Illinois Press, 1986.

Gerberding, G. H. *The Lutheran Catechist.* Philadelphia: Lutheran Publication Society, 1910.

Gerrard, Thomas J., Rev. *The Church and Eugenics.* London: P. S. King and Sons, 1912.

Glazer, Nathan. *American Judaism.* Chicago: University of Chicago Press, 1989.

Gluck, Sherna, ed. *From Parlor to Prison: Five American Suffragists Talk About Their Lives.* New York: Vintage, 1976.

Goldstein, Sidney E. *Meaning of Marriage and Foundations of the Family, a Jewish Interpretation.* New York: Bloch, 1940.

Gordon, Linda. *Woman's Body, Woman's Right: A Social History of Birth Control in America.* New York: Penguin, 1976.

Gould, Lewis L., ed. *The Progressive Era.* Syracuse, N.Y.: Syracuse University Press, 1974.

Grand, Sarah. "The New Aspect of the Woman Question," *North American Review* 158 (March 1894), 270–276.

Grant, Madison. *The Passing of the Great Race; or, the Racial Basis of European History.* New York: C. Scribner, 1916.

Gray, A. Herbert. *Men, Women, and God: A Discussion of Sex Questions from the Christian Point of View.* New York: George H. Doran Company, 1923.

Gray, Madeline. *Margaret Sanger: A Biography of the Champion of Birth Control.* New York: Richard Marek, 1979.

Haller, Mark H. *Eugenics: Hereditarian Attitudes in American Thought.* New Brunswick, N.J.: Rutgers University Press, 1963.

Handlin, Oscar. *Al Smith and His America.* Boston: Little, Brown, 1958.

Harris, Barbara J. *Beyond Her Sphere: Women and the Professions in American History.* Westport, Conn.: Greenwood Press, 1978.

Hasian, Marouf Arif, Jr. *The Rhetoric of Eugenics in Anglo-American Thought.* Athens: University of Georgia Press, 1996.

Henderson, Charles R. *Education with Reference to Sex.* Chicago: University of Chicago Press, 1909.

Herberg, Will. *Protestant, Catholic, Jew: An Essay in American Religious Sociology.* New York: Doubleday, 1960.

Higham, John. *Send These to Me: Immigrants in Urban America.* Baltimore: Johns Hopkins University Press, 1984.

_____. *Strangers in the Land: Patterns of American Nativism, 1860–1925.* New Brunswick, N.J.: Rutgers University Press, 1994.

Himes, Norman E. *Medical History of Contraception.* New York: Gamut Press, 1963 [1936].

_____. *Practical Birth Control Methods.* New York: Modern Age Books, 1938.

Hofstadter, Richard. *The Age of Reform: From Bryan to FDR.* New York: Alfred A. Knopf, 1955.

_____. *Social Darwinism in American Thought.* New York: George Braziller, 1959.

Hopkins, Charles Howard. *The Rise of the Social Gospel in American Protestantism, 1865–1915.* New Haven, Conn.: Yale University Press, 1940.

Huffman, J. A. *Building the Home Christian.* Marion, Ind.: Standard Press, 1935.

Hume, Maggie. *Contraception in Catholic Doctrine: The Evolution of an Earthly Code.* Washington, D.C.: Catholics for a Free Choice, 1991.

Hutchinson, E. P. *Legislative History of American Immigration Policy, 1798–1956.* Philadelphia: University of Pennsylvania Press, 1981.

Hutchison, William R., ed. *Between the Times: The Travail of the Protestant Establishment in America, 1900–1960.* New York: Cambridge University Press, 1989.

Johnsen, Julia E., comp. *Selected Articles on Birth Control.* New York: H. W. Wilson, 1925.

Jordan, David Starr. *The Blood of the Nation: A Study of the Decay of Races Through the Survival of the Unfit.* Boston: American Unitarian Association, 1903.

Kennedy, David M. *Birth Control in America: The Career of Margaret Sanger.* New Haven, Conn.: Yale University Press, 1970.

Kevles, Daniel J. *In the Name of Eugenics: Genetics and the Uses of Human Heredity.* Cambridge, Mass.: Harvard University Press, 1995.

Kirk, Maurice Massimo Livi Bacci, and Egon Szabady, eds. *Law and Fertility in Europe: A Study of Legislation Directly or Indirectly Affecting Fertility in Europe, Vol. 1.* Ordina Editions.

Lader, Lawrence. *The Margaret Sanger Story and the Fight for Birth Control.* Westport, Conn.: Greenwood Press, 1955.

Landman, Isaac, ed. *The Universal Jewish Encyclopedia, Vol. 2.* New York: KTAV Publishing House, 1969.

Lasch, Christopher. *Haven in a Heartless World: The Family Besieged.* New York: Basic Books, 1977.

Latz, Leo J. *The rhythm of sterility and fertility in women; a discussion of the physiological, practical, and ethical aspects of the discoveries of Drs. K. Ogino (Japan) and H. Knaus (Austria) regarding the periods when conception is impossible and when possible.* Chicago: by the author, 1932.

Laughlin, Harry H. *Eugenics Record Office, Bulletin No. 10A, Report of the Committee to Study and to Report on the Best Practical Means of Cutting Off the Defective Germ-Plasm in the American Population — The Scope of the Committee's Work.* Cold Spring Harbor, NY: 1914.

Leuchtenburg, William E. *The Perils of Prosperity, 1914–1932.* Chicago: University of Chicago Press, 1958.

Linkh, Richard M. *Catholicism and European Immigrants.* New York: Center for Immigration Studies, 1975.

Ludmerer, Kenneth. *Genetics and American Society.* Baltimore: Johns Hopkins University Press, 1972.

Maier, Walter Arthur. *For Better, Not For Worse: A Manual of Christian Matrimony.* St. Louis, Mo.: Concordia Publishing House, 1939.

Malik, Kenan. *The Meaning of Race: Race, History and Culture in Western Society.* Washington Square, N.Y.: New York University Press, 1996.

Marchant, James. *Birth Rate and Empire.* London: Williams and Norgate, 1917.

_____, ed. *The Control of Parenthood.* New York: G. P. Putnam's Sons, 1920.

Marcuson, Isaac E. *Central Conference of American Rabbis Thirty-Seventh Annual Convention,* vol. 36. n.p.: 1926.

_____, ed. *Central Conference of American Rabbis Yearbook,* 1927.

Marsden, George. *Fundamentalism in American Culture: The Shaping of Twentieth Century Evangelicalism, 1870–1925.* New York: Oxford University Press, 1980.

Marty, Martin E. *Modern American Religion, Volume 1, The Irony of It All, 1893–1919.* Chicago: University of Chicago Press, 1997.

_____. *Modern American Religion, Volume 2, The Noise of Conflict, 1919–1941.* Chicago: University of Chicago Press, 1991.

_____. *Protestantism and Social Christianity.* New York: K. G. Saur, 1992.

Mazumdar, Pauline M. H. *Eugenics, Human Genetics and Human Failings: The Eugenics Society, Its Sources and Its Critics in Britain.* New York: Routledge, 1992.

McCann, Carole R. *Birth Control Politics in the United States, 1916–1945.* Ithaca, N.Y.: Cornell University Press, 1994.

McClorey, John A., Rev., S. J. *The Republic and the Church: A Series of Lenten Lectures Mainly on Divorce and Birth Control.* St. Louis, Mo.: B. Herdee, 1927.

McKeown, Elizabeth. *War and Welfare: American Catholics and World War I.* New York: Garland, 1988.

McLaren, Angus. *A History of Contraception, from Antiquity to the Present Day.* Oxford: Basil Blackwell, 1990.

_____. *Sexuality and Social Order: The Debate Over the Fertility of Women and Workers in France, 1770–1920.* New York: Holmes and Meier, 1983.

McShane, Joseph M., S.J. *"Sufficiently Radical": Catholicism, Progressivism, and the Bishops' Program of 1919.* Washington, D.C.: Catholic University of America, 1986.

Meyer, Adolf, ed. *Birth Control Facts and Responsibilities: A Symposium Dealing with This Important Subject from a Number of Angles.* Baltimore: Williams and Wilkins, 1925.

Meyer, Donald B. *The Protestant Search for American Realism, 1919–1941.* Berkeley: University of California Press, 1960.

Miller, David. *The Secret Life of the Jew: His Life — His Family.* Oakland, Calif.: by author, 1930.

Miller, Robert Moats. *American Protestantism and Social Issues, 1919–1939.* Chapel Hill: University of North Carolina Press, 1958.

Miller, Stuart Creighton. *The Unwelcome Immigrant: The American Image of the Chinese, 1785–1882.* Berkeley: University of California Press, 1974.

Montgomery, Harry Earl. *Christ's Social Remedies.* New York: G. Putnam's Sons, 1911.

Moore, John F. *Will America Become Catholic?* New York: Harper and Brothers, 1931.

Moore, R. Laurence. *Religious Outsiders and the Making of Americans.* New York: Oxford University Press, 1986.

More, Adelyne. *Uncontrolled Breeding; or, Fecundity versus Civilization, a Contribution to the Study of Over-Population as the Cause of War and the Chief Obstacle to the Emancipation of Women.* New York: Critic and Guide, 1917.

Myrdal, Gunnar. *American Dilemma: The Negro Problem and Modern Democracy.* New York: Pantheon, 1975 [1944].

Nearing, Scott. "Race Suicide v. Overpopulation," *Popular Science Monthly,* January 1911, 81–83.

Nelson, E. Clifford, ed. *The Lutherans in North America.* Philadelphia: Fortress Press, 1975.

Newcomer, Mabel. *A Century of Higher Education for Women.* New York: Harper and Brothers, 1959.

Noll, John Francis. *Catechism on Birth Control.* Huntington, Ind.: Our Sunday Visitor Press, 1938.

_____. *The Catholic Church v. the Federal Council of Churches of Christ in America.* Huntington, Ind.: Our Sunday Visitor Press, 1931.

Noonan, John T. *Contraception: A History of Its Treatment by the Catholic Theologians and Canonists.* Cambridge, Mass.: Harvard University Press, 1966.

Northcote, Hugh. *Christianity and Sex Problems.* Philadelphia: F. A. Davis, 1916.

Nuechterlein, Louis. *Concordia Pulpit for 1940.* St. Louis, Mo.: Concordia Publishing House, 1939.

O'Brien, David J. *American Catholics and Social Reform: The New Deal Years.* New York: Oxford University Press, 1968.

O'Brien, John A., Rev. *Legitimate Birth Control: According to Nature's Law, in Harmony with Catholic Morality.* Huntington, Ind.: Our Sunday Visitor Press, 1934.

Olson, James S. *Catholic Immigrants in America.* Chicago: Nelson-Hall, 1987.

Ozment, Steven. *When Fathers Ruled: Family Life in Reformation Europe.* Cambridge, Mass.: Harvard University Press, 1983.

Petersen, William. *Malthus: Founder of Modern Demography.* New Brunswick, N.J.: Transaction, 1999.

Pfotenhauer, F., *Der Lutheraner.* N.p.: N.p., 1911.

Pick, Daniel. *Faces of Degeneration: A European Disorder, c.1848–c.1918.* New York: Cambridge University Press, 1989.

Pierpont, Raymond, ed. *Report of the Fifth International Neo-Malthusian and Birth Control Conference.* London: William Heinemann, 1922, 301–302.

Pivar, David. *Purity Crusade: Sexual Morality and Social Control, 1868–1900.* Westport, Conn.: Greenwood Press, 1973.

Potter, Charles Francis. *The Story of Religion.* New York: Simon and Schuster, 1929.

Randall, J. Herman and J. Gardner Smith, eds. *The Unity of Religions: A Popular Discussion of Ancient and Modern Beliefs.* New York: Thomas Crowell, 1910.

Ranke-Heinemann, Uta. *Eunuchs for the Kingdom of Heaven.* New York: Doubleday, 1990.

Rauschenbush, Walter. *Christianity and the Social Order.* New York: Macmillan, 1914 [1912].

Ravitch, Diane, ed. *The American Reader: Words That Motivated a Nation.* New York: HarperCollins, 1991.

Reed, James. *From Private Vice to Public Virtue: The Birth Control Movement in American Society.* New York: Basic Books, 1978.

Reilly, Philip R., M.D., J.D. *The Surgical Solution: A History of Involuntary Sterilization in the U.S.* Baltimore: Johns Hopkins University Press, 1991.

Riddle, John M. *Contraception and Abortion from the Ancient World to the Renaissance.* Cambridge, Mass.: Harvard University Press, 1992.

_____. *Eve's Herbs: A History of Contraception and Abortion in the West.* Cambridge, Mass.: Harvard University Press, 1997.

Ripley, William Z. "Races in the United States," *Atlantic Monthly,* December 1908, 745–759.

Robertson, William H. *An Illustrated History of Contraception: A Concise Account of the Quest for Fertility Control*. Park Ridge, N.J.: Parthenon, 1990.

Robinson, Caroline Hadley. *Seventy Birth Control Clinics: A Survey and Analysis Including the General Effects of Control on Size and Quality of Population*. Baltimore: Williams & Wilkins, 1930.

Robinson, William J. *Birth Control; or, the Limitation of Offspring by the Prevention of Conception*. New York: Critic and Guide, 1917.

Roosevelt, Theodore. *The Foes of Our Own Household*. New York: George H. Doran, 1917.

Rose, June. *Marie Stopes and the Sexual Revolution*. Boston: Faber and Faber, 1992.

Rosenberg, Charles, and Carroll Smith-Rosenberg. *Birth Control and Family Planning in Nineteenth Century America*. New York: Arno Press, 1974.

Rosenberg, Rosalind. *Beyond Separate Spheres: Intellectual Roots of Modern Feminism*. New Haven, Conn.: Yale University Press, 1982.

Ross, Edward Alsworth. *The Principles of Sociology*. New York: Century, 1920.

_____. *Standing Room Only?* New York: Century, 1927.

Ross, Eric B. *The Malthus Factor: Population, Poverty and Politics in Capitalist Development*. New York: Zed Books, 1998.

Rothman, David J. ,and Sheila M. Rothman, eds. *Birth Control and Morality in Nineteenth Century America: Two Discussions*. New York: Arno Press, 1972.

Ruethers, Rosemary Radford. *Religion and Sexism: Images of Women in the Jewish and Christian Traditions*. New York: Simon and Schuster, 1974.

Ryan, John A. *A Program of Social Reform by Legislation*. New York: Paulist Press, 1919.

_____. *Social Reform on Catholic Lines*. New York: Paulist Press, 1914.

_____, and Moorehous F. X. Millar. *The State and the Church*. New York: Macmillan, 1922.

St. John-Stevas, Norman. *The Agonising Choice: Birth Control, Religion and the Law*. Bloomington: Indiana University Press, 1971.

Sanger, Margaret. *An Autobiography*. New York: Norton, 1938.

_____. *Happiness in Marriage*. Garden City, N.Y.: Blue Ribbon Books, 1926.

_____. *My Fight for Birth Control*. New York: Farrar and Rinehart, 1931.

_____. *The Pivot of Civilization*. New York: Brentano's, 1922.

_____, ed. Sixth International Neo-Malthusian and Birth Control Conference, Vol. IV, Religious and Ethical Aspects of Birth Control. New York: American Birth Control League, 1926, 18–19.

Sarna, Jonathan D., and David G. Dalin. *Religion and State in the American Jewish Experience*. Notre Dame, Ind.: University of Notre Dame Press, 1997.

Schlesinger, Arthur M., and Fred L. Israel, eds. *History of American Presidential Elections, 1789–1968*, vol. 3, 1971, 2585–2590.

Schneider, Dorothy, and Carl J. Schneider. *American Women in the Progressive Era, 1900–1920*. New York: Facts on File, 1993.

Shapiro, Thomas M. *Population Control Politics: Women, Sterilization, and Reproductive Choice*. Philadelphia: Temple University Press, 1985.

Sklare, Marshall, ed. *The Jew in American Society*. New York: Behrman House, 1974.

Slawson, Douglas J. *The Foundation and First Decade of the National Catholic Welfare Council*. Washington, D.C.: Catholic University of America Press, 1992.

Smith-Rosenberg, Carroll. *Disorderly Conduct: Visions of Gender in Victorian America*. New York: Oxford University Press, 1985.

Soloway, Richard A. *Demography and Degeneration: Eugenics and the Declining Birth Rate in Twentieth Century Britain*. Chapel Hill: University of North Carolina Press, 1990.

Sorin, Gerald. *Tradition Transformed: The Jewish Experience in America*. Baltimore: Johns Hopkins University Press, 1997.

Spalding, Henry S., S. J. *Talks to Nurses: The Ethics of Nursing*. New York: Benziger Brothers, 1920.

Spaulding, Clarence A. *Twenty-Four Views of Marriage*. New York: Macmillan, 1930.

Spitzer, Walter O., and Carlyle L. Saylor, eds. *Birth Control and the Christian: A Protestant Symposium on the Control of Human Reproduction*. Wheaton, Ill.: Tyndale House, 1969.

Stephenson, Alan M. G. *Anglicanism and the Lambeth Conferences*. London: SPCK, 1978.

Stephenson, George M. *A History of American Immigration, 1820–1924*. New York: Ginn and Company, 1926.

Stevens, Doris. *Jailed for Freedom*. New York: Schocken Books, 1976.

Stoddard, Lothrop. *The Revolt Against Civilization: The Menace of the Under Man*. New York: Charles Scribner's Sons, 1923.

_____. *The Rising Tide of Color Against White World-Supremacy*. New York: Blue Ribbon Books, 1920.

Stopes, Marie. *A New Gospel to All Peoples*. London: A. L. Humphreys, 1922.

_____. *Radiant Motherhood*. London: G. P. Putnam, 1920.

Stouffer, Samuel A., and Paul T. Lazarsfeld. *Research Memorandum on the Family in the Depression*. New York: Arno Press, 1972.

Strong, Josiah. *The Challenge of the City*. New York: Young Peoples Missionary Movement, 1907.

Suksdorf, Henry F. *Our Race Problems*. New York: Shakespeare Press, 1911.

Sulloway, Alvah W. *Birth Control and Catholic Doctrine*. Boston: Beacon Press, 1959.

Szasz, Ferenc Morton. *The Divided Mind of Protestant America, 1880–1930*. Tuscaloosa: University of Alabama Press, 1982.

Taylor, Graham. *Religion in Social Action*. New York: Dodd, Mead, 1913.

Tentler, Leslie Woodcock. *Seasons of Grace: A History of the Catholic Archdiocese of Detroit*. Detroit, Mich.: Wayne State University Press, 1990.

Thompson, Warren S. *Population: A Study in Malthusianism*, Ph.D. dissertation, Columbia University, 1915.

Tobin, Kathleen, and Schlesinger. "The Changing American City: Chicago Catholics and the Birth Control Movement, 1915–1935," *U.S. Catholic Historian*, Spring 1997, 67–85.

Todd, John. *Serpents in the Dove's Nest*. Boston: Lee and Shepard, 1867.

Tone, Andrea, ed. *Controlling Reproduction: An American History*. Wilmington, Del.: Scholarly Resources, 1997.

Trumbull, Charles. *Anthony Comstock, Fighter*. New York: Fleming H. Revel, 1913.

Wade, Raymond J., ed. *Journal of the Twenty-Ninth Delegated General Conference of the Methodist Episcopal Church*. New York: Methodist Book Concern, 1924.

Wade, Wyn Craig. *The Fiery Cross*. New York: Simon and Schuster, 1987.

Ware, Susan. *Holding Their Own: American Women in the 1930's*. Boston: Twayne, 1982.

Wells, David F. *Reformed Theology in America: A History of Its Modern Development*. Grand Rapids, Mich.: William B. Eerdmans, 1985.

Wells, H. G. *The Outline of History, Volume I*. New York: Doubleday, 1971 [1920].

_____. *Social Forces in England and America*. New York: Harper and Brothers, 1914.

Wentz, Ross. *A Basic History of Lutheranism in America*. Philadelphia: Fortress Press, 1964.

Wertz, Richard W., and Dorothy C. Wertz. *Lying-In: A History of Childbirth in America*. New Haven: Yale University Press, 1989.

White, Ronald C., Jr., and C. Howard Hopkins. *The Social Gospel: Religion and Reform in Changing America*. Philadelphia: Temple University Press, 1976.

Wiebe, Robert. *The Search for Order, 1877–1920*. New York: Hill and Wang, 1967.

Wittke, Carl. *The Irish in America*. Baton Rouge: Louisiana State University Press, 1956.

Woloch, Nancy. *Women and the American Experience*. New York: McGraw-Hill, 1994.

Yarros, Rachelle S. *Birth Control and Its Relation to Health and Welfare*. Chicago, Ill.: Birth Control League, 1925.

# Index